LIFT

THE NATURE AND CRAFT
OF EXPERT COACHING

BRUCE R. DOREY, PHD

ISBN 978-1-7326168-0-6 Trade paperback
ISBN 978-1-7326168-1-3 Kindle
ISBN 978-1-7326168-2-0 EPUB
ISBN 978-1-7326168-3-7 Hardcover

Library of Congress Control Number: 2018956222
Langer Bell Press, Charlottesville, Virginia, 2018

Editor: Anne M Carley, Chenille Books.
Designer: Abigail Wiebe, Next Leaf Publications.
Cover design: Joe Daugherty, Eyedea Advertising & Design Studio.
Chapter heading maps and Figures 1.0 and 1.1: Deanna Griffin Dove.
Figure I-1: Sidney Harris. Reproduced with permission of ScienceCartoonsPlus.com.
Figure 1.2: Tom Fishburne. Reproduced with permission of Marketoonist.com.
Figure 4.0: DILBERT © 2005 Scott Adams. Used by permission of Andrews
McMeel Syndication. All rights reserved.
Propeller image in Parts licensed from Can Stock Photo / happyroman.

Learn more at brucerdorey.com

instagram.com/bruce_r_dorey
facebook.com/brucerdorey
twitter.com/bruce_r_dorey
linkedin.com/in/brucerdorey

To Karen
and
In memory of a dear friend, Ron Hanlon

Look deep into nature, and then
you will understand everything better.

Albert Einstein

∞∞

To me there has never been
a higher source of earthly honor or distinction
than that connected with advances in science.

Isaac Newton

∞∞

The difficulty lies not so much in
developing new ideas as in
escaping from old ones.

John Maynard Keynes

CONTENTS

LIST OF FIGURES

ACKNOWLEDGMENTS

Shortly before I started writing the book in earnest, a friend and client committed suicide. This was a great guy, ten years older than I, very accomplished, well educated, healthy and happy (outwardly) with a nice wife and great kids. We had worked closely together years before and I would never have predicted suicide. More accurately, until my fiftieth birthday I simply could not even relate to what must be the crushing despair and the inconsolable internal dialog of someone seeking a way out. But this tragedy proved to be an eerie foretelling of what was a disturbing increase in middle-aged suicide.

I turned fifty during the worst economic depression of my lifetime and like many somewhat privileged baby boomers, I began to experience a different kind of life. What had been a fairly consistent upward trajectory, with a stable career, began to stutter and even miss a beat. My self-worth was tightly commingled with the reputation I believed I had, or more importantly, with the reputation I thought I could have, and the person I thought I could be...one day.

As a self-absorbed baby boomer, I looked for satisfaction in what I had and how I felt. But what I found, somewhat by accident, was that deep satisfaction and an elevated feeling of self-worth and purpose, a LIFT, came from contributing to someone who wanted to learn.

It was also clear that more and more gen-Xers authentically wanted to learn and move into more senior management positions. While executive/leadership coaching was becoming more mainstream, little was being done to address the intergenerational transfer of skill and working knowledge at the senior management level. Now that baby boomers are retiring and moving out of management positions, there will be significant pressure on the next generation.

As a true engineer, I was given to think in practical terms of systems and of cause and effect. I wanted to know how we baby boomers could help coach and prepare the next generation of senior management. I also wanted to understand the reasons why so many baby boomers (including myself) seem desperate and anxious, so much so they were killing themselves at an alarming and increasing rate?

So I started to search for answers. For me that meant reading everything I could find. What began as curiosity became a kind of desperation-fueled manic period of about three years during which I cut way back on coaching and consulting, and essentially woke up, read, and read, and read, until I began to write.

As a new author, the process of writing was more than daunting and far more challenging than I had anticipated, but also far more therapeutic and satisfying. To say it was an extraordinary process doesn't seem to express the appropriate sentiments. I feel so grateful and appreciative to many people for their help and encouragement.

When I thumb through the finished book now, I return to specific times and vividly recall the moments of insight or realization, which were almost always connected with the specific individuals I am acknowledging.

I'm also reminded of the nights I would go to sleep feeling defeated, only to hustle out of bed the next morning to capture a new thought or piece of the story which was somehow revealed overnight.

My sister Karen deserves special mention since it was her guidance, unconditional love, and encouragement which gave me energy and perspective. My father's and mother's love and support were the rocks on which I could rely.

Anne Carley's hours and hours of expert coaching, editing, and encouragement were essential, and I am grateful.

Alynn Morina, Mark Hatton, Scott Cameron, Surendar Balakrishnan, Professor Ed Hess, and Dr. Neil Strauss were wonderful sounding boards and provided important editing and content assistance.

A warm thank you very much to the following people who helped to review, edit, or discuss the manuscript: Gary Antonio, Doug Bloom, Matthew Carter, Evan Clarke, Jeremy Clarke, Lindsay Clarke, Lisa Clarke, Jen Dalton, Nathalie Delmas, Dr. Murtazali Dibirov, Jennifer Fox, James Gambrel, Mark Govechinkov, Jon Greenwald, Ron Hanlon, Sean Hanlon, Tyler Hatton, Sam Kempf, Brian McCay, Paul McClean, Katie Newcombe, Beth Oddy, Vanessa Parack, Mike Pawelski, Michael Rice, Danielle Righter, Paul Santucci, Jeanne Schlesinger, Bill Shanahan, Steve Shiro, Debika Shome, Ray Sprouse, Al Ward, Tom Watson, and Matt Yoder.

—BRD

PREFACE

"It's your aircraft."

"My aircraft," answers Jeffrey Skiles, the 49-year-old second-in-command (SIC).

The captain has just handed Skiles the controls of the Airbus A 320. From his "right seat," typical for an SIC, Skiles begins to push the thrust lever engaging the two massive engines. It's a chilly January afternoon in New York, as US Air Flight 1549 begins take-off. The experienced pilots know that the cold, heavy air enables the engines to create more thrust, accelerating and lifting the 155,000 pound plane much faster than on a warm day.

Each 60,000-horsepower[1] high-bypass turbofan engine uses fan blades to slice into and carve out this heavy air, pushing it backward. Seen from the front of the massive engines under the wings, the fan blades may look like small propeller blades, but they function differently.[2] The fans push the air backward, compressing it into a smaller and smaller space. The air then comes bursting – or accelerating – out the back of the engine, much like water in a garden hose when you put your thumb over it. This backward acceleration of the heavy, more massive air, creates what Sir Isaac Newton called an action or a force.[3] This force drives the plane forward, because, just as Newton said in his third law of motion,[4] "for every action, or force, there is an equal and opposite reaction."[5]

Now, at 1525:51 (3:25 p.m.) on January 15, 2009, the plane is climbing. Skiles hears his captain give LaGuardia air traffic control their current altitude, and confirm they'll be climbing to 5,000 feet. Skiles has flown the route from New York to Charlotte, North Carolina many times, and this afternoon he enjoys the view of Citi Park, the home of the New York Mets.

Then, just ninety-five seconds after takeoff, in the top right corner of his field of vision, Skiles sees dark spots moving very quickly in his direction.

The plane is traveling at just over 300 feet-per-second (204 mph) – that's the length of a football field in the time it takes to say, "football field."

The flock of Canada geese is traveling slower, at about 73 feet-per-second, (50 mph). While it catches Skiles's attention, he's not startled, having seen birds many times before.

However, Skiles said later, "I barely blink and they were upon us. …The cockpit windscreen of an A320 is large and as I looked out the front, all I saw was birds."[6]

He feels the first impact a fraction of a second before he hears a loud BANG/THUD. "The plane shuddered. …"

Skiles next hears a THUD THUD, followed by multiple collisions, as the geese – each bird weighing as much as 18 pounds – strike the nose, windshield, cabin, and wings. Some birds are pulled directly into the jet engines, and once one of the small fan blades is toppled, domino-like, it causes a chain reaction destroying the interior of the engine.

"It sounded like tennis shoes in the dryer," recalled a passenger.

Almost immediately there's the smell of an electrical fire. … It was all over in a second or two.

The windscreen is covered in remains.

"My aircraft."

With that comment, Chesley ("Sully") Sullenberger, the captain, calmly and purposefully takes back control of the plane from his second-in-command.

It's hard to imagine a situation with a greater concentration of stress. With the skyline of Manhattan now clearly in his view beyond the George Washington Bridge, and warning systems audibly blaring and blinking in the cockpit, the amygdala in Sully's brain – home to his "fast-thinking" conscious and unconscious systems – is tripped, firing off powerful chemicals into his bloodstream to prepare for urgency and danger.

All this makes it even more difficult to focus. A cacophony of shouting automated voices and warning alarms are all demand Sully's attention. Meanwhile, as he pilots the plane from the cockpit, the lives of 154 people are literally in his hands. The engines will not restart, and the Airbus keeps dropping.

Like all commercial pilots, Sully and Skiles are prepared for emergencies, having trained with simulations and virtual pilot testing systems, but a water landing with no thrust in either engine is unlike anything the simulator has ever thrown at them. Over the next 195 seconds, Sully and Skiles, heroically and under extremely stressful conditions, maneuver the highly automated digital "fly-by-wire" aircraft safely onto the Hudson River between Midtown Manhattan and Weehawken, New Jersey. After impact, the three flight attendants manage to lead everyone to temporary safety on the wings of the plane. Then, adding to the myth-like quality of the story, in what soon became known as the "Miracle on the Hudson," small watercraft from both the New Jersey and New York sides of the river mobilize to bring every single passenger to dry land and emergency care.

A Paradox

Flight 1549 illustrates a paradox:

As our machines and artificial intelligence become more powerful and more automated, we are setting up situations in which we will need to be more prepared for extreme complexity, with more at stake. At the same time, our most experienced and skillful employees are leaving the work force in record numbers.[7]

As we work more closely in and with robotic augmentation, we'll need more Sullenbergers, more expert men and women so familiar with the systems, the science and the environment in which they work that they aren't tripped up by cognitive overload. In this case, it was Sully's deep knowledge of the aircraft's systems, his skill as a pilot, and his knowledge of the physics of lift which were critical. Far from being helpful to the pilot and co-pilot of Flight 1549, automated systems were a distraction and a hindrance; their effect was to ratchet up the psychic pressure and chaos in the cockpit.

To demonstrate the paradox of the benefits and hazards of increased automation, consider a few salient points from Flight 1549:

First, with no thrust from either engine, Sully had no options, and no time to run through checklists, searches, or scenarios. The plane was on a fixed glide path, obeying only the laws of nature, and it was going down. It wasn't behaving like a typical glider, by the way. In his book, *A Higher Duty*, Sully explains, "There was speculation in the media that my experience as a glider pilot thirty-five years earlier had helped me on Flight 1549. I have to dispel that notion. The speed and weight characteristics of an Airbus are completely different ... from the gliders I flew. It's a night and day difference."[8]

Newer commercial aircraft are more efficient and have better glide characteristics compared with older aircraft, but, with no thrust, landing – on dry land – is still difficult. Many commercial pilots now, when starting descent from very high altitudes, allow the planes to follow a controlled descent, saving fuel. But, as you may recall from your last flight, the pilot uses some thrust near the point of touchdown to soften the landing. Also, the landing gear behaves like a shock absorber, further softening the impact.

The flight simulation software used by the Airbus engineers who designed the aircraft determined theoretically that the airplane would be descending at three feet per second. However, in reality, the plane was coming down at twelve feet per second: that's more than the height of the room in which you may be sitting, each second. Hitting the relatively flat water of the Hudson River was going to be like hitting concrete. The flight simulators were not programmed to simulate a total loss of thrust at a low altitude, and certainly not on water.

Consider next-generation aircraft flying more passengers with more highly mediated and automated on-board controls. Just as robot-assisted surgery still depends on a human surgeon to supervise – and intervene if necessary – saving lives in unexpected aircraft emergencies, at least for the foreseeable future, will depend on a human expert pilot like Sully. The airplane does not fly autonomously.

As Sully explains, "The plane is never going somewhere on its own without you. It's always going where you tell it to go. A computer can only do what it is told to do. The choice is: Do I tell it to do something by pushing on the control stick with my hand, or do I tell it to do something by using some intervening technology?"[9]

To make matters more difficult, multiple systems were now demanding attention – the ground proximity warning system's synthetic voice was repeating, "PULL UP! PULL UP! PULL UP! TOO LOW! TOO LOW!" and another system was shouting, "CAUTION! TERRAIN! CAUTION! TERRAIN!" To add more chaos to the cacophony, the video screens directly in the pilot's field of view were flashing and scrolling out vital aircraft information and emergency procedures.

Patrick Harten, of the New York Terminal Radar Approach Control, was communicating with the plane as this was all happening. Harten commented later, during his testimony to Congress, "People don't survive landing on the Hudson. I thought it was [Sullenberger's] own death sentence. I believed at that moment I was going to be the last person to talk to anyone on that airplane."[10]

Harten's belief was reasonable. If a water landing is too steep, the plane dives nose first and buckles – breaking apart and disintegrating. Too shallow, and the tail will drag, causing the nose to be slammed down hard into the water and likely disintegrating the front of the aircraft and/or causing a catastrophic cartwheel and break-up. If one side dips, causing a wing to touch the water, the nose of the plane slams into the water and the plane cartwheels and breaks apart.[11]

Commercial pilots like Sully or Skiles are essentially multitasking most of the time as they fly these complex machines. This situational awareness requires a wide variety of deep contextual knowledge, a master's knowledge that is only acquired after years of deliberate practice and hard work. Humans are still better at situational awareness than computers and robots. Masters – at anything – know when to focus and be mindful. They have learned to automate through practice and experience, during the good days and the bad. "Automate," in this sense, means to become highly skilled, so deeply familiar with a procedure or process that it becomes second nature and requires little to no conscious effort to implement, like riding a bicycle or driving a car. This mastery is essential with more and more complex machines and information systems, which require rapid bursts of focus.

Second, and not widely reported, is the extraordinary work of the flight attendants, done in largely "automated" states, suppressing panic and following their decades of training and preparation. Seconds after impact, the 41°F river water began flooding the cabin. Within a minute, the frigid water was waist deep at Doreen Welsh's position near the rear of the aircraft. Welsh, a flight attendant with 39 years' experience, noticed a passenger running toward her.

Adrenaline was coursing through the passenger's body. Under its powerful fight-or-flight influence, she pushed Welsh, 58, aside, in an attempt to exit by the rear cabin door. Although the passenger did manage to get the door open, most importantly Welsh calmly and forcefully grabbed her; then lifted and pushed her and other passengers – many in shock and some badly injured – out of their seats and to the exits over the wing. Welsh knew that the odds of survival were far better on the wing than in the water.

In addition to her safety responsibilities, Welsh had more than an adrenaline-crazed passenger to contend with. She'd been hurt. Only a minute or two prior, upon impact with the water, a metal vertical support beam drove up through the reinforced cabin floor, puncturing and ripping the skin, tendons, and muscle of Welsh's left shin, creating a deep V-shaped gash 5 inches long by 2 inches wide. Her injury would require surgery.

Welsh and the other crew somehow suppressed their own panic responses; their practice and training kicked in. Their preparation was the difference. They automatically, efficiently, and altruistically moved the passengers onto the wings, out of the icy water, saving all 155 lives. Stampedes on dry land can kill, but in an aircraft sinking into frigid water with constricted pathways to exit, there is even less margin of error.

The crew knew about the research that reveals the real reasons people die in cold water (below 15°C or 59°F) are not hypothermia or loss of consciousness. In the case of Flight 1549, had they not been directed to safety on the wings, the passengers would have lost dexterity in their hands, and become unable to hold their breath. They would have drowned in the river or died from heart failure. Inhaling the cold water, scrambling over others, and attempting to swim all would have increased their risk of death.[12]

Flight 1549 serves as a compelling example of our paradox. However, the next generation of artificial intelligence and more highly automated machines will pose greater and greater challenges, requiring more – not less – human expertise. Not only will rapid task switching be required, but deep contextual knowledge and an overall understanding of the systems (flight systems in this case) and the fundamentals of the applicable science (here, the physics of flight) will also be required to make accurate operating choices in real time.

Metis & the Craftsman Culture

Field research on commercial pilots revealed no software program, robot, or algorithm existed in 2009 (nor does one at this writing) that could have made the complex set of decisions – nor piloted so expertly – as Sully did. Captain Sullenberger was on his own.

After the fifteen-month investigation into the water landing, the Chairman of the National Transportation Safety Board declared that Sully's actions that day "provided the highest probability that the accident would be survivable."[13]

Captain Sullenberger's performance involved something beyond skill and good luck, beyond just a situational awareness. He demonstrated a deep knowledge of the context, including the environment in which he worked. Not only a modern adaptation to a modern problem, this deep knowledge was given a name by the Ancient Greeks. In *The Iliad*, nearly three thousand years ago, they called it metis ("MET-iss").

Metis encompasses something we value dearly today in fields like education, medicine, aviation, many areas of business, and in numerous kinds of art, craft, and sport.

Metis includes the hard-learned competencies of working alone, with groups of people, and, increasingly, with technology. Captain Sully, with forty years' experience as a pilot and 19,663 hours – that's ten years – sitting in the cockpit, clearly personifies the concept of metis.

Extraordinary acts like landing USAir Flight 1549 are credited to experience, luck, God-given skill, or divine intervention. All of those may be part of the answer. However, these explanations do not provide any foundational knowledge on which to build. They ignore the vast, extraordinary, and wildly complex collection of human capabilities which enable a master to gain and use metis.

Although pilots have an apprentice–master culture of ongoing training, many emerging "creative" careers and technology jobs do not. Also, as Sully clearly explains in his book, because of displacement, pilots in particular feel marginalized and undervalued. In Sully's words, "We've been through pay cuts, givebacks, downsizing, layoffs. We're the working wounded."[14] This hardly seems appropriate. By contrast, it would make more sense to learn from the knowledge and metis of these masters, and help them transfer it to their successors.

It is the intention of this book and of my work to shine a bright light on the value and importance of metis – which is far more than just algorithms and knowledge management – and to suggest a framework for transferring it between the generations.

Metis includes knowledge and skill, but also a way of relating to the work we do, and to the people with whom we work. It is a way of being that is forged in the craftsman culture.

At present, just as Captain Sullenberger handed the airplane to his junior officer, Skiles, as the plane took off, the baby boomers are now handing over control of the corporations, institutions, and governments to the next generations.

Are we doing a good job helping them transition from apprentices or journeymen to masters?

Enjoying their new promotions, do the younger workers recognize when they still need help? Note how in a crisis Sullenberger's superior experience and training – his metis – saved the lives of the passengers and crew of Flight 1549. Second-in-command Skiles, with his own extensive training and experience, did not dream of opposing his captain when Sully took control of the flight back from Skiles with the familiar words, "My aircraft."

LIFT

This book focuses on a few simple ideas, the chief one being that we are not merely observers or caretakers of nature. From our humble beginnings, we too are of nature.

At some point in the past few decades, it became clear that many of our "new" and brilliant ideas, were in fact modeled from Mother Nature. "[S]olar cells copied from leaves, steely fibers woven spider-style, shatterproof ceramics drawn from mother of pearl...,"[15] and on it goes. Biomimicry is a relatively new branch (forgive the pun) of natural science, which is inspired by and learns from nature, her designs, processes, and systems. "[It] introduces an era based not on what we can extract from nature, but on what we can learn from her."[16]

Essentially, we can use nature as a template and a teacher. Biomimicry and science in general strive to understand how nature – Mother Nature as well as human nature – works. As we'll see throughout this book, lift is a familiar and early example of a force of nature that humans modeled, to learn from Mother Nature's genius.

In this book on coaching I make the case that we can learn and coach naturally and effectively by examining and understanding our own human nature. Perhaps in this way LIFT is aligned with Socrates's claim:

"The unexamined life is not worth living."

THE CRAFTSMAN CULTURE

The near-catastrophe that was USAir Flight 1549 demonstrates another idea central to this book. We can assume that
artificial intelligence technology will continue to march forward,
performing more and more of the routine operations in our society,
and displacing highly skilled humans into more supervisory roles.
But as Sully elegantly demonstrated in those 195 seconds over the
Hudson, these supervisory roles will require extraordinary human
performance and skill – the work of a master – to get us out of the
highly complex situations that newer technology will get us into.

This idea of the craftsman culture returns to a focus on understanding a few foundational principles and how they will help you
improve and do good work – working to improve on your strengths,
and then to master your skills and competencies, before jumping
to leadership. Leadership without an apprenticeship, and without
a mastery of the quality of the work itself, results in dis-ease and
anxiety.

Enormous personal and social benefits can flow from a structured
career path using the apprentice-to-master model of development.

In addition, the craftsman model includes the ongoing training
and development of the next generations of managers and leaders
– especially significant in light of impending demographic trends.

METAPHOR

We communicate by relying on simple metaphors. It may be
obvious, but these metaphors are based on our understanding of
actual behavior[17] within our natural physical world.

If these principles are misunderstood and if our language mis-
uses the metaphors, the results are unpredictable and most often do
not produce the desired outcomes.

For example, for many years we used a foundational concept
that our brains were like hardwired and fixed computer files. This

old, mechanistic metaphor explained that what went into memory was stored intact in a particular part of the brain, just waiting to be retrieved upon command. Our misunderstanding of the human brain and memory system has led to years of frustrations, discouragement, failure, and even injustice.

In this book, we intend to provide some new key principles, and four core practices of the Expert Coach. These practices will enable you, as a coach, to think through problems, and understand both why they happened, and how you can improve the situation, in ways a hack or an app cannot.

The Crisis in Personal Well-Being

LIFT includes an array of concepts around personal well-being at work and the transfer of knowledge, skill, and metis through coaching and skills development. The chief assertion is this: Our current models and processes of self-help and our single concentration on leadership coaching are objectively failing. Even more disconcerting and ironic are the data demonstrating that the people most negatively impacted are those who have the most to offer, with their decades of experience, skill, and metis.

I say this based on two objective measures of personal well-being: (1) The dismal and essentially unchanging data on employee engagement and leadership effectiveness in business,[18] and (2) our mental condition based on current levels of depression, anxiety, and even suicide rates.

This book applies to us as individuals and as members of companies and organizations: Our current methods of self-help, coaching, and training are insufficient to keep up with the technology we have developed, not to mention the next generations of technology.

As the menu-driven controls of dumbed-down machines like ATMs are encroaching into more of our lives, we are concurrently moving away from the physical and mental aspects of learning and mastering. In doing so, we are not accessing the extraordinary capabilities and potential we have developed as humans. The tail is wagging the dog.

As a mechanical engineer, I've been trained to understand and rely on a few basic principles and laws of physical science in nature, along with the associated mechanical models and metaphors. Fortunately, some widely appreciated psychologists and authors, including Daniel Kahneman (*Thinking Fast and Slow*), Timothy Wilson (*Strangers to Ourselves*), A. David Redish (*The Mind Inside Your Brain*), and Matthew D. Lieberman (*Social*) use scientifically accurate and consistent mechanical models and metaphors to describe their ideas. Their research and writing apply nicely to the way we behave and learn at work, and will be explored throughout this book.

WHY NOW?

As we work with and even in (as in the case of an aircraft) robotics and computer-aided machines, artificial intelligence and knowledge management are becoming more and more intertwined with our lives. From money managers to medical professionals, warehouse workers to widget makers, our working people now and in the future must interact with information, smart machines, and technology.

A study of Flight 1549 makes it clear: Five seasoned, skilled, and well-trained human beings working together with (and without) the most advanced commercially available technology at that time, up against the harshest forces on the planet, performed far better than any machine or group of machines could have, in the same scenario.

It is the intent of this book to do more than merely bring an awareness to the value and importance of metis. One key intention is to offer a way to get outside of our own heads and to manage and reclaim our own attention – not allowing it to be hijacked by powerful online agents – so we invest it in the clear understanding of the precious few foundational principles at the heart of all behavior.

Also, by marshalling our attention and working to improve our unique individual strengths and the quality of the work itself, we can simplify the way we experience the daily firehose of information.

Admittedly, merely suggesting that something must be done to change the current path and buck these current trends is too simplistic and naïve, especially considering the power and momentum of the largest and wealthiest technology companies, driving us each day to rely even more on their immediate access to information and social interconnections which they mine for their enrichment.

So rather than make a feckless plea that we abandon the status quo of coaching, this book simply offers an additional way of coaching which may, over time, help to make meaningful change.

As for our fraught relationship to technology, perhaps psychologist Richard Sennett provides a valuable observation. In his book, *The Craftsman*, he explains, "Technology often creates or invents tools which cannot be or are not used properly for years and even decades."[19] For example, European knife technology in the sixteenth century was not used to its full potential for nearly a century.[20] Similarly, perhaps, we have just begun to learn how to work with artificial intelligence and robotic technology, and will in time develop more effective ways.

Meanwhile, understanding your way forward as an apprentice or an Expert Coach amid the rapid and dramatic changes of today can seem overwhelming and confounding. Perhaps the very best advice comes from someone with an extraordinary grasp of the basic physical principles of the world in which we live. American physicist Richard Feynman said:

Fall in love with some activity, and do it!

> Nobody ever figures out what life is all about, and it doesn't matter.
>
> Explore the world. Nearly everything is really interesting if you go into it deeply enough.
>
> Don't think about what you want to be, but what you want to do.
>
> —Richard Feynman[21]

LIFT is a product of my working life: three decades of observation and research as an entrepreneur, business executive, and business coach.

Put simply, the metis of the Captain Sullys of our world is not only valuable to our coworkers and customers, but also to the fabric of all our families, communities, and organizations.

On an individual level, this is a practical book offering some of the more important research in behavior and effectiveness, in order to demonstrate how it can be applied in coaching and managing. It's not about getting off the grid or rejecting technology. In LIFT, we look deeper into the digital version of craftsmanship and coaching while learning to work with some of the basic foundational principles. We examine the metis that each of us develops, and the degree to which it influences – and can influence – others.

This book is based on the premise that perhaps the most important and valuable knowledge gained in your life, and specifically life at work, cannot be done in isolation, interacting only with a screen. This knowledge can't be "learned" or coached by studying general abstract linguistic distinctions, videos, or even virtual reality simulators. This metis can only be learned and developed – consciously and unconsciously – by "doing," by applying our minds and bodies to the task in an apprentice–journeyman–master model.

While only a few basic foundational principles and laws are required for most of the things we do every day, we do need a clear and accurate understanding of these principles. It is when we understand and work with nature's laws that we are able to build and accomplish amazing things. Trying to dominate and control nature has proven insufficient, to say the least.

This book is designed to start the metaphoric flywheel that Jim Collins writes about in *Good to Great*, creating a push from which to develop momentum toward a twenty-first century craftsmanship mindset and culture. LIFT does, however, rely on a shared understanding of the basic concepts and principles of nature – be that human nature or Mother Nature – which are critical to your business or craft and to your own well-being. Join me as we explore the ways to make lift happen.

Bruce R. Dorey
Charlottesville, VA
18 September 2018

INTRODUCTION

Two men in suits are delivering a load of consulting-speak to a frowning, white-haired CEO behind the desk:

"We think you need to integrate your global supply chain – move assembly overseas and accelerate inventory velocity. ..."

The camera tightens on the CEO. He draws a deep breath. First his eyes soften, and then his entire face brightens into a broad smile as he says, "Great! Go do it."

The consultants look confused and then exchange vexed glances. One of them speaks up:

"We don't actually DO what we propose. ... We just ... propose it."

This 30-second UPS television commercial concludes as the two men walk through an unimpressive office building lobby toward the camera; one of them, with a look of disdain, talks into the cell phone tucked under his chin, "Can you believe that guy?!"

The other consultant is too busy inserting an earbud to acknowledge his colleague's indignant comment.

A voiceover then explains that UPS will actually do something, and goes on to give details.

What makes this commercial funny, even a decade after it originally aired, is what makes any good joke funny. It's the "kick in the discovery,"[1] when our thinking is suddenly turned around. As the commercial opens, we begin with a familiar story, starring the "grumpy old boss." The arc of the story is not moving in a good direction for our consultants. Then the story makes a U-turn when the grumpy old boss turns out to be a good guy and gives them what they presumably want.

We know that business consultants are hired to provide a service their clients are unable to perform in-house. But when the consultants come out and acknowledge that "we don't actually do..." we catch ourselves, and realize we've tacitly accepted this idea that "not doing something" has become a legitimate offering – another big U-turn.

This ad captures the idea that doing something – physically doing something to improve the quality and effectiveness of your work – is the old way, and the hard way, to accomplish and succeed. The consultants are offering something else – something for nothing. That, too, seems to be part of our nature.

The urge for instant gratification – a hyper-efficiency at the extreme – is all about getting something for nothing. We see it in our fables like the goose that lays the golden eggs or the genie who rises from the bottle to grant your wish. Unlike the CEO in the commercial, we want to believe that if you're really sharp, enlightened, and you "get it" – you just have to transform the way you think, change your mental models, shift your mindset, adopt a new way of standing, or add distinctions to your vocabulary. Something for nothing, seen this way, is the efficient route to success.

We want to believe that one day, someday, we'll find such a magical solution. This kind of transformation may feel modern, but it relies on a very old metaphor, one we've used for centuries. Even the cleverest among us, Sir Isaac Newton, was no match for the promise of this metaphor.

Back in the seventeenth century, after he'd dispatched the three laws of motion, redefined gravity, and co-invented calculus, which proved the aforementioned laws,[2] all in his twenties, Newton spent much of the rest of his life trying to transform lead[3] into gold. In Newton's day, alchemy relied on a belief in this magical *transformation* metaphor, and because the science explaining how Mother Nature's systems work together was not yet understood, Newton got nowhere.

Throughout LIFT, we'll be looking at what transformation really is and what it is not. It's useful to note that the metaphor of transformation explains both what will happen and how it will happen. For example, when liquid water becomes water vapor, we say it has gone through a transformation. That's *what* happened. Then, self-referentially, to explain *how* it happened, we use the same verb: the liquid was transformed to a gas. What we sometimes forget is the foundational science that underlies the possibility of such a change, and the enormous amount of energy that is required to produce that profound change. Try as he might, Sir Isaac Newton couldn't transform lead into gold – regardless of his motivation, his "why," or his "possibility." Even with a lot of time and energy, he could not do it because the foundational science wasn't there.

And, although it looks quick and simple to us, it took Mother Nature a lot of energy to transform the caterpillar into a butterfly, over eons of evolution. In short, nature's rules of transformation must be followed.

We *know* there is a natural balance, and that you can't get something for nothing. We know that our results are based on what we're willing to do, the work we put in. The UPS commercial, with its well-placed blow to the funny bone, reveals a deeply held belief or something we just seem to "know." Yet men and women lie, cheat, and steal regularly when they are under the influence of the powerful urge to attain something for nothing.

At the same time, when we are not in the grips of that urge, most people share a sense of existential fairness, or balance; the idea that getting something for nothing is neither just, nor right. For example, when someone else tries to get something for nothing by cutting in front of us in a long line or queue, or shortchanges us in a trade, they'll probably elicit from us a fast, almost primal, emotional response.

In this book, we look at the degree to which the urge for getting something for nothing has leached into coaching and managing, and we offer a new way, the Craft of Expert Coaching. While it is new in the context of the twenty-first century, it returns us to a way of working which naturally evolved over generations: the craftsman culture. Over time, a focus on craftsmanship, and on *doing*, has slowly been eased out, and not solely because of technology. It is also the result of the magic of metaphors and good stories. In this book, we look at how we can reintegrate the best of the past with the brightest new findings and research.

LIFT is dedicated to the huge cohort of baby boomers and gen-Xers now staring at the uncertain horizon of their future. They, like Captain Sullenberger and the masters of earlier generations, will be transferring the control, not just of an aircraft, but of our industries, governments, and institutions to the next generations. Like Sully, they have extraordinary knowledge and skill – metis – gained from their 10,000 plus hours.

If you are a baby boomer, you may have become the master craftsman in your field. You will recognize in your own work the places where the key elements from the familiar craftsman model can support you. The LIFT model offered is not some fictional utopia of a craftsman's workshop; instead, it's practical, designed to save time and anguish. We're not inventing a new context or creating a new reality, and we're not asking people to develop new habits – if any of that is even possible in our fast-paced world with our equally fast automated responses.

This book is about *doing*: coaching and managing, and doing so in harmony with nature.

Lift is a central metaphor in this book, because it is one of nature's most powerful and useful forces. The basic principles of lift have been known for thousands of years, and have been used to move sailboats and turn windmills.

Lift is a unique metaphor because it models an emergent or resultant force. In fluid dynamics (a branch of the physics of flight), lift is the result of the wing moving through the air. But lift does not exist in a stationary wing, nor does it exist in a specific location in the air – it emerges only when a wing moves through the air, where the wing and the air meet.

While calculations of aerodynamic lift can be complex, a deep understanding of Mother Nature's fundamental systems, and a few of her laws, are all that are required to use lift effectively.

As Doug McLean explains,[4] essentially lift is the result of three key forces, all of which need to be present. Understanding lift requires an understanding of Sir Isaac Newton's second *and* third laws, as well as of the fundamental concept of a field.

When you stick your arm out the window of a car at high speed, you understand the first of these forces; you turn your hand up and down and feel the shifting force. Like your hand, a wing directs the air downward, and just as Newton said in his third law, for every force (or action) there is an equal and opposite force or reaction. So, part of the lift comes from this reaction.

Most of us understand the concept of a field, which is the area around an object, like a magnetic field or the field that surrounds a cell phone tower. The other two forces that influence lift are the result of the velocity fields and pressure fields above and below the wing. These two fields support each other in a reciprocal cause-and-effect relationship, an interaction in accordance with Newton's second law of motion.[5]

To create lift, all three elements need to work together; one or two will not do it.

Similarly, lift is also part of the reason an airplane propeller works; the propeller blade acts like a lifting airplane wing as it pulls or lifts the plane forward.[6]

The field metaphor is very useful in physics and, as we'll see, in human behavior as well. I build the case that much of our experience and behavior is a result of what is going on around us in the fields that surround us as we live and work, whether we know it or not.

Many of the key abstractions which we use in coaching and managing, like leadership, collaboration, and alignment, are also resultant. Just as lift results or emerges from doing something – the interaction of wing with air currents, velocity fields, and pressure fields – similarly, leadership, collaboration, and alignment result from doing something. We interact with the "fields" around us. The key abstractions don't magically appear simply because we have language for them or an understanding of them.

This book is meant to be practical, not theoretical. We reclaim the art and craft of understanding and doing good work, and through practice and expertise, gain a sense of pride and meaning. The focus is on learning the things you naturally do well and then working hard on your unique contribution, letting yourself shine.

It is our light, not our darkness that frightens us... and as we let our own light shine, we unconsciously give others permission to do the same. As we are liberated from our own fear, our presence automatically liberates others.[7]

—Marianne Williamson

We will identify four practices of the Craft of Expert Coaching which operate in alignment with our human nature and in harmony with Mother Nature.

We consider the value of a community with Expert Coaches who are there to help you master your work, and to lift you up when you are down.

LIFT's basic ideas are consistent with positive psychology in that they address aspects of improving performance, helping to engender an objective and scientifically sound concept of inner work life.[8]

The Craft of Expert Coaching deals with the small issues every day before they become big issues. Through examining the influences inside their heads and in their surroundings, the Craft of Expert Coaching uses existing, proven methodologies to help give people the lift they may need.

Magical Thinking & the Transformation Metaphor

We are becoming habituated to fake news, alternate realities, and "truthiness."[9] A recent cover story in The Atlantic, "BELIEVE, Conspiracy Theories, Fake News, Magical Thinking. How America Went Haywire,"[10] addresses questions on the minds of many in America and around the world. Author Kurt Andersen explains that, since the 60s, "Americans have had a new rule written into their mental operating system: *Do your own thing, find your own reality, it's all relative...* . We Americans have given ourselves over to all kinds of magical thinking, ...all of us free to reinvent ourselves by imagination and will. ... [T]hose more exciting parts of the Enlightenment idea have swamped the sober, rational, empirical parts."[11]

This same phenomenon occurs in business coaching and consulting today. I make the case that it is found in the metaphor of "transformation," a word granted magical powers in the 60s and 70s.

By definition, if something has transformed, there will have been an objective change in the form, structure, appearance, or character.[12] In the physical sciences, we understand the "how to" process of transformation. The transformation of liquid water to gas (water vapor) for example, requires an increase in temperature.[13] The "how to" is clearly and objectively understood. In fact, it is common knowledge even for young children.

But in the larger world outside physics, we believe that *somehow* things will be, well, better – after the transformation. Similarly, in the case of a business transformation, *somehow* there will have been a dramatic improvement in business results.

Transformation as a business or coaching strategy is a seductive "catch-all" phrase, and in some cases the younger sibling of a miracle. It's an impressive-sounding word, but one which few people understand or apply in the same way, and it has been let in the front door by some very clever consultants, coaches, and self-taught gurus. They begin their mischief by delivering an impressive performance amid claims of great "transformational" success (often with anecdotal stories like the four-minute mile but little objective proof). Like the famous Vegas illusionists Penn and Teller, they perform convincingly, and their illusions appear to make something "magically appear" in the controlled environment of a seminar or board room. However, that new car, or those sustained breakthrough results, will not magically appear from behind the curtain on an assembly line.

"I THINK YOU SHOULD BE MORE EXPLICIT HERE IN STEP TWO."

Figure I-1 Artist: Sidney Harris. Reproduced with permission of ScienceCartoonsPlus.com

In fact, Penn and Teller are very good at what they *do*. They are masters of their craft – and they will tell you the only way to do what they do is by dint of deliberate practice[14] and hard work. They, more than most, don't believe in magic, or in something for nothing.

When you can do something well, you are able to do it, as Sully did, even during highly stressful situations. You will not be stricken with panic or anxiety; you can focus, and become immersed in what you are doing, in the moment.

The quality of practice and repetition of a person learning their craft or trade is not the same as the kind of repetition criticized in the well-known quip, "Doing the same thing over and over and expecting a different result is the definition of insanity." Some coaches and consultants hang their hats on this quotation, which has been attributed to Albert Einstein, Ben Franklin, and Mark Twain.[15] While it may be accurate in certain situations, it's not the whole story. We can't simply ignore the value of technique and skill, and the lessons learned through dedication and commitment. Repeated effort is essential on the path to mastery, whether that is rolling out a new QA program or presenting a new idea.

A true transformation is possible if the underlying knowledge is present. So, because we have the knowledge of the atomic structure of the water molecule, we can reliably reproduce the transformation from liquid to vapor and back again. As the old saying goes, "Once you know how, it's easy." Writing becomes easy when we do the work to learn the foundational principles of the language, including all 26 letters of the alphabet. If we only know a few letters, however, we will struggle.

Perhaps the most common response to the question, "How're you doing?" is "BUSY." The data support this, as we are working more hours per week, and far more of them outside of the office.[16] However, in the context of craftsmanship, people with little skill and experience who are trying to do a good job often look and are very busy, flustered, and anxious, even harried. They make their job look very difficult. By comparison, someone who is good at their job, (and has the results to prove it), makes it look easy. I have found this to be true in almost all aspects of activity.

One of the inherent advantages of the craftsman culture is the certainty of the path forward. While it is unlikely you will work for just one company in your life, you can still focus on building your career, not just taking the best paycheck. By focusing on what you do well, the daily process of making progress and improving your skills is in and of itself rewarding. In skill development, we appreciate this familiar path of learning: moving from a beginner to a C player, then to a B player, an A player, and on to becoming a master.

An important part of this process of learning and improving is working with experts or masters, because there seem to be no substitutes for personal connection and coaching. When someone is reaching out for a helping hand, or offering one, an important by-product of the exchange is the lift of spirits that emerges from the connection, for both participants.

The Path Ahead

Performance and behavior research in the past few decades reveal spectacular new models and processes which are highly relevant to coaching and managing. Simply stated, we've learned that we process information and make decisions using two different ways of thinking: an automated fast way of thinking and a more deliberative slow way. This research upends many long-held beliefs, and their associated metaphors and methods, in coaching and managing. It may also explain why "leadership" in America gets such poor survey results,[17] and why, for decades, employees have been disconnected and disengaged from their jobs.

In Part One of LIFT, we look at the origins of business coaching, and at its so-called technology which was borrowed from real psychology and simplified for public seminars. We also examine the seductive nature and power of a good story, and how many of these good stories rely on flawed metaphors and magical thinking.

Because coaching has developed outside of the rigorous evaluation process found in academics and science, a number of practices, which are essentially hoaxes or myths, still exert great influence. In fact, many training textbooks for new coaches and managers recite these same myths, and have done so for decades. We examine one such myth, the four-minute mile, and use it to reveal how our innate biases have led us off track.

However, other research has validated some early practices from the craftsman culture, and demonstrates the importance and value of the apprentice-to-master process for the next generation of

managers and leaders. Extraordinary new research into our unconscious minds has revealed some stunning results, of which we as
managers and coaches must be aware. Sully "knew" what to do. He
didn't run the numbers or follow a prescribed algorithm. Over his
almost 20,000 hours in the cockpit, his conscious and his unconscious had been sweeping up information and learning all the time.

We'll provide a high-level view of the workings of the adaptive unconscious, which plays an enormous role in our behavior as
coaches and managers. Here we'll also survey the power of our environment to influence our behavior – and how it relates to coaching
and managing.

In 2005–2006, the book and the movie *The Secret* debuted, and
produced a world-wide phenomenon in "self-help" and coaching.
Coaching got some new tools, and a powerful new metaphor. We'll
shine a light on some of the biggest myths that grew from *The Secret*
– and still influence the coaching field.

Next, we'll begin pulling together some of the concepts introduced earlier. We'll examine metaphors in more detail and see their
invasive influence on our behavior and performance.

We'll then look at Renaissance craftsmen and their similarities
to today's knowledge workers and creatives. The focus on the skill
and quality of "doing" something requires a deep understanding of
one thing, and we see this most clearly with professional athletes,
musicians, and entertainers today, who have spent years and years
honing their skills. These real masters often express their love for
the art, game, or the work they do – and this is not a coincidence.
Mastery brings meaning, and meaning brings self-confidence and
deep satisfaction – a kind of self-lift in spirits and experience.

Another central theme of this book is that the development
of your work as craft is emotionally healthy for you and for the
entire organization. Today people practice crafts, sports, and hob-
bies to combat anxiety and create satisfaction, because they do not
bring a crafts approach to their jobs. I suggest that whether it be

a professional skill, a trade, an art form, or the craft of teaching or managing, the practice as a craft provides an intuitively fulfilling and healthy way to live.

> All craftsmanship is founded on skill developed to a high degree... . As skill progresses, it becomes more problem-attuned...whereas people with primitive levels of skill struggle just to get things to work. At its higher reaches, technique is no longer a mechanical activity; people can feel fully and think deeply about what they are doing, once they do it well.[18]

—Richard Sennett

In Part Two of the book, we'll move into the practical aspects of the Craft of Expert Coaching, and ways to introduce it into your organization or coaching practice. The approach is constructed on the solid foundations of positive psychology and the real world business research and data from, among others, businessman and former psychology Professor Robert Hogan, and his wife Dr. Joan Hogan; Harvard professor Theresa Amabile; the multidecade research and work of Professor Donald O. Clifton, (Clifton StrengthsFinder), and Professor Daniel Goleman's research and data on emotional intelligence.

With this book, I hope to build confidence in, and spur into action, those men and women who have worked hard to become masters in their jobs and careers. You have much to share. With the coming changes in workforce demographics, we will need Expert Coaches to help train the next generation of leaders and managers. I offer LIFT as a guidebook for the journey.

NATURE

PART ONE

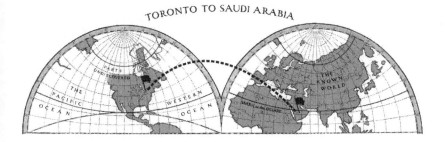

CHAPTER I — NATURE & TRANSFORMATION

I have worked most of my life in a field that relies on the phenomenon of transformation.[1] So, let's begin with a look at this natural wonder – in physics, in business coaching, and even in my own life. We'll be examining the metaphor of transformation throughout this book, and we need to begin with some basic, undisputed science.

In 1982, when I graduated from engineering school, large-scale commercial air conditioning was only about sixty years old. The technology uses a liquid-to-gas transformation to capture and then pump the heat out of large enclosed spaces. Air conditioning permitted the creation of new towns and cities in the now-wealthy regions of the Middle East, which had been previously uninhabitable sunbaked desert.

So, as a newly graduated – and broke – engineer, I was lured to Saudi Arabia by an urge for quick riches, perhaps the same urge that led men and women to the Gold Rush. While it was not as simple as a "something-for-nothing" path, it looked like a shortcut, and I was tempted by the same urge.

I believed that in a few years I could save enough money to distinguish myself from my peers, and ultimately to BE a lone business tycoon, like Jay Gatsby, Blake Carrington, or even Donald Trump. My dream was not what I was going to do but who I was going to BE.

Also, the notion of living in an exotic warm environment, free from office politics, had enormous appeal to a loner like me. Moving to the Middle East from Canada was an ideal solution to accommodate my nature, because at that stage of life I lacked confidence and any sense of who I was.

It wasn't particularly difficult to get a job with a major US air conditioning company in Saudi Arabia, the largest, wealthiest, and fastest growing country in the Middle East. But I was still thrilled when I was hired by The Trane Company. After spending eight months in Athens, working for Trane's Middle Eastern head office while waiting for a visa, I moved to Al Khobar.[2] With a population of about 20,000, it was the largest of three towns, grouped closely together on the Arabian Gulf, near the ARAMCO[3] compound in Dhahran.

We supplied the large-scale air conditioning systems for the new hospitals, desalinization plants, and oil company buildings going up in the Eastern Province. The first few years were grueling and disorienting, but I loved just being part of the process, creating these huge structures rising out of the stark desert.

Early on, I would often drive the beat-up old two-lane oil-paved highway through mostly empty desert from Al Khobar to Al Jubal, and then on to Al Khafji, where much of the new construction was happening.[4] Sometimes I'd need to stop to let a train of camels meander across the road, or negotiate around a newly formed sand drift. But far more frequently, I'd encounter an abandoned white Mercedes, either damaged from a collision with a pack of wild dogs, or simply left on the side of the road, presumably out of gas. Anyone who traveled in the Kingdom during this time saw the strange but frequent occurrence of the abandoned white Mercedes.

Al Khafji was a small, dusty, unaffected town with typical rectangular mud-and-lime adobe structures. Corrugated metal overhead doors opened and closed the small shops lining the modest main street. One lunch excursion was memorable, in a macabre kind of way. I'd stopped at a small café which displayed a large Pepsi sign alongside the images of a chicken and a goat. I had just placed my order for *hares*, a tasty dish of porridge with lamb, when a big white Mercedes skidded to a stop just outside the front door. An older barefoot Bedouin jumped out and flung open the trunk. He leaned in and pulled out a good-sized live sheep, which he escorted and dragged through the middle of the café. Maybe because it all happened so fast, I didn't connect the dots until I heard a couple of gunshots and the high-pitched whine of a small chain-saw. I realized I'd just seen my lunch being ushered in.

As a loner, I'd learned to live in my head, in my own world. Initially, I found I was happiest when I could get lost in these inimitable and diverse cultural experiences. While I longed to be alone, I found that when I was inside my own head I would inevitably cycle through the same arguments and get caught in the same self-fulfilling negative loops. After several years, the novelty of my new surroundings receded and I was restless and truly lonely. The truth was that I envied those friends and colleagues back home who were doing all the things I was delaying, like settling down and starting a family. In fact many of them were building successful careers and making lots of money, in some cases more than I, and were enjoying a healthy life around family and friends. I learned to put up a good front and portray that what I was doing was the better, faster track.

But, sadly, I didn't focus on doing a good job and learning the "nuts and bolts" or the trade-craft of my industry. Like a typical baby boomer, I believed individual leadership and management (rather than doing good work) were the only way to the American dream, so I focused on the management side of the business, working with our Saudi partners and the odd collection of non-Saudis who lived and worked in the Kingdom.

Ironically, in high-level negotiation, I was no match for someone with real "hands-on" experience who clearly understood how a piece of equipment behaved in the harsh Arabian climate. I could be out-negotiated based on their knowledge and real experience of what did and did not work; I thought negotiation was just about the money. Years later, when I returned to the Middle East, I realized I had accumulated a lot of knowledge about how to relate to and work with the wide variety of nationalities who typically worked in the Middle East. More importantly, I learned to trust and hire those who actually did the work in that environment and knew the trade–craft.

The Physics of Transformation

We all have observed that children come to know their native language before they are taught spelling, sentence structure, or verb conjugation. They learn by being exposed to it in their environment. In this way, they get to know their language, without understanding the principles or being able to explain why they use language as they do. Similarly, we come to "know" through our experience that cooling is happening.[5]

Whether you recognize it or not, you experience an actual transformation when you get out of a shower or tub, and feel your skin get cold. You've learned by being part of it, not by thinking abstractly about the principles. This "knowing" occurs with no language, words, or formal training as to the nature of heat transfer.

Let's look a little closer at what happens. The basics are simple: Transformational cooling starts with a heat source, and we know that heat always moves away from the source; it always flows from hot to cold. The water on your skin evaporates when your body heat warms the tiny water droplets, and, like water heated in a kettle, the water turns to vapor. The water on your skin "takes" or draws the heat from your body, and the heat transforms the structure of the water from liquid water to vapor. You feel a chill because the vapor, now floating outside your body, holds the heat energy. This process of evaporation in thermodynamics is a real transformation; it's the underlying science of air conditioning in which a real molecular change happens as the liquid becomes a vapor (also referred to as a gas).

While the mechanism is straightforward conceptually from a physics or chemistry perspective, the applications are pure genius. Your home air conditioner or heat pump uses the same natural process.[6] In a standard home air conditioning system, the hot air (the heat source) is sucked from outdoors and from rooms in your house by a fan inside the air conditioning unit in your basement or attic. This hot air passes over a coil (the thing that looks like a car radiator), and the heat from the hot air travels to the cold liquid refrigerant inside the coil. (Remember, heat always travels from hot to cold).

Next comes nature's elegant phenomenon: the hot liquid refrigerant inside the coil, transforms into a gas, and as it does this it removes A LOT of heat from the hot air (the heat source). The heat is transferred and now held, or stored, in the hot refrigerant gas inside the coil; and the air, now cooled, is blown back into your home. The hot refrigerant gas is then pushed/pumped through a pipe or tube outside your home to your outdoor air conditioning unit, called a condenser. Even when it is 110°F outside, the refrigerant gas is designed to be hotter than the air outside, so that the heat can flow from hot to cold (less hot). You may have noticed that when you stand beside a condenser outside your home, you can feel the heat being pumped out.

After the heat is removed from the refrigerant, the cold refrigerant, now a liquid again, is then pumped back to the indoor air conditioner/cooling coil and the cycle continues.

The process of transformation in air conditioning involves a real physical change in molecular structure, and this change removes an enormous amount of heat relative to the volume of refrigerant, which makes it so elegant and useful. But the key to the entire process is the actual physical change: a liquid transforms into an objectively different form – a gas.

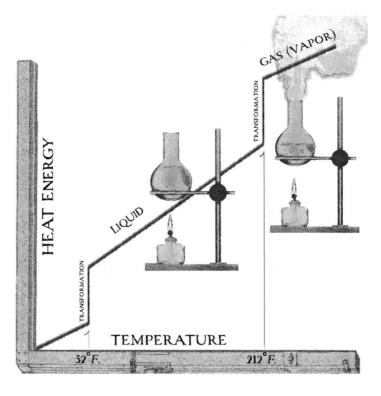

Figure 1.0 The step up from liquid water to gas vapor
at 212°F – a physical transformation

When a liquid is heated (at a constant pressure), it takes in heat at a steady state, which would be demonstrated by a straight line sloping upward, like the straight line in the middle portion of Figure 1.0, between 32°F and 212°F. But a sudden change occurs when the liquid gets to the boiling temperature and changes or transforms into a gas. Right at that point, the amount of heat energy the water takes in jumps, or steps up.

When it steps up, in the change from liquid to vapor, an immense amount of heat is taken in from the heat source.

Air conditioning systems essentially harness this huge removal of heat energy. But it doesn't happen without supplying another kind of energy – and A LOT of it. Electrical energy, typically purchased from the power company, is required to increase and decrease the pressure of the refrigerant gas so that it reaches the right conditions for a physical change.[7] In the real world from which the metaphor of transformation was created, energy – and therefore transformation – is not free, and does not magically happen.

For this reason, commercial air conditioning in warm climates is the most expensive use of energy – definitely not a something-for-nothing situation. It takes far more energy to cool a building than to run all its lights, elevators, doors, and computing systems combined.

The Law of Conservation of Energy

With the discovery of the conservation of energy, the extraordinary interconnectedness and symbiosis of nature began to come into focus for us. We began to understand that as humans we could no longer separate ourselves from our natural environment. Nowadays, even if we don't think of ourselves as scientists or environmentalists, we're seeing more clearly that we're all a part of nature, no longer able to disconnect from it or dominate it.

The psychoanalyst Erich Fromm proposed that we humans are born with biophilia, an innate love of nature, perhaps even a genetic "passionate love of life and of all that is alive."[8] For example, when the audience members at a 2009 TED talk were asked to close their eyes and imagine themselves in a place of beauty and tranquility, they all, to the person, pictured somewhere outdoors in nature.[9]

The law of the conservation of energy inspired a great unification in natural systems, since it proved[10] that all things in our universe, both living and non-living, follow a few essential laws with respect to the flow of heat as energy (thermodynamics).

As mentioned earlier, Sir Isaac Newton in 1687 famously published the three laws of motion and universal gravitation, which even centuries later are still valid and useful.[11] Remarkably, by understanding just these simple laws, we can build and send a machine to the surface of Mars, and we can routinely place a tiny machine inside someone's body to ensure their heart keeps beating.

Although Newton also worked on the laws of conservation of energy, it wasn't until the early 1840s that the German physician and physicist Julius von Mayer offered an original version of the conservation of energy, declaring that "energy can be neither created nor destroyed." Von Mayer's statement is now known as an early version of the first law of thermodynamics.[12]

Even as recently as one hundred and seventy years ago, scientists thought of heat in terms of a hypothetical (imaginary) weightless fluid they called "caloric." Then, in 1843, another German physician, Hermann Ludwig Ferdinand von Helmholtz, wrote a paper called "On the Conservation of Energy."

His research helped us understand that energy was not some magical stuff or "life force" which exists inside of certain living things, as the theory of "vitalism" suggested. Helmholtz instead proposed a general law that applied to energy in both non-living and living systems.

Helmholtz, a brilliant young physician as well as an accomplished mathematician, was also one of the first to attempt to bring together physics and psychology. "His paper was in the language of mathematical physics and the mastery and elegance of the exposition was unexpected in a person without formal training in this area."[13]

CONSERVATION OF ENERGY

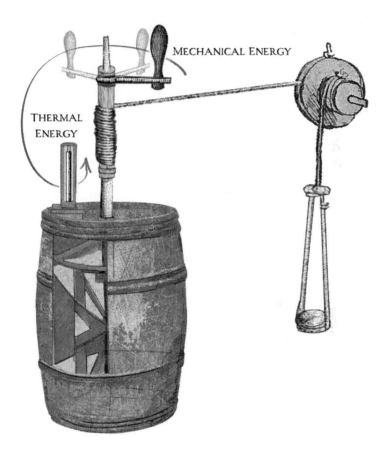

Figure 1.1 Joule apparatus

The point is, Helmholtz did not simply dream up an interesting idea about transformation and energy conservation with an easy to remember metaphor. Instead of a dreamed-up idea, he used existing science to show that energy merely changed from one form to another; instead of a metaphor, he used mathematics to back up his theory. Then a few years later, in the late 1840s, James Prescott Joule, the son of a wealthy English brewer, through experimentation validated the work and mathematics of Helmholtz, and independently discovered the mechanical equivalent of the law of conservation of energy.

Joule devised experiments to demonstrate that the energy from heat and the energy from motion were one and the same.

He built what is now called a "Joule apparatus," in which a descending weight hanging from a string threaded through a pulley is attached to a winding drum that can spin a paddlewheel in a barrel of water.

When the weight descends and the drum turns the paddlewheel, the water in which the paddlewheel is immersed, heats up.

Joule empirically demonstrated that the mechanical energy (human arm energy) required to turn the crank and lift the weight from the ground was equal to the heat energy of the water when the weight dropped back to the ground. He showed that the mechanical energy – the energy required to lift the weight – was conserved, even as it became the heat energy in the water. No energy mysteriously disappeared[14] and no energy magically appeared. It had only changed its form, from mechanical energy to heat energy.[15]

For another illustration of the conservation of energy, we'll consider your home air conditioning system again. When it is running, it uses the electrical energy you purchase from the power company to transfer or pump the heat energy out of your home. That electrical energy will be equal to the amount of heat energy you pumped out of your house, plus the energy used to run the air conditioner.[16] If you did a detailed analysis, you'd see that the law of the conservation of energy is upheld.

This understanding is essential to the basic ideas of LIFT.

Hemholtz and Joule learned that what we call energy is real and measurable, not an odd collection of incongruent ideas and beliefs, impossible to quantify, measure, or predict. Their scientific breakthroughs about the conservation of energy in the 1840s popularized a simpler and more holistic concept of energy. No longer a partly magical force retained only by humans or living spirits, energy had come to be understood as a single, quantifiable concept that follows precise rules.

One of those ideas is that nature and all her intricate and symbiotic systems flow together in a harmonious dance. They do so based on what we have found to be a few inarguable principles; we call them scientific laws.

What is important for our discussion is that, before we understood how nature actually worked, we used a variety of metaphors that called upon spirits and angels, often quoting Biblical scripture; or requiring the existence of bizarre substances like caloric or phlogiston.[17]

In the absence of knowledge, the metaphors completed a logical story – a story that made people feel good.

Transformation Management & Coaching

Not just a term from the study of science, transformation is a commonly used concept in management and leadership coaching, where, however, the term and the metaphor remain largely disconnected, and transformation is randomly used for an infinitely wide range of treatments or changes.

The definition of transformation, as it is often used in coaching, varies from one Large Group Awareness Training (LGAT) weekend seminar to the next. A common theme concerns the possibility, or realm of possibilities, created by and in language – specifically a declarative speech act. In leadership coaching, transformation is attainable only in language and by "sharing" and using certain speech acts to talk about a possibility. In fairness, some LGATs talk about the need for action, in alignment with the possibility. But often, little more is said about what to do after the declaration.

An Amazon search for books on transformational coaching produces about 50,000 books, and a search on business transformation yields 2.5 million books. But in the context of business, what does that word transformation actually mean? In business, what is the difference between transformation and change, or between transformation and re-engineering? When executives say "transformation," what do they *really* mean?

Often, the word confuses three fundamentally different categories of effort. As Scott Anthony explains in a 2016 *Harvard Business Review* article, one common meaning is "doing" something differently – like using the Cloud, or going digital. But when an organization uses new tools to solve the same old problems, while it may improve results in the short term, it is still doing the same thing only faster and maybe cheaper. It's not a transformation. Costs are always projected to be lower and customer satisfaction projected to be higher; but the essence of the company isn't changing in any material way. And, "in a quickly changing world, playing an old game better is simply insufficient."[18]

Similarly, we see a so-called core transformation that is really just doing something in a new or different way. Take Netflix. "Netflix has shifted from sending DVDs through the mail to streaming video content through the Web. It also has shifted from simply distributing other people's content to investing heavily in the creation of its own content, using its substantial knowledge of customer preferences to maximize the chances that content will connect with an audience."[19] Again, same business, same outcomes, and same metrics; just a product-line extension and a different way of acquiring content. Soon, the rest of the pack will imitate these steps and find new ways to improve and compete.

The third common definition of transformation is the strategic transformation where the essence of the company objectively changes, like Apple moving from a computer manufacturer to an entertainment provider, or Google moving from search engine to designer of driverless car technology.

But are any of these real transformations? The changes outlined above fall into several well-known categories of business strategy, and are addressed by Michael Porter's competitive forces, which have been around for decades.[20] Upon closer examination, most so-called transformations are just changes, often simply in technology or business process.

Figure 1.2 Artist: Tom Fishburne.
Reproduced with permission of Marketoonist.com

In the Craft of Expert Coaching, we acknowledge the value of declarative language, but we also build the case that there is far more to mastery and leadership than transformational language. No expert professional in almost anything would accept the notion that you can "get it," or master your profession, through linguistic distinctions alone. While in some cases the process may begin with a declarative statement, becoming an expert or a master requires much more.

In the context of Expert Coaching, the expert or master authentically and naturally develops and earns mastery through observing and doing, over time. In other words, what is distinct about the Craft of Expert Coaching is that, to become an expert and achieve higher levels of performance, you will need to learn to DO and then to practice with a purpose.

When we use the word "transformation" as a metaphor, we imply that the target of the metaphor will react and behave in the same way as the transformation in nature from which the metaphor developed. We know that when liquid water transforms to a gas, it changes its physical structure and physical properties.[21] Before the transformation, there is liquid water, and after, there is simply no liquid water – the liquid water hasn't changed; it has transformed into something else. We can also prove that a transformation has taken place using objective scientific measurements. In short, there's no mystery or magic in the underlying physical science of the transformation.

With the transformation metaphor, however, especially as it's applied in business management and coaching, we have a lot less science and a lot more mystery and magic. Again, I am not comparing humans to machines, or to natural phenomena; I am saying the word transformation is a metaphor, based on naturally occurring phenomena and processes.

Using the transformation metaphor inaccurately is like using any other metaphorical concept inaccurately.

Let's say you hire a delivery company that claims to "fly" around the country delivering your packages, only to find out they use trucks and do not actually leave the ground. Then what? What would your reaction be?

When you challenge them, they innocently explain they simply use flying as a metaphor. They claim that because of their unique perspective and ability to break through limiting beliefs, they deliver very fast.

But, you contend, flying is flying, and it implies an entirely different way of travel, with far different results.

While their service might be faster in special circumstances, like short distances around congested cities and airports, flying a package from New York to Seattle will be faster than "flying" in a truck.

You may think you don't use metaphors, that you're not "right-brained" or "visual," and that you don't think "that way;" however as we'll see later in more detail, we all use metaphors – all the time. In fact, we cannot help but use them.[22]

One of the key ideas offered in LIFT is that when we use metaphors, we need to understand the underlying actual physical principles, as well. This way, we can transfer the metaphorical concepts effectively. Things get cloudy, though, when we discuss the confluence of physics and philosophy, even using simple metaphors.[23]

The field of coaching was heavily influenced by the popular human potential movement started in the 1960s and 70s, and revived a quarter century later by the hugely successful movie and book, *The Secret*. In the next chapter, we'll look in some depth at the evolution of coaching in the face of these influences.

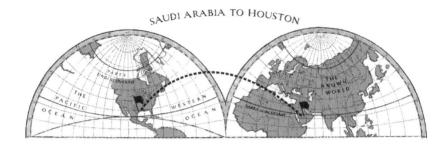

CHAPTER 2 — THE NATURE OF RETAIL TRANSFORMATION

I had a master plan. First, I would earn enough money in Saudi to pay off my student debt; then I was going to start a real estate investment company, as my first step on the road to becoming someone who mattered – someone rich. While I didn't have a lot of free time in Saudi, the time off I did take in the evenings was devoted to studying real estate investing, searching for the perfect place to build my empire, and dreaming of the company and life I would build. Houston, Texas was the city I chose, hoping to take advantage of bargain apartment properties that had been foreclosed upon after the Savings and Loans disaster of the 1980s. I had no family or even friends in Houston, nor had I ever been there.

After eight months in Athens and nearly six years in Saudi, with some cash in the bank, I moved to Houston.

Following the advice of the how-to books I'd been reading, within the first five years, I'd bought eight small, beat-up apartment buildings "inside the loop" near Houston's Museum District and Medical Center, neighborhoods that I thought were undervalued.

My nest egg had grown to over a million dollars, but I was becoming increasingly disenchanted with the day-to-day hard work necessary to run and build the business. I was getting impatient and I thought my goal was to BE the wealthy successful guy.

An old friend from school called me out of the blue and essentially told me to take this amazing self-help seminar called "The Forum." The Forum was the central seminar offered by Werner Erhard's company, at the time called Erhard Seminar Training. The Forum was the next generation of "*est*," a pop psychology phenomenon from the 1970s that gained popularity when Hollywood celebrities like John Denver, Diana Ross, and Valerie Harper publicly endorsed it.[1]

The word "transformation" was associated with Erhard Seminar Training, which became the most successful Large Group Awareness Training (LGAT) in the USA. In the 1980s, when I came across Erhard's organization, they were transitioning to new ownership, amid reports on *60 Minutes* alleging some pretty nasty stuff. Frankly, I didn't see the *60 Minutes* program, and was somewhat oblivious to the accusations against the founder, Werner Erhard. I assumed, with a name like "Werner" he was a German philosopher–guru. I was young and ambitious and wanted fast results. My friend had just taken the Forum in the Northeast, claiming he was immediately "transformed." A low-key engineer, he was so uncharacteristically insistent about this that I became interested – and a little suspicious. But, hey, I was in luck: there was a "special guest seminar" the next Tuesday at the Houston Galleria Marriott.

About two hundred and fifty well-dressed men and women sat in theater-style seating in a ballroom at the hotel. The atmosphere before the presentation was light, breezy, and excited. Loud bursts of laugher sporadically erupted and there seemed to be a lot of hugging.

But the important part of the experience for me that evening was the attractive twenty-something woman in charge of "enrollment" or sales. She was gorgeous, outgoing, and friendly to me; I was smitten.

That night, called the "Evening Session," was held on the Tuesday after a weekend-long Forum seminar. The person who invited me, my friend in the Northeast, was playing the "guest game," he later told me. And I was his long-distance guest.

At 7:00 p.m. sharp, a well-dressed man confidently strutted on stage, to what approached a standing ovation. He was gracious and well spoken, but used and repeated several unfamiliar phrases, like "declaring a future," "standing for a possibility," and "running a racket." I thought it might be Erhard himself, but it was not. What snared me early in his presentation was the claim that we were all simply focusing on the wrong thing. He confidently told us we had studied only prescriptive methods: those how-to books, and recordings like the ubiquitous Tony Robbins 30-Day programs that focused mainly on action steps.

Instead, our hosts claimed that night, success at whatever it is you want to pursue would not be attained by doing more of what you are doing now.

To live life fully and get what you want, the Forum speaker told us, a transformation is required. You transform who you are "being" relative to the issue, not what you are doing. The seminar leader referenced ontology, explaining they were engaged in an ontological transformation. I didn't understand at the time, but it sounded impressive. It also was the first time I was called a "human doing," since I was only focused on doing, while, according to our hosts, success and accomplishment came from humans who were focused on being. It sounded logical. ...

It became clear, after the session started, that this was no ordinary free seminar. This was slick; it was a good performance. The session began with members of the crowd "sharing." Many of them talked about getting "it." The "it" they were talking about was apparently transformation, or enlightenment. This "it" wasn't a change or improvement, but a new way of thinking, or more accurately a new way of being. It would, they claimed, naturally create a new and better way of behaving, resulting in a "life that you love." Forget busting my ass in Houston's 90 degree heat doing the work! I liked this new way of thinking; it teased my urge for getting something for nothing.

I later understood more about ontology, and learned that it did in fact come from German-speaking philosophers: Martin Heidegger (German, 1889–1976) and Ludwig Wittgenstein (Austrian, 1889–1951). Also, in the context of coaching, a philosopher and biologist from Chile, Humberto Maturana (1928–) was instrumental in forming the concepts of biological existence and "being." But the framework for the ontological philosophy can be traced to Chilean Fernando Flores (1943–).[2] Flores completed his PhD at Berkley, under John Searle, whose work will be discussed in more detail in a subsequent chapter. Flores is considered the originator of the Ontological Coaching approach.[3]

In the mid-1970s, Werner Erhard (born John Paul "Jack" Rosenberg in Philadelphia) integrated Flores's work into the *est* training and later created the Forum.[4] Flores originally developed those odd phrases used in the Forum like "declare yourself as a possibility," and have "conversations for action."[5]

The Guest Game

What I didn't know at the time was that to complete the Forum seminar and really get "it," participants had been challenged to share what they got from the seminar – or share what they heard from others – and invite a guest to this evening session like the one I was attending. At the event, it was critical that you "authentically" share something personal, demonstrating your vulnerability in such a way that the person you invited was moved and inspired to register and make their down payment on the spot. If you brought a guest, and they registered, then clearly you got it, if not, well...no one really talked about that. As I came to learn, these guest events were, from the perspective of Erhard's organization, the lifeblood of the company. Each volunteer and employee was on a serious mission to register as many guests as possible that night.

Thirty minutes into the evening session, about twenty of us guests were separated from the main seminar and ushered into a smaller room. A trained volunteer was there "to answer any questions we have about the seminar." It sounded like an informal Q & A.

This room was a smaller version of the seminar room – same director's chair in the front, same tables and brochures. It looked like the people who set up the room had OCD; the pens were perfectly spaced and lined up in a chevron design, just like the main seminar room.

As the session started in the smaller room, it was clear this wasn't going to be an informal Q & A. This, too, was a performance. The leader, a well-dressed and well-spoken young man about my age, set up the discussion in a professional and clear way. He let us know several times there would be an opportunity to register if we chose to do so. He made a point of saying that tonight we would have a choice about our futures.

What I didn't know was the person leading the session was selected to speak that evening based on his most recent results in other similar guest sessions. "Results" meant only one thing: sales ... period. Sales or "registration" statistics were fastidiously tracked and a source of pride and stature at the Werner Erhard and Associates offices referred to as "the Center." Also in the room with my group were men and women assistants trained in "enrollment" whose results were good, just not as good as our leader's. Before the seminar, they had met as a team, and aligned on a registration goal for the evening and made a registration promise to the staff. Each volunteer team member had also made a promise as to the number of registrations they would personally obtain, and were allocated

guests accordingly. Attaining this goal was by far the most important result for the evening.

At the onset of the small group session, we were asked to think
of something we really wanted to accomplish, but were currently
struggling to achieve. Saving money, losing weight, or getting a new
job and making more money were the topics, off-handedly offered.

The performance was fast-paced and well rehearsed with no
room for questions or deviation, (questions would be addressed
one-on-one at the end of the performance). It delivered a series
of simple insights and metaphors which were impressive and difficult to refute. When it ended, as with any good performance, the
audience members sat there, wanting more. Our attention had been
masterfully captured.

It began simply enough. Our speaker drew a circle, or pie chart,
on the whiteboard. One small slice was allocated to all the things
that you know, and that you know that you know. A second small
slice was defined as all the things that you know you don't know,
like a foreign language. This left the final, largest slice of the pie,
which was all the knowledge that you don't know, but don't know
that you don't know. The bottom line was made abundantly clear.
It's what you don't know that you don't know that stands between
you and your goals, not your skill level, grit, or deliberate practice. I
assumed this was an original concept, since there was no acknowl-
edgment of any source material; but it was another borrowed concept, a simplified version of the competence model developed by
psychologist Thomas Gordon in the 1960s.[6]

We were paired up with people who looked like fellow guests.
My partner was an eighteen-year-old who listened to my goals, and
told me, "It's really not your fault, but you are working on the wrong
thing, you're just doing." His cool confidence and misdirection
paralyzed me as he calmly explained. "Now, if you really want to
accomplish your dream goal, you have to discover what's in the way,
or what's stopping you." He went on to say that what was stopping

me was something I didn't know, and didn't even know that I didn't know...and that taking their seminar was the only way to determine for myself what stood in my way. He calmly asked, "So are you ready to register – to actually start to move toward the dream?"

After a little hesitation trying to sort out what had just been proposed – and as I saw others standing up and walking to the registration table – I said "Yes." My partner quickly rose, and invited me to join him as he walked to the table.

I later discovered I was on the receiving end of the most effective objection-killer sales closing technique I'd ever experienced. If executed right, in the right environment there is almost no way out. This slick and fast closing technique was part of the "leader trainee program" (in which I later participated) and was a tightly scripted algorithm which the volunteer trainees drilled and practiced weekly for six months in marathon Friday-evening meetings. The technique was nothing new or radical, but was executed well, and offered a scripted set of options, in a controlled environment.

For example, if someone did not register at the first request or decision gate, like I had, the volunteer would ask them to talk about the dream goal they had put at stake, and ask, "Why is it important to you right now?" They would refocus the discussion to include the guest's dream goal, making it vivid and real. They would authentically share with the guest their own emotional story (which they had practiced over and over) about their own dreams and the breakthroughs they had as a result of the seminar. This reframed the opportunity to register to a simply binary choice: Keep doing the same old thing or follow your dreams.

Finally, for those guests who still didn't register, the algorithm branched to another gate, the "Hail Mary" close, which was surprisingly effective. It was so simple: "By the way, whatever is stopping you from registering right now is stopping you in all areas of your life...just saying."

Erhard was a superb salesman and packager of existing material. He understood enough about "engineered environments," and
their influence on behavior to integrate them into his programs.[7]
The large rooms in which the seminars took place were typically
ballrooms in hotels, with the windows blocked out and the clocks
removed. Participants in the Forum seminar were asked to agree to
wait to leave the room until a break was announced. Door monitors
sat on both sides of the exit doors for the entire three days plus an
evening – roughly forty hours total. In this controlled environment,
with no windows or clocks, and restricted access, real-world dis-
tractions were out of play.

In the small Q & A rooms like the one I was in, the choreography and the authentic shares were practiced and well-rehearsed.
When one guest would get up and follow someone back to a registration table, it started a group trend in behavior. LGAT programs
were designed to take advantage of this. The conformity that occurs
when people go along with the behavior of others to feel accepted
by the group is well known in psychology, and generally falls under
the broad category of normative social influence. In the 1950s,
psychologist Solomon Asch's research demonstrated the power of
normative influence on group behavior.[8] His experiments showed
that the social pressure created by the opinions (and actions) of
others in a group influences the decisions and behavior of individual members.[9]

The sales closing effectiveness was impressive; the retention of
customers after they participated in the paid weekend Forum seminar was not.

A few weeks later, I attended the whole forty-hour Forum
weekend seminar, and almost immediately developed a love–hate
relationship with the program and the organization. On the one
hand, I found a group who were putting in long hours, and doing
something to become better people. Many of the men and women I
met seemed genuinely fulfilled by taking personal responsibility for

their actions and life. On the other hand, I disliked what I found to be deceptive and almost constant high-pressure sales tactics.

To be fair, many thousands of people loved the *est* training and the Forum, and seem to very much appreciate what they found to be useful personal development tools and exercises.

While I am critical of particular individuals and some of the methods and tactics, I have a profound respect for those who authentically participate to develop this most beautiful expression of human nature: coaching and lifting others. My experiences in the LGAT seminars ultimately enabled me to work with and engage my affinity for coaching, which has certainly brightened my life and helped me deal with some challenging issues.

During a one-on-one exercise in the seminar, I was recounting something I had learned from a challenging time in my life, and I felt my partner was really listening, not just waiting for her turn to talk; she was appreciating what I had to say. While it may sound trivial, it was profound for me. During these exercises, I seemed to transcend my normal fears and anxieties about fitting in and talking with others. I wasn't teaching or convincing; I was just talking about my life and what I came to understand. It was a flow-like[10] experience of being in "the zone," and continued to happen during one-on-one discussions throughout the weekend. It was during these one-on-one discussions that a peak experience would emerge, lifting my spirit and my mood. I felt "up," regardless how long and hard the day may have seemed. The experience was undeniable, and it was exhilarating.

Although I had been secretly checking my watch, waiting for the next break, these types of discussions felt different, and time flew by. I felt more connected and alert, and I felt accepted. It was a temporary experience, which I later referred to as "lift," and it happened only while I was actively engaged in the discussion about myself or the partner with whom I was talking. Thinking about the logic or mechanism of the experience on the drive home, or explaining it to someone else did not do it for me.

I had just read a popular book at the time (early 1990s) called *Flow*, by Hungarian American psychologist Mihaly Csikszentmihalyi. This experience, this lift, was the closest thing I had to a flow-like experience, outside of sports. It was intoxicating. It allowed me to transcend my clumsy and uneasy experience in social settings, and cut through my anxiousness and awkwardness around people. The feeling that I could actually contribute to someone was new, extraordinary, and profoundly uplifting. It was so powerful and intense for me that I thought I had found what I really wanted to do in life. Being a real estate mogul was no longer it.

In the Forum, the conceptual models they called the "technology" were simple: black and white, with no shades of gray. It went like this: Something happened. We made it mean something. This meaning was then burnt into our memory and reinforced... forever. With this one simple model, they told us, we could effectively identify the stories that ran our lives.

This led to perhaps the most popular and effective aspect of the so-called technology: the not-so-new idea of taking responsibility for your actions by contacting someone important to you and making amends. Although it resembled the practices of twelve-step programs that had been around since the 1930s, it was still an exercise that many people appreciated.

I was not the only one who found the weekend program to be an entertaining performance, with pockets of one-on-one discussions that I found profound. The overall experience revealed valuable insights. But the Erhard organization was another story entirely, and most certainly did not display virtuous leadership characteristics or healthy personal growth. Like others whom I interviewed for this book, I resented the non-stop sales efforts that made up much of the final day of the seminar.

Maybe the best way to describe *est* and the Forum was written by Dr. Joe Vitale in his introduction to the 2009 book, *The Book of est*, by Luke Rhinehart. Werner Erhard himself wrote the foreword.

> The problem is est is not a religion, not a therapy, not an academic course, and not a belief system. It might be best described, if it can be described at all, as theatre – living theatre, participatory theatre, encounter theatre.[11]

The seminar was a cross between Judge Judy, Dr. Phil, and Oprah. But after hours and hours in the controlled environment of the seminar room, the concepts and ideas seemed so simple. My energy waned. Then, every hour or two, someone made an interesting point or got snarly, and I would perk up. It was like being fed a salty snack. I wasn't really nourished, but got a temporarily satisfying boost when the leader caught a participant in a well-designed, Judge-Judy-style "gotcha." It was thought-provoking, like all good theater, but it was less clear how useful this so-called technology or performance therapy really was.

Over the next few months I attended more seminars and the Center became my social hub. It attracted a young, single, and vital group of people who, like me, were influenced by celebrity endorsements and a belief that the work being done by Werner Erhard was literally saving the world. Acquaintances told me it wasn't a good place to meet women. Of course, it seemed so for me. I went as often as I could to hang out with the woman I'd met a month ago and now wanted to marry.

Large Group Awareness Training (LGAT)

The real sources of what became the Human Potential Movement and the LGAT programs are difficult to isolate and briefly outline. However, it is widely agreed that Los Angeles and

San Francisco were the smoking cauldrons from which the most successful of these programs emerged.

In 1950, *Dianetics*, by science fiction writer L. Ron Hubbard, became the number-one best-selling book, according to the *Los Angeles Times*. Hubbard was a celebrity guru with advocates like Cecil B. de Mille and Ernest Hemingway.[12] In 1951, Hubbard left Los Angeles for Phoenix, Arizona. Claiming to have found something more powerful than Dianetics, Hubbard moved on to Scientology, which used "scientifically validated evidence" of the existence of the human soul.[13]

In the early 1960s, Scientology was very active in California, and the newly renamed Mr. Erhard was taking classes and studying Scientology with Peter Monk, a franchised "Scientology auditor."[14] Early in 1970, when a Texas company called Mind Dynamics offered lectures in the San Francisco Bay area, Erhard and Monk attended a lecture together.

Mind Dynamics was an assemblage of self-help concepts and "mind-cure" principles presented by an Englishman and former Unity School of Christianity schoolmaster named Alexander Everett. The promise of this work was wide-ranging, from improving IQ scores and eliminating insomnia, to even curing cancer.[15] (Everett, years earlier in Texas, had worked with Jose Silva, founder of Mind Control, which taught how to relax and harness the brain's alpha waves.[16]) Notable other Mind Dynamics leaders at the time were the four co-founders of Lifespring – perhaps the next most popular LGAT after *est* – John Hanley, Robert White, Randy Revell, and Charlene Afremow.

In January of 1971, Erhard became a Mind Dynamics franchise holder in San Francisco. Erhard completed his Mind Dynamics training and led several seminars for them, but by the end of 1971, Erhard left and started *est*. This was roughly seven years after he claimed to have started his intense studies in Scientology, self-help, Zen, and Mind Dynamics;[17] as we'll discuss later in the book, seven years has been the typical apprenticeship time period, ever since the Middle Ages.

While Erhard may have claimed that he "got it" in a single epiphany while driving over the Golden Gate Bridge one day, he had invested at least seven years of apprenticeship.

LGAT Technology

As a mechanical engineer, what captivated me was the claim made at the first evening session that a "technology" existed to address the key questions and issues of self-discipline and will-power I had wrestled with for years. The use of the word technology made it trustworthy, because it implied the application of scientific principles to address practical problems.

I wanted this technology to resolve the same question that kept bedeviling me: How is it that I can "know" what to do, and yet simply not do it consistently?

When I faced the important aspects of my life, like staying on a financial budget, or a fitness program, I impatiently strayed off course. I was already convinced it was a matter of my weak will-power. But then the Forum made it crystal clear: The problem was the feeble relationship most of us "assholes" had to our word. Now I had hope, because the *est* technology addressed this.

Over the next year I volunteered more and more, eventually joining an internal leadership development program. I had been dating the enrollment manager and was now certain I wanted to marry her.

During the leadership development program, I learned "enroll-ment" – or how to be successful at selling the program. In our class of about fifteen men and women, we had an inside joke: the key to enrollment and getting a registration was being authentic; once you learned to fake that, you had it made. The class was competitive and the score card was simply the number of registrations you brought in. I came to learn that the key to registration relied on getting someone to commit to something emotionally charged – something big and important to them. As we'll see in a later chapter, we engaged the person's fast-thinking processes. It was then our job as their "coach" to hold them to account, to have them "honor their word." The coach was not pressuring them to register but was "taking a stand for them" and helping them get what they really wanted. The mischief came from manipulating the situation so that the emotionally charged commitment included registering for another seminar.

It was simple cause and effect. As the coach, you were innocently just holding them to account for what they said they wanted. Later in my working life as a "coach" and transformational consultant, I saw how easy it was to create this cause and effect and to misuse it. The discussion went something like this:

> *Coach*: What is it that you really want? Something you may think is too big, but if you achieved that, it would be amazing. Another way to say it is, what would be a breakthrough for you? How would you measure it, and by when do you want to accomplish it?
>
> *Client*: Doubling sales this year would be a breakthrough and is something I really want.
>
> *Coach*: OK, are you willing to make a commitment to that? Are you willing to go for it and throw your hat over the fence? To take a stand for the possibility that you could do it?
>
> *Client*: Well I guess… but, I don't know how to do it. I've never even increased sales by more than ten percent.

Coach: That is a good thing to notice because you will never get what you want, doing the same thing over and over.

Client: Well then, yes this is what I really want.

Coach: OK, but instead of focusing on doing, because doing the same thing over and over is the definition of insanity, you must focus on transforming who you are being.

Client: How do I do that?

Coach: By taking the next seminar ... (or working with a coach who understands transformation and transformative language...hint...hint. ...)

This tried and true model is still used, over and over.

Later that year, I sold my real estate investment and management business, a business I had been planning and dreaming about since high school, although I retained most of the real estate. I joined a management consulting firm, which, although not legally connected to Erhard, grew out of the Werner Erhard technology.

When I reflect on this period of my life, I can see the degree to which I was influenced by people in the environment. Inside the engineered environment, it all made sense, even the things that didn't feel right. I can also see how the promise of love colored my perception and beliefs. After all, as I was told, this technology allowed me to find the woman of my dreams – because there are no coincidences. Looking back, I can see how often I was locked in, and then held to account from the results of my first impulses and quick decisions. Later in LIFT we'll see more about how our System 1 fast thinking automatically produces these rapid, emotional decisions, and why it's so valuable to have someone outside yourself, like an Expert Coach, who has your best interests at heart.

When I look back on this time, I often think about the Maya Angelou quotation:

> "I've learned that people will forget what you said, people will forget what you did, but people will never forget how you made them feel."[18]

It worked for a while, but somehow it didn't feel right.

The Power of Language

The technology of the Forum was ultimately focused on the power of language, which wasn't just used to describe a preexisting world, but to create the world. Something existed only if you had language for it.

An integral component to the seminar was the work of Fernando Flores, mentioned earlier. His work was relatively new and essentially developed from the work of the Englishman John Austin (1911–1960) and then the American John Searle (1932–), who wrote an important philosophical book, *Speech Acts*, in 1969. Searle, a professor of philosophy and language at the University of California at Berkley, worked with Fernando Flores while Flores developed the work later adopted by the Forum. (Nowhere in the Forum seminar did they mention the names of Searle, Austin, or Flores.)

At the Center, the staff members seemed to be hyper-effective as they employed these somewhat stilted and unnatural speech acts. It appeared they had found a powerful new way to communicate, which was important for me because I struggled with this. However, as I spent more time at the Center in between seminars, out of the public eye, I saw staff members subjected to overt and caustic reprimand from superiors. Their "open and honest communication" which seemed to work so beautifully in the engineered environment of the weekend seminar, had degraded into a righteous, mean-spirited dressing-down. Intuitively I knew this was wrong – but perhaps I had just never had anyone speak with me openly and honestly? So, I let my intuition slide.

I finally got what I thought I wanted: After a brief engagement, the enrollment manager and I were married. The day we returned from our honeymoon, I found out that my new wife had been promoted to manager of the Center. The previous manager, also in her twenties, had been fired after about eight months, a typical tenure for this position.

The Dark Side of Alignment

An important part of *est*, the Forum, and many LGATs was the concept of "alignment." The idea was logical and efficient, with plenty of music and sports metaphors to back it up. For example, when the symphony conductor – the leader – announces what you will play, you play it, with no discussion or consensus building; as a member of the symphony, it is your job to get aligned. Similarly, using a football metaphor, when the quarterback calls a play, team members do not get to vote on it, they get aligned and do what the quarterback says.

These practical metaphors of real-world alignment made sense. But the metaphors did not accurately reflect the situation in the different context of the Forum. The way they used alignment seemed intuitively wrong and self-serving; it sounded and felt more like, "You'll do it because I am the leader and I said so."

Today, far fewer consultants and coaches rely on this nefarious 1970s interpretation of alignment, bypassing the healthy process of deliberation, debate, and discussion.

Alignment, like lift, is an emergent phenomenon, not pre-scriptive, and although it may take a little longer and may be diffi-cult, it's a necessary process when working with a team of people. Leadership and transformational coaching, which use alignment in the "because I said so" way, may force alignment in the short term, but this interpretation does not develop leadership characteristics important to motivating and retaining good people, and, worse, it creates resentments and division. This is not a concept that trans-fers well to corporations developing leaders and vying for talent.

But the metaphor and concept I saw most damaging, particu-larly to my kind-spirited twenty-five-year-old wife, was the concept of a "clearing." The metaphor was so powerful it diverted attention from the underlying transaction (at least for me, for a while). The metaphor goes like this: trees are removed to create a clearing in the forest where a helicopter can land. A helicopter needs a clear-ing, in the same way results need a clearing to land in our lives. As the argument goes, we become a "clearing" through the use of lan-guage both verbally and nonverbally – essentially, as a result of our thoughts. While "the clearing" metaphor appears in Heidegger's work, he used it in a different context. Within the Forum, it was just another version of the Law of Attraction, which we'll address in more detail later.

So as it related to producing results, and making sales, staff members like my wife received a targeted number of guests from her boss. It was her job to get aligned, like the conductor or quarter-back. Then, she coached volunteers to each make an unreasonable promise, so their combined total would add up to the promise she made to her boss. These promises were certainly not based on any-one's past performance. The specific number most probably would need to be a breakthrough to accomplish. So, metaphorically, you throw your hat over the fence,[19] and "stand for" a personal trans-formation to produce these results. But at the end of the night, the reckoning was simple: You had promised to deliver X, and if you did not, it would be perfectly acceptable for the team leader to "hold you to account," which included a good dressing-down, often in a public place.

If my wife had a bad night at the Center and fewer guests registered than what she had targeted (or promised), she was deemed to have been "not effective" that evening, and we could be sure her "clearing" was off. This meant that she was "a clearing for bad results": in other words, she was attracting these poor results at the Center. The question then became, "Why?" It took late-night marathon conference calls with her bosses to coax the answers out of her. These "processing" calls were brutal, and often resulted in tearful admissions of her so-called failings. I watched a spirited, beautiful, healthy young woman transform – but it wasn't into someone happier or healthier. If this was transformation, I no longer wanted it.

To make a long and unpleasant story short; I got the girl and honored my word to support her "commitment to the work" – but after a few long years, I'd had enough. I drifted away from the Center, my "transformation" job, and my wife.

I became ill, and for several months had a recurring case of pneumonia. I continued to travel and work as a transformational consultant, only because I had given my word to stay. I was miserable. My family, and friends outside of my job and the *est* network, from whom I also drifted, were all moving forward nicely in their careers, and now when they called me an "est-hole," it hurt.

I felt lost. I also felt like a bigger failure because I wanted to quit and I was forcefully reminded that if I did, it would be one more time I didn't honor my word. On the other hand, I couldn't simply honor my word and stay. Looking back, what was most disappointing for me was the way I gave up on coaching. That experience of lift I got from coaching had been compromised and corrupted. I had not made progress on my willpower, either, because I was too busy taking seminars and volunteering. The "declarations" I had made during the many seminars were now further evidence of my lack of willpower, now that the personal transformation I commit-ted myself to had not happened.

Meanwhile, my health was deteriorating. A tumor had grown and was now completely blocking the tube connecting my wind-pipe to the superior (upper) lobe of my left lung. During what had become a somewhat routine visit to the doctor for more antibiotics, the X-rays – and then CAT scans – showed a golf-ball-sized tumor. I had little time or choice. A thoracotomy, more accurately a lobec-tomy (removal of a lobe of the lung), removed the entire superior lobe of my left lung.

It was very early, still dark and raining, when I drove alone to the hospital. After an hour of paperwork and basic tests, I lay in a cold and noisy ward for what seemed like another hour, when a kindly older woman wheeled me to a cold, bright operating room where I was sedated.

To perform the lobectomy, the surgeon made an incision of about eighteen inches starting three inches from the spine at the top of my left shoulder blade, to just below my ribcage on my left side, at about a forty-five-degree angle. To gain access, the surgeon broke a rib, and then used a rib retractor to create the space to remove the entire lobe, about the size of a small birthday balloon.

The lungs are well protected in the body, and as anyone who has had pleurisy or broken ribs will tell you, just breathing hard or coughing is very painful when they are disturbed. During the first few months after the surgery I was in more continuous pain than I had ever experienced. I was taking oxycodone three times every day and while it did dull the pain, it also made me depressed. I now lived alone and spent much of my days inside my head, blaming myself and others for what I felt were careless mistakes in my career and relationships.

It was a dark time. My mother had just been diagnosed with a form of brain cancer that was spreading quickly to multiple sites in her brain. She was most certainly going to die within months. By the time she did pass, nine months later, my wife and I had started the formal process of a divorce.

Home alone, drugged, and increasingly depressed, I was still wrestling with the questions that haunted me in my head. How can I improve or transform my willpower? Why can some people like Tony Robbins and all the celebrities endorsing his programs just "decide" – basically just give their word – and get what they want in life? Why couldn't I?

During this time, my father reached out to me. Although he had just lost his wife of nearly forty years, he intuitively knew that I was struggling. While he did not recommend a course of action, he helped me untangle my own thoughts, and get outside of my incessantly self-critical internal dialogue. Over the next few months he came to spend time with me and we talked. ... I began to trust myself and appreciate my values. With his support, I did not act on impulse, and learned to pause and deliberate; I considered what I needed to do for my own spirit and for my career.

Trane, my employer in the Middle East, had a large manufacturing plant a few hours by express train from Paris. We used this plant for some products in Saudi because of the favorable exchange rates and shipping costs back in the 1980s. I was fortunate to have traveled to Paris many times during my time in Saudi, and, on weekends, I often had the pleasure of wandering around the 6th and 7th Arrondissements. I felt at home in these small, quaint neighborhoods, and knew I wanted to live there.

When I was recovering from the surgery, I had this dream of starting the new millennium sitting at a café in Paris. In my dream, I wasn't just a tourist, but a regular patron.

So, after months of looking online at apartments in Paris, it started to sink in. I was going to do this! One night, with a settled mind, I booked a perfect little apartment on the Left Bank. This was no stake in the ground or hat being thrown over the wall; this was a deliberate and conscious act. I slept well for the first time in years.

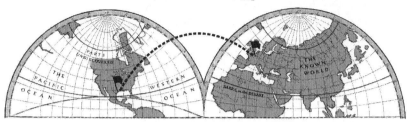

CHAPTER 3 — NATURE AS TEACHER: METIS

My tiny Paris apartment was at 12 Rue du Bac, on the Left Bank, close by the foot of Pont Royal, the bridge that crosses the Seine and delivers you to the Tuileries – the gardens of the Louvre. I lived in a seventeenth-century building, said to have been the home of bakers for the King. Rumor had it that tunnels in the cellar once ran under the Seine to the royal family's palace. Most mornings I got up before dawn and hauled my backpack down five flights of an oval spiral stairway with uneven wooden steps. The stairway led to a small foyer with an old, beautifully carved double wooden door. Stepping outside, I turned right to Rue de l'Université, which became Rue Jacob and, in ten short minutes, took me to the Boulangerie Paul, a bakery on Rue de Seine. The shop was part of a larger chain of bakeries, but unlike most American chains, this was a real neighborhood bakery run by a master. I was greeted with cheery "Bonjour," as I opened the door to the muffled sound of a hanging bell supported by a decorative brass "L" bracket.

On shelves and in cases, the pastries, quiches, and sandwiches were artfully displayed, demonstrating the pride and profession-alism of the shop. Being part of the environment, and breathing in the exquisite smells, lifted my mood immediately. Most mornings I got a *pain au chocolat* – a croissant-like pastry with a cube of dark chocolate inside – and, if my timing was right, the center of the croissant was warm and moist, the chocolate partially melted. In Paris that September, many mornings presented an overcast sky with a light rain. The warm *pain au chocolat*, a hot cup of rich dark French roast coffee, and the order and pace of the shop were comforting and calming. The shop itself seemed to give me energy to get to my own work for the day.

The baker and her two or three apprentices – "the rascals" as she called them, in a beautiful Parisian accent – ran the shop and cleaned up after customers. Before clearing a table, they made eye contact, not as a perfunctory checklist item, but with interest, to ensure everything was OK. Their attention to detail and respect for their work was captivating.

They had a purposeful way of visiting each table, with a light touch at some, and a thoughtful conversation about the texture of the bread that day or the quality of the new apples they just received with the patron at the next. Absorbed in their routines and detailed knowledge, they drew my attention, relieving me of the ongoing self-critical dialogue in my head. It was somehow calming to watch the baker's deliberate choreography as she glided from the ovens to the counters. It felt good to be in the presence of intentionality and a practice. The baker and her apprentices demonstrated an appreciation for doing something well for the sake of the craft.

In Paris, I learned the degree to which the craftsman culture and the guild society were integral in forming this beautiful city. The baker as a craftsman served as a good microcosm. Even the process of making bread has been used as a metaphor for raising children and training apprentices for centuries: It simply takes time for the dough to rise, in the same way it takes time for an apprentice to learn. At the Paul bakery, the master baker and apprentices

arrived around 4:00 a.m. and began making bread from scratch –
with just flour, water, salt, and yeast.[1]

The process of bread making starts by mixing these ingredients
in the right portions, forming the dough into a ball, and letting it sit
for perhaps an hour or two (depending on temperature and humid-
ity), to grow on its own. The bread then rises or inflates, like the
ego of an apprentice, sometimes doubling in size. The baker then
"knocks" it down to size. Interestingly, the French word used for the
knocking-down process is *étirage*[2] which means stretching out, a
word commonly used in conversations about training and teaching
a skill. After the *étirage*, the flattened dough is again formed into
a ball, left to sit for another hour or two to grow on its own, again,
just like the baker's apprentice, gradually learning and incorporat-
ing the new experience and knowledge.

In the world of cause and effect, the dough rises through the
Maillard reaction, a chemical reaction the protein undergoes when
combined with sugar and heat energy.[3] As the sugar is digested,
it creates carbon dioxide and alcohol. The trapped carbon dioxide
expands or inflates the glutinous ball, altering the dough. *Étirage*
releases the trapped carbon dioxide and deflates the dough, allowing the process to start over – providing more density, strength,
and character. The baker explained to me in her wonderful accent
that each time the dough is allowed to "sit" and grow on its own,
it becomes stronger, containing less sugar and starch, more protein
and flavor – more character. The loaf of bread needs time to develop
on its own, just as the apprentice needs time to develop and pick
up what is in the environment, both consciously and unconsciously.

The ongoing craftsmanship process is not a blind disciplined
routine or mindless tradition; it is based on actual cause and effect
– a natural process with a useful purpose, a practice also supported
by current neuropsychology. For thousands of years, this process of
breadmaking has been used as a metaphor for life.[4]

The breadmaking metaphor, born from observations made over time, now bears with it the deep purpose and meaning of the gestalt or set of practices on which it is based.

The Creative Craftsman

After the Industrial Revolution in the late nineteenth century, even a city like Paris began bypassing the craftsman model, adopting a lower-cost Frederick Winslow Taylor–inspired model. Taylor, an American mechanical engineer, (1856–1915) was perhaps the first management consultant. In Taylor's model of "scientific management," the work is separated into discrete tasks, and each employee's specific task operates as one part of a larger process. The goal is to find the lowest cost and lowest skilled labor to build a product or provide a service, essentially eliminating the need for an apprenticeship. The employee, an unskilled laborer, only needs to know one simple task.

Not surprisingly, this practice showed signs of strain by the 1940s and 50s. In *The Organizational Man*, William Whyte describes workers performing discrete tasks, in layer upon layer of management, together forming a "generation of bureaucrats, with all their creativity sucked out of them."[5]

However, and perhaps unexpectedly, more recent advances in technology and automation have reintroduced opportunities for craft and a renewed appreciation of the importance of context expertise or domain knowledge. More large companies have begun using outside experts in place of full-time employees to do higher skilled jobs requiring considerable industry expertise. Although it's still early for this trend inside larger corporations, it opens new opportunities for highly skilled independent contractors like accountants, designers, and writers to provide services once done exclusively in house. The reduced costs of administrative support lowers barriers to entry into all sorts of enterprises and have spurred an increase in individual and small crafts or boutique businesses.

In his book, *The Rise of the Creative Class*, Richard Florida outlines the spectacular rise in the number of independent contractors, as "creatives," who now offer their unique skill and domain knowledge to a wider variety of companies. Previously shut out by the high costs of operating a small business, before the days of mobile hand-held computers, creatives now can work anywhere. In 2010 in the United States, more than forty-one million individuals operated creative and specialized small businesses[6] – from craft beer makers to specialty insurance and financial management firms – bringing a high degree of knowledge and skill while focusing on a unique slice of the market. Healthcare professionals, lawyers, architects, and engineers are also opening more niche enterprises to serve specific needs. They offer to the larger organizations their knowledge, experience, and craftsmanship. These solopreneurs and boutique businesses are in demand because they understand the nuances. They know the context and can efficiently cut through tricky issues.

In a word, what they develop and sell is their metis.

What Is Metis?

Metis, which we touched on in the Preface, deserves a closer look now. For centuries, leaders in business, the professions, trades, crafts, and government throughout much of the world followed a shared, unwritten apprenticeship. New workers learned their craft and were trained as apprentices under a craftsmanship model. This was an inherently logical and accepted practice, but today far fewer professions and occupations follow this path.

So, the question emerges: does it make sense – or is it even possible – for us to make a course correction now, and adopt the best of the traditional craftsmanship model?

I argue that, because we are in the early stages of a massive shift in the demographic makeup of the workforce, and we're increasing our use of artificial intelligence technologies, the time to make this transition is now.

As we are transferring management and leadership to the next generations, it is our responsibility to transfer the metis, and that can only take place through mentoring, or Expert Coaching.

I recommend the term "Expert Coach" as the most effective replacement for mentor, since the term mentor has an abysmal reputation in corporate America. The term Expert Coach better identifies what internal senior managers and leaders will need to become before they transition out of the work force.

The Expert Coaching I refer to is equivalent to the master's role in the development of a journeyman or apprentice. Expert Coaching transfers more than just knowledge and skills; it encompasses the additional abilities to cooperate and build relationships, and to "get along" both in the work environment and with the customers and vendors. The Expert Coaching role may also include leadership development, one competency among many that successful executives use.

Developing and maintaining relationships to improve social collaboration and organizational effectiveness is a powerful adaptive practice, which may be our greatest innate ability as *Homo sapiens*. "It is our ability to socially cooperate in a flexible way which separates us."[7] The ways in which we cooperate and communicate socially have been and continue to be a powerful adaptive advantage, and one that only gets transferred person to person. In *The Wisdom of Crowds,* James Surowiecki demonstrates our effectiveness as social collaborators; those skills enable us as groups (or in crowds) to become far more effective and accurate in decision making and predicting than we can be individually.

This craftsmanship process may bring to mind a quaint medieval scene, where life was lived at a slower pace within a small, embracing community; it may also imply a so-called "working-class" trade or craft, presumed to be separate from and beneath those of us herded through a university system. But Richard Sennett, in *The Craftsman,* brings a fresh, insightful perspective:

> The craftsman may suggest a way of life that waned with the advent of industrial society – but this is misleading. Craftsmanship names an enduring, basic human impulse, the desire to do a job well for its own sake. Craftsmanship cuts a far wider swath than skilled manual labor; it serves the computer programmer, the doctor, and the artist.[8]

Sennett may accurately identify the human impulse which endures, but the role of the master craftsman as an integral part of our communities and economy has faded from popular business culture. Perhaps the craftsman culture made sense only during periods of slower technology adoption or change? From medieval literature, we know that this culture was real and thriving for centuries, certainly up to the Industrial Revolution in the late eighteenth century. But, in our time, is the craftsmanship culture still a viable model or is it merely a romantic distraction, just one more version of the good old days when the grass was greener? Is doing a job well for its own sake an outdated luxury, an irrelevant concept, in our rapidly evolving new creative class?

As a way to answer these questions, I would like to expand on my introduction to the term metis, the word from the ancient Greek:

> A type of intelligence and of thought, a way of knowing; it implies a complex but very coherent body of mental

attitudes and intellectual behavior which combine flair, wisdom, forethought, subtlety of mind, deception, resourcefulness, vigilance, opportunism, various skills, and experience acquired over the years. It is applied to situations which are transient, shifting, disconcerting and ambiguous, situations which do not lend themselves to precise measurement, exact calculation or rigorous logic.[9]

This expanded definition, from authors Jean-Pierre Vernant and Marcel Detienne, offers a glimpse into the "situation" twenty-five hundred years ago. Describing "situations which are transient, shifting, disconcerting and ambiguous, situations which do not lend themselves to precise measurement, exact calculation or rigorous logic,"[10] the authors bring to mind circumstances we find ourselves in today. In short, metis has always been, and will continue to be, an important asset, not to be underestimated.

The term metis has an Indo-European foundation, and is thought to have been used in measuring, or creating measured plan. The word then developed from ancient Greek religion: Zeus was a *Mêtieta*, or "wise counsellor." The Stoics referred to metis as the embodiment of "prudence," "wisdom," or "wise counsel." This kind of knowledge, and its practice, were written about by Homer in both *The Iliad* and *The Odyssey*.

Homer specifically referred to it and explained its value in *Iliad* 23.[11] Nestor, King of Pylos, described as a wise older man, demonstrates the common use of the word in a pep talk to his son before what must have been an important chariot race. He assures his son he has the horsemanship skills, developed through training and practice, but...;

> "Antilochus, since you are dear to Zeus and Poseidon and since they have taught you all manner of horsemanship, there is no great need for me to teach you. Well you know how to make the turn around the stile. But, to be sure,

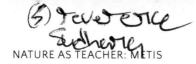

your horses are the slowest in the race. For that reason, I expect, there will be sorrow for you. But although the other men have horses that run faster, they don't know more than you do about how to make a metis. So come now, dear boy, and store up all kinds of metis in your mind, so that prizes don't escape you."[12]

Nestor knows his son has studied the "how to's" of chariot racing, but he explains this will not win the race. To win, Antilochus "must gain metis for himself... by metis does one charioteer surpass another."[13]

Metis includes "knowing" how to read an opponent, how to read a situation, and how to win. Learned only through deliberate practice, imitation, preparation, winning, and losing, perhaps metis encapsulates the original ten-thousand-hour rule.

Particularly interesting about Homer's reference is that, in the same way that Captain Sullenberger demonstrated metis, *Iliad* 23 specifically refers to metis as the knowledge and mastery required to captain a ship: "[A] helmsman has to guide aright a swift ship that is buffeted by winds."[14] Or a ship that has lost both engines and has no place to conventionally land, like US Air Flight 1549.

In *The Social Animal*, David Brooks refers to metis as a kind of sixth sense: the kitchen smarts of a master chef, or the intuition developed by a Marine sweeping the occupied streets of Iraq.

Metis was used to build the rituals, practices, and hierarchy that conferred a certain order, respect, and honor on those willing to do what it took to journey through the ranks. These practices and processes chaperoned a young man, or woman, working alongside the journeyman or master. They offered an opportunity for a young person to build a life and raise or lift themselves up through the context of the craft or trade. It was not only the craftsmen, but all in the tribe or village community, who appreciated and paid respect to the masters. It took a major motion picture[15] to reacquaint us with a modern-day master. The same apprenticeship process enabled

Mastery Center

Captain Sullenberger – in an almost impossible situation – to masterfully perform his craft.

Metis gets built into one's character and self-confidence. It's more than the ability to perform the skill or craft, and includes all that it took to move from an apprentice to a journeyman and then to a master. Sennett is quick to point out an additional benefit for those who choose this path: it is "also the way to secure deep inner satisfaction, to earn respect and self-worth."[16]

Also, and perhaps the most difficult to explain, is the sheer pleasure, or positive, *flow*-like therapeutic experience, of doing something well for its own sake.

Metis is about mastering – DOING – something. While it may, and often does, include a specific mindset, it is more about the execution, the art, and the craft of doing something very, very well. Master craftsmen and women have ups and downs like the rest of us. They have days when their mindset may not be so optimal, but the master will still execute.

"Metis is about finding an elegant solution to difficult problems instead of relying on brute force."[17] An Expert Coach with metis can help an entrepreneur – who may not have the most money or the latest technology – to outsmart competitors and win.

What makes the craftsman system elegant and sustainable is that metis includes the duty of a master to pass on the essence of what it takes to become a master: how to learn; how to seek out metis and appreciate your 10,000 hours in the pilot's seat; how to collaborate, manage, lead, inspire, and bring out the best in others.

In ancient Greek society, boys of citizens were given a mentor at an early age. These boys also had to become an apprentice in a craft, even if they were not going to pursue it later in life. Implicit in becoming a master is an understanding of what it takes to apprentice and to appreciate the value of metis.

Perhaps the strength and success of the Greek society resulted from this appreciation of the importance of training the next generations through the craftsman model. Grandfathers played an important role, as important as the father's, and were expected to participate deeply in the education and training of their grandsons. The training in, and practice of, a craft develops strict rituals for the process of passing metis on to the next generations. Take, for example, the simple statement, "It's your airplane."

Sully is such a powerful example for us, because it was his first instinct, after the flight made him a hero, to write a book entitled *Highest Duty: My Search for What Really Matters,* just the kind of message one would expect from a master.[18]

But what are the conditions and opportunities for the craftsman model today? Based on Sully's comments in his book, the craftsman model in commercial aviation is being second-guessed and is even in danger of being rendered obsolete.

However, we can circle back and answer the question posed earlier in the chapter: "Is doing a job well for its own sake an outdated luxury, an irrelevant concept, in our rapidly evolving new creative class?"

Richard Florida's research offers us some hope. He points out that the creative class has grown from just twelve percent of the population in the 1800s to 32.6 percent in 2012.[19] While some agricultural labor and manufacturing workers moved into the service class, which has also grown, the data are clear that the creative class, as defined by Florida, is growing.

Florida explains, "The distinguishing characteristic of the Creative Class is that its members engage in work whose function is to create meaningful new forms."[20] In other words, the creatives value work in which they find meaning. They are also more inclusive and diverse as a group, with more women (52 percent) than men.[21]

Doing a good job is more important and relevant to this group than the preceding working class tethered to a robotic set of tasks on an assembly line. Florida points out that this group values a meritocracy, and "favors hard work, challenge and stimulation."[22] In addition, this creative work is not easily performed by machines as it requires the valuable human capabilities of specific domain knowledge, experience, and metis.

Metis Through the Ages

For centuries, both skill and metis have been transferred within a master-to-apprentice structure: mother to daughter, father to son, and so on, through interaction, through "doing," modeling, and imitating both the skills and the way of being. While the data point to 10,000 hours, a master will tell you that he or she also had one or more mentors, or Expert Coaches.

According to Edith Hamilton, the Ancient Greek thinkers Aristotle, Socrates, and Plato didn't teach and mentor by assigning readings. Instead, they transferred metis using dialogue, and modeling practices, dispositions, and propensities to their students.[23]

Now, in our current social and business world, how do we deliberately transfer important behavioral practices, habits, and mindsets?

Sennett explains:

> It is a negotiation between autonomy and authority (as one must in any workshop); how to work not against resistant forces but with them (as did the engineers who first drilled tunnels beneath the Thames); how to complete their tasks using "minimum force" (as do all chefs who must chop vegetables); how to meet people and things with sympathetic imagination (as does the glassblower whose 'corporeal anticipation' lets her stay one step ahead

of the molten glass); and above all they know how to play,
for it is in play that we find the origin of the dialogue the
craftsman conducts with materials like clay and glass.[24]

The master must first learn the craft, start at the bottom, and
learn the skill, or the "doing." Only after becoming an expert can we
think about managing and leading others. Leadership, if it is to be
effective, must be earned – not taught in artificial settings.

The extraordinary progress and accomplishments of ancient
Greek society are almost unfathomable. Their advancements and
contributions to art, education, entertainment, engineering, law,
mathematics, medicine, and politics are mind boggling. It's not
as though they merely took existing concepts and technology and
improved them; they actually created and successfully adapted revo-
lutionary concepts in politics, theater and entertainment, medicine,
and science. The Greeks were said to be addicted to innovation[25]
as well, but what is most remarkable was their ability to question
their own reality, and give up superstition or dogma. The Greeks
also held what are again popular beliefs around the importance of
fitness and mentorship.

The Greece that rose in 450 BCE was arguably the greatest civilization to have lived, and reasons for this greatness can be deduced
from the foundations on which its society was built. One of those
central foundations was the notion of craftsmanship.

One could also build a case for sixteenth- and seventeenth-century Europe as the period with most radical change and growth in
knowledge, and contributions to thought and science from giants
like Copernicus, Galileo, Descartes, Spinoza, and Sir Isaac Newton.
These leaders shattered a metaphoric glass ceiling – the long-held
notion that the heavens were filled with perfect crystal spheres. The
repressive fear imposed by the church was thereby shattered as well,
which enabled the rest of society to realign their stars in science and
philosophy and change their futures. Newton acknowledged that
he stood on the shoulders of giants; he recognized that the work

done during this period was built on the foundation of other great thinkers.

Ancient Greece was different in a couple of important ways. Greece was in no way the continuation of a specific social structure with social norms, and, unlike seventeenth-century Europe, it was not built on the shoulders of giants. Societies that preceded Greek society, at least for the prior millennium, had a common mindset of fear and subservience to the unknown magical and mystical powers of the dead and the afterlife.[26] Evidence of this is permanently marked on our planet's surface: pyramids preserved as the ancients intended for their dead gods and deities. Ancient Persians, Indians, Egyptians, Ethiopians, Incas, and Maya all built pyramid-shaped tombs to preserve their dead or from which to offer their dead.

The Egyptians spent lifetimes working for the afterlife, and in China, in 250 BCE, the Qin Dynasty built an entire city with a six-thousand-man "army" of terracotta sculptures, all to protect the emperor in this mythical spirit afterlife. While these cultures have differences, their common and overarching mindset was one of reverence to the unknown, magic, and the spirit world. Priests, and the "high priests" with direct access to the Pharaoh, had the power. They didn't understand the science or the actual cause and effect, but it is presumed they effectively used metaphorical concepts of magic, mysticism, and divine intention, in place of real knowledge, to exert control. We will see later in the book that we continue to use this strategy. The high priests' special magical powers and knowledge of the gods were jealously guarded, isolating others in their societies as well as those outside.

Also, the cultures of ancient Egypt and Mesopotamia, both geographically significant for Greece, left almost no evidence in their art, crafts, or writings that they led lives of joy. There were no games, no comedies, and little evidence of play or the demonstration of uplifting human experiences.[27] Each culture made almost no separation between spirituality and leadership.

Greece, on the other hand, separated the church and politics. Greek citizens had something very new and yet extraordinarily human: the freedoms to think and to learn. Now, we must note that the contradictions are clear: the Greeks owned slaves and gave little power to women.

What was so extraordinary in the small town of Athens, located in the far western region of the settled and civilized world? What was the spark, and what fanned the flames?

Through a self-reinforcing process of mastery and craftsmanship, the Greeks understood and celebrated the ability to lift the human spirit through connections with others.

During the writing of this book, the very experience I believe the ancient Greeks hoped to engender was played out on one of the biggest stages in the world. It was August 17, 2016, during the Summer Olympic Games in Rio de Janeiro, Brazil. During a heat for the five-thousand-meter race, New Zealand's Nikki Hamblin and the United States' Abbey D'Agostino became entangled and tripped up in the pack; both went down. Then, each athlete offered a helping hand, a lift: first Abbey D'Agostino bent to lift Nikki Hamblin who had fallen, then Hamblin lifted D'Agostino after she collapsed from the pain of a torn ACL. These acts of human kindness and selflessness transcended borders, geographically, racially, politically, and religiously. They lifted millions, reminding us to appreciate, in our unique desire to contribute to others, the gift of being human. Both athletes claimed they would never forget those moments. Was this the experience the Greeks were out to create when they invented the completely new practice they called the Olympics?

What was it about the Greeks that created this extraordinarily advanced, intellectually adventurous, and prolific society? Was it just astonishingly good fortune that masters like Socrates, Plato, Aristotle, and others happened to have lived during that time or was it something else? Was it also just lucky that Socrates mentored

Plato, Plato mentored Aristotle, and Aristotle mentored Alexander the Great?

I contend that the key was the Greek culture of craftsmanship and mastery, from which we can benefit today.

How Do You Know What You Know?

Just as children know their native language because they've grown up with it in the environment, we all absorb much of what we know about getting along with others, for example, simply because we've lived in our environment and interacted with others. In his bestselling book, *All I Really Needed to Know I Learned in Kindergarten*, Robert Fulghum demonstrates this important point, which resonated with millions of people. Filled with bite-sized wisdom, Fulghum's book builds the case that, before we learn to read and write, we learn the important aspects of human cooperation.[28]

This is a central point throughout LIFT because things like leadership, collaboration, friendship, and relationship management are first learned without the written word or formal education. We continue to learn when we are in different environments (or contexts).

Executives and leaders "know" much of the important stuff from doing what they do, and being present in their environment. As we will see, our unconscious is gathering some eleven million pieces of information a second, with only a small portion of that consciously managed.[29] Why would the body capture this information if it had no use for it?

One theory proposes that we gather this information as part of the knowledge we use consciously and unconsciously to collaborate for survival and reproduction in the dizzying complexity of life. This may be one reason that Expert Coaches – executives with experience and domain knowledge – are believed to be more effective to an organization than coaches with no domain or industry expertise.[30] Some portion of the eleven million pieces of information these experienced coaches have swept up is part of their metis – the sum total of what the Expert Coach "knows," that adds to their ability to understand complex situations.

In the next chapter, we will examine the origins and foundations of business coaching in America.

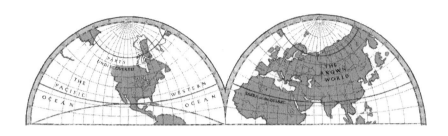

CHAPTER 4 — LEADERSHIP COACHING: THE CURRENT CLIMATE

A fundamental assumption throughout LIFT is that the profession of business and leadership coaching is attracting a wide range of qualified, smart, and ethical individuals. In spite of that, the evidence is consistent: Current leadership performance in US businesses is perceived to be poor. While there may be a number of ways to investigate why, I determined the most pragmatic method would be to look at the methods and the foundational materials being used to teach and train leadership coaches – the people largely responsible for training our business leaders.

So I conducted research. My own background as a former executive with a Fortune 100 company provided me access to dozens of executive coaches and senior executives who use coaches, as well as hundreds of leadership and coaching seminars, books, and experts. Then, two years after starting to write this book in 2015, I completed a coaching program at Georgetown University, which enabled me to study the curriculum and source materials currently in use. I also had the opportunity to interview a number of coaches.

Experience has taught me real leadership is important, and my experience is supported by the rigorous research findings of smart successful people like Jim Collins. Based on the handful of Fortune COO/CEO's whom I know well, I've found these leaders are empa-, thetic and have a healthy self-awareness. They are all willing to face up to their own human nature – their personal strengths and weaknesses.

I also strongly believe there is a place for leadership coaching; however in any organization, far more people are not actually "the leader." This is why I advocate for at least equal emphasis on skill development and collaboration.

One practice of the Craft of Expert Coaching is the use of validated assessment instruments. Such tools allow the coach to have stable baselines and accurate reference points for individuals interested in improving their performance, competency, and leadership.

I use and recommend four independent assessments,[1] all of which have been widely employed for decades and are validated, written, and tested by business-focused psychologists.[2]

While third party validated assessments are being more widely used in coaching, a majority of the roughly 17,500 coaches in the United States who identify themselves as business and leadership coaches[3] do not rely on or associate with any of these four assessment instruments. How did this majority learn their craft?

Author and researcher Vikki Brock, PhD, has compiled perhaps the most broadly comprehensive history of business and leadership coaching. In her book, *The Sourcebook of Coaching History* (2012), Brock builds the case that "the impact of large group awareness training (LGATs) starting in the 1970s, in the coaching field cannot be overstated." The largest, most influential of these was Erhard Seminar Training or *est* which we introduced in Chapter Two.

Brock explains that, "[j]ust as Erhard is credited with popularizing personal development, Thomas Leonard is credited with popularizing coaching."[4] Leonard worked for and with Erhard for years, and essentially repurposed Erhard's material for coaching. "Leonard codified the coaching curriculum so that it could be taught telephonically... Leonard articulated, simplified and in essence 'commodified' the principles of Landmark, making it possible to teach them to anyone anywhere."[5]

Thus, Erhard's work in personal development was translated into business leadership development, making it more acceptable and more congruent with the hierarchical corporate culture. Cleverly rebranded, leadership development conferred prestige, and was used to retain promising managers, or reward a leader without a pay raise.

In our current popular culture, coaching is associated with sports, and dates back centuries, where it grew from the training of a master or a journeyman. In the highly skilled professions like surgery and aviation, as well as some of the more hands-on trades, this kind of coaching is still much as it was centuries ago. In this context, effective coaches have domain expertise: a distinct knowledge and metis gained from the practice and mastery of their trade or profession.

By contrast, in much of mainstream business since the 1970s and 80s, the term "coaching" has been repurposed so that it's now considered to be its own category – with the advantage of being industry-agnostic. Business, or executive, leadership coaching became the standard; it was all about individual leadership.

Early in the twentieth century, leadership was simply one of the roles of a manager or business owner. Developing this view, after the Second World War, Peter Drucker was recognized as the father of modern American management with his seminal book, *The Practice of Management*, in 1954. Although Drucker believed that management was itself an important and noble endeavor which included a measure of leadership, he did not, throughout most of his career, focus much on leadership. In an interview with Forbes in 2004, Drucker said:

> You know, I was the first one to talk about leadership fifty
> years ago, but there is too much talk, too much emphasis
> on it today and not enough on effectiveness.[6]

But for some in the mid-twentieth century, a proficiency in leadership alone became enough. It was just the right tool to help them skip over rungs on the way up the corporate ladder. In the post-war expansion and baby boom, large conglomerates like General Foods and General Electric grew dramatically, managing a more and more diverse portfolio of businesses.

During this period of rapid growth, it was believed that gifted and brilliant leaders did not need experience or skill in the businesses they led. After all, the thinking went, leadership is leadership. By the 1970s, leadership had ascended and was no longer considered simply a part of mere management. Leadership was becoming something more powerful and exciting.

In this way of thinking, a manager or high-potential employee needs to improve their leadership abilities. Skill competency and performance are no longer as important, and suffer by comparison to leadership competencies.

In this model, leaders are coached by leadership experts, with no particular knowledge or expertise in the technology or current market demands. Trainees are simply coached to lead, sometimes by coaches who don't know the first thing about their client's industry or technology. Does that mean those chosen for leadership coaching are already highly competent doing their jobs and managing their teams? Have those selected for leadership coaching demonstrated they have earned the respect of the organization they will lead? Leadership at one time was considered an emergent quality, one which was earned not anointed. Leadership was not so much an individual set of skills or a "way of being," but rather a quality that was cultivated and grown in the hearts and minds of others.

Leadership Report Card

The Gallup Organization's *2017 State of the American Workplace* is a survey of more than 195,600 employees in a variety of industries. The results for leaders and their coaches are not good. Just twenty-two percent of employees strongly agree their leadership has a clear direction for their organization. Further, only fifteen percent of employees strongly agree that leadership makes them enthusiastic about the future in the organization, and a mere thirteen percent of employees strongly agree their leadership communicates effectively with the rest of the organization.[7]

According to Gallup CEO Jim Clifton, "These figures indicate an American leadership philosophy that simply doesn't work anymore. One also wonders if the country's declining productivity numbers point to a need for major workplace disruption."[8]

Gallup isn't the only one. Each year, the US Government Office of Personnel Management (OPM) conducts a mandated survey, the NARA Employee Viewpoint Survey.[9] One of the highlighted improvements from 2015 to 2016 was the score for question Q53: "In my organization senior leaders generate high levels of motivation and commitment in the workforce." In 2016, thirty-eight percent of respondents strongly disagreed or disagreed with the statement. So, well over one-third of those surveyed were critical of senior leadership's ability to motivate employees. Even more concerning, this was a significant improvement over the previous year, when a full forty-seven percent strongly stated their leadership did not generate high levels of motivation and commitment. While the newer result was highlighted as a win, it is still a startlingly poor reflection of how employees anonymously rated their leadership. This is another piece of evidence – and a loud message.

Because of the impending labor shortage when the boomers retire, organizations will struggle to hire and retain top talent. Out of necessity, companies will, to some degree, rely on coaching. But additional research, in line with the Gallup data, finds that only twenty-three percent of employees receiving coaching feel that it's effective.

The Gallup survey does not indicate that heavily weighted leadership coaching is producing better leaders. Nor is this coaching producing more satisfied employees,[10] if we are to believe some of the top business professors in some of our finest universities. A growing number of these professors are writing books and articles highlighting the long list of consistently poor job satisfaction and leadership scores over decades of surveys.

One of these seasoned and well-respected business professors is Barbara Kellerman, leadership professor at Harvard Business School and founder of the Center for Public Leadership. She writes that the leadership industry "has failed over its roughly forty-year history to in any major, meaningful measurable way improve the human condition." In fact, Kellerman adds, "the rise of leadership as an object of our collective fascination has coincided precisely with the decline of leadership in our collective estimation."[11]

Other prominent professors speaking out are Jeffrey Pfeffer of Stanford and Robert Sutton, an engineering professor also at Stanford. They offer solid research and compelling evidence. It's not as though business professors are taking their time to write articles targeting other business service fields like accounting or project management; they're targeting leadership coaching for a reason.

In 2015, Professor Pfeffer's book, *Leadership BS*, received acclaim from the best and the brightest in the management industry. Jim Collins (*Good to Great*), Google's Laszlo Bock, and Wharton professor Adam Grant all endorsed the book and the message.

Pfeffer's book sets out to prove four things:

1. The leadership industry is large and prominent, but not withstanding its magnitude and reach,

2. workplaces in the United States and around the world are, for the most part, (as there are obviously exceptional places on best-places-to-work lists), filled with dissatisfied, disengaged employees who do not trust their leaders;

3. leaders at all levels lose their jobs at an increasingly fast pace, in part because they are unprepared for the realities of organizational life, and thus,

4. the leadership industry has failed and continues to fail in its task of producing leaders who are effective and successful, and it has even failed to produce sufficient talent for leadership vacancies.[12]

Nonetheless, an entire consulting and coaching industry has developed around leadership coaching. With a focus solely on leadership, this subcategory grew in much the same way as Taylor-style scientific mass production. As we saw in Chapter Three, Frederick Winslow Taylor broke down processes into the basic tasks which could be done by the least skilled employee, necessitating that they learn only one task or skill and not the industry or context. This trend seems to have migrated up to management, anointing some as leaders, enabling and encouraging them to move from one enterprise to another with little or no knowledge of any actual product, service, or industry. Logically, executives in these environments came to believe that the important characteristic they brought to the table was this new "skill" called leadership.

There is little to no mention of business skill development or deliberate practice methods by early coaching practitioners. Neither Erhard nor his devotees focused on or wrote about business skill improvement or expertise. The contrast is clear, and it is simply the difference between doing and being: Compared to transformation, doing was boring. In the world of mass-produced leaders, there was no room for an apprentice.

Da Vinci & the Abbreviators

A true master like Leonardo da Vinci underscores the value of the apprenticeship model and skill development. One of the essential points in LIFT is the simple idea that metaphors are a powerful way to communicate and transfer concepts and processes. When the metaphor of transformation is misapplied, it is generally because of a failure to honor the natural physical phenomenon. So, when the term is misapplied in coaching or managing, it communicates a process which is at best unclear, and at worst impossible – absent magic or delusion.

To demonstrate this idea, in the first chapter we dug into the basic concept of the transformation of liquid water. There were two key points in this discussion: First, that transformation is a precise, well-understood naturally occurring process which can be reliably reproduced and effectively used, for example in air conditioning. In the transformation of water,[13] as you know, the water does not merely change; after the transformation, there is simply no water, at all. The second point is that to reproduce a transformation is both complex and costly, in terms of energy. It's not merely a shift in perspective or thinking.

According to Fritjof Capra, author of wonderful books such as *The Science of Leonardo,* da Vinci's notebooks revealed that he often refers to "abbreviators" with great disdain.[14] He uses the term to describe, for instance, the artists who, in sketches of the body, abbreviated key anatomical features. Rather than drawing the actual elbow joint, they might use a symbolic representation, like a mechanical hinge. He also refers to reductionist philosophers of the day as abbreviators.

> The abbreviators of work do injury to knowledge and to love... [O]f what value is he who, in order to abbreviate the parts of those things of which he professes to give

complete knowledge, leaves out the greater part of the things of which the whole is composed...?[15]

To da Vinci, an abbreviator looked at the beauty of life, and the human body, and reduced it to a mechanism,[16] as Descartes would do centuries later. Abbreviators also looked at a natural process like transformation and reduced it to magic or necromancy, to manipulate the outcome and to validate their own ideas. Leonardo was strongly opposed to the idea of spiritual or mystical intervention, or necromancy, often cited by his contemporaries as the cause of unexplained natural phenomena:

Of all human opinions that is to be reputed the most foolish which deals with the belief in Necromancy, the sister of Alchemy, which gives birth to simple and natural things. But it is all the more worthy of reprehension than alchemy, because it brings forth nothing but what is like itself, that is, lies... but this Necromancy the flag and flying banner, blown by the winds, is the guide of the stupid crowd...[17]

With an insatiable curiosity and a deep respect for the brilliance of Mother Nature's designs and natural processes, da Vinci believed nature's ingenuity to be much greater than man's, and felt we would be wise to respect nature and then learn from her. He also believed in the interconnectedness of all things and exhibited a kind of systems thinking.[18]

Today, transformation, as it is typically used in coaching and managing, has been so abbreviated it has completely lost any connection to the phenomenon from which it was named. Transformation can refer to any number of new linguistic creations which are merely changes, or are based in some magical or supernatural "physics."

Figure 4.0 DILBERT © 2005 Scott Adams.

Of the two and a half million books on transformation currently listed on Amazon, how many do you think da Vinci would label as abbreviations? What would Leonardo have to say about language as the source of mastery?

Leadership from Language – Speaking & Listening

As we've seen, the human potential movement of the 1970s encouraged the idea that leadership in business was just personal development in a different environment, and therefore it, too, was just about language. There was no need for skill development, craft knowledge, or industry expertise; business leaders were learning skills in the "domain of speaking and listening."[19]

It then followed that mastery of business leadership existed in language. The go-to example parroted in many of the LGAT seminars is now referred to as "The Great Eskimo Hoax." This story claimed that the reason the Eskimos are so successful at surviving in a harsh Arctic environment is that they have many more words for snow (some claimed 32 and some, several hundred). Because they had more words and therefore more distinctions for the snow, they had attained mastery.

But with some field research – physically going to the Arctic and interviewing native "Eskimos" – this was found not to be true. In fact, according to award-winning linguist and Harvard professor Steven Pinker in his book *The Language Instinct*, "Contrary to popular belief, the Eskimos do not have more words for snow than do speakers of English. ... Counting generously, experts can come up with about a dozen."[20]

Instead, the explanation for their expertise is rooted in common sense, and now supported by neuropsychology. The Eskimos are effective with snow because of their years of experience working with and in snow. The training and metis passed to them by masters was comprised of far more than language, and is not teachable by someone without this metis.

Relevant for this discussion is the fact that much of the foundational leadership coaching literature and methodology still used today relies on the foundation of language, which comes directly from Erhard and his early associates and devotees.[21]

Popular coaching textbooks, some now in their third edition, were written by early devotees. These books are prominent in their categories, and some are used in leading coaching programs as assigned texts. However, each relies on the idea that coaching and leadership exist in the distinctions in language.

These texts, listed below[22] all borrow heavily from the LGAT seminars, in many cases using identical terminology that originated thirty or more years ago. All are peppered with the recognizable jargon; the books make a point of spelling out exactly the same set of "distinctions" used in communications, often with the same anecdotes that were used, first in *est* and then the Forum.

Clearly, coaching has longstanding roots in LGAT technologies and therefore in language and transformation. Then, in 2006, arrived the phenomenon of the book and movie called *The Secret*, which we'll address in more detail in Chapter Eight. The message of *The Secret* strayed even further from expertise of the profession or craft. Not only was craft not important, but a plan or method was not important, either. As Jack Canfield – now a best-selling leadership coach – says in *The Secret*, "It's not our job to figure out how; the how will show up out of a commitment and belief."[23]

These notions swept the popular culture, and coaches were not immune. "Leadership" experts in *The Secret*, like chiropractor John Demartini, referred to wildly inaccurate interpretations of laws of physics, while, as in the LGAT seminars, employing a simple metaphor to which we could all relate. *The Secret* used a TV tower metaphor, and Erhard used the metaphors of the clearing and of transformation, as the means to get something for nothing.

Importantly, many of the "teachers" who contributed to the book and movie, *The Secret,* were also trainers and practitioners of Erhard's material, and presumably understood the power of a good metaphor. Chiropractor Joe Vitale, who wrote the introduction to *The Book of est*, (to which Erhard wrote the foreword), also played a significant role in *The Secret*.

These concepts were propagated by relying on the easily available metaphors of the TV tower, or the clearing in the forest, but also importantly on the inarguable, irrefutable "greatness" of the human spirit – the inner quality of human beings given by God. In effect, rather than basing their programs on real science, or even our everyday understanding of reality, these coaches celebrate the *vis viva*, life force, reminiscent of vitalism, which went out of favor with rational thinkers three hundred years ago.

These stories and myths may have been propagated with good intentions. But by using simple metaphors and anecdotes based on inaccurate, unproven "laws," coaches influenced by *The Secret* and its ilk are promoting and playing into the idea that we can get something for nothing. The consistently poor results speak for themselves.

Expert Coaching, the type of coaching I introduce in this book, is distinct from conventional executive coaching as it is taught and practiced today. Expert Coaching is best implemented by those with domain expertise and skill in our institutions and businesses, and will be essential as we transfer the knowledge and develop the skills necessary to help fill the leadership roles in the next decade.

Business Skills Coaching

As part of the Craft of Expert Coaching, I'm suggesting that we use coaching as it was designed and is still used today in critical fields like medicine: coaching people to collaborate, learn, and improve their skills and performance, not merely to lead.

Creating a coaching competency in an organization is certainly not a new idea. It was proposed in one of the most important business strategy books of the past 75 years,[24] *The Fifth Discipline* by Peter Senge, and more recently in Bob Kagan's important book, *An Everything Culture*.

This type of coaching works because, like many aspects of human behavior, particularly in learning and skill development, it is accepted and congruent with our natural intergenerational relationships. Through history, coaching has been a natural part of the developmental process of becoming an adult. Coaches or masters "took on" apprentices and trained them in both the craft and the culture, not just to improve their work, but also to manage, lead, and collaborate as part of the guild or team.

There are wonderful benefits to be gained from focusing on "doing" your work well. Doing good work will take the focus off your self-centered concerns and shift it to the quality of work and the skill or competency it demands. A focus on doing work well requires and builds mindfulness and self-confidence, which brings meaning to work. The natural process of learning through trial, error, and practice provides the ultimate satisfaction and rewards.

I've casually mentioned the ten-thousand-hour rule so far in the book primarily because it conveys deep meaning to those familiar with it. The well-known term was made popular by Malcolm Gladwell in his book, *Outliers: The Story of Success*, and then in the song, "10,000 Hours" on the 2012 chart-topping album *The Heist*, by Seattle musicians Macklemore and Ryan Lewis.

The concept came from a Swedish psychologist, K. Anders Ericsson, who is well known for his own deliberate practice and success as an author, researcher, and authority on the development of expert performance – or expert "doing."

In his 2016 book, *Peak: The Secrets from the New Science of Expertise*, Ericsson explains that the popularly understood ten-thousand-hour rule is an oversimplification and does not accurately portray the results of his research. He explains that to become an expert in some fields, like becoming an expert violinist, requires far more than 10,000 hours, and other skilled professions or trades may require less.

Ericsson's work is important to the Craft of Expert Coaching because he focuses not merely on the leadership aspect, but also on skill development within professions. Ericsson builds the familiar case that no one is born an expert. He also makes the important point that experience or time on the job is not enough. It takes a specific kind of "deliberate practice" and it also takes a predictable amount of work, so that those at the very top of their field reliably have invested more of their time toward purposeful, deliberate practice.[25] In simple terms, Ericsson believes in training competencies, so that C performers can move up to B performers, and B performers to A.

Even though the research from Ericsson and others is clear, in corporate America today there is little opportunity to chart a course of business skills improvement in your area of interest. In many entry-level "management" jobs, new hires are left on their own to "learn the ropes" and to prove themselves. Other than basic training in the organization's internal systems, there is little skills training.

LIFT will provide a more complete picture of the context of coaching and illuminate why employees seem to think so little of their current leadership. Having reviewed the concepts used to train coaches, I suggest we start training and coaching all employees to improve their skills, building on their talents and interests where possible.

This book, and the principles of the Craft of Expert Coaching, argue for a new focus on the practice of business skills: developing skill in your field, and doing your work well, for its own sake. There is plenty of evidence, which we will discuss later, to demonstrate that we experience meaning and authentic satisfaction in our work through deliberately practicing and making progress, day after day.

While leadership is valuable, it is not authentically learned or practiced until a person first earns their position as a leader through performance, the way an apprentice would.

Getting "It"

I lived for almost three years in the picturesque 7th Arrondissement of Paris, across the Seine from the Tuileries Gardens at the Louvre where I would walk most days. I had found a small private American graduate school in the 10th – another beautiful neighborhood, home to Les Invalides and the Eiffel Tower. What the school may have lacked in academic reputation it made up for in location, ambiance, and an eclectic group of top professors and students who also appreciated the locale. It allowed flexibility as I worked on a graduate degree with a wonderful American professor as my advisor. In my dissertation, I reviewed the pertinent literature on organizational climate and leadership.

I had become an advocate of the best-selling business book by Jim Collins, called *Good to Great*, and I conducted primary research on three of the eleven companies which Collins and his team determined had made the transition from good to great.

I, along with millions of others, connected with the book because of the use of a few powerful metaphors. Collins's metaphors allowed me to keep his concepts uncluttered; they allowed me to more easily recall and apply the material in detail.

For those unfamiliar with *Good to Great*, Collins used the metaphor of the fox and the hedgehog, borrowed from Isaiah Berlin's 1953 essay.[26] In this business metaphor, the fox is the person or company that changes strategy frequently and is always chasing after the next big shiny thing. While the fox may be good at many things, it is the hedgehog that knows one important thing, and is "great" because of its focus on that one important thing.

Collins also employed another important and powerful metaphor, of a flywheel, to provide a complete picture of the process of learning a skill, or making progress on a project.

> No matter how dramatic the end result, the good-to-great transformations never happen in one fell swoop. There was no single defining action, no grand program, no one killer innovation, no solitary lucky break, no miracle moment. Rather the process resembled relentlessly pushing a giant heavy flywheel in one direction, turn upon turn, building momentum until a point of breakthrough and beyond.[27]

Collins's metaphor accurately describes the difficulties and extra effort required just to get the flywheel to move, and the relative ease required after enough time and energy have been invested, when the wheel is spinning quickly.

Collins's book, *Good to Great,* sold over four million copies in many categories. To me, the book's great appeal was that it was based on real evidence. Collins, a faculty member at Stanford, used a large team of researchers who pored over thousands of articles, transcripts, and megabytes of financial data to help him explain why some companies make the leap from a good company to a great one, outperforming the average traded stock by many multiples.[28]

I liked Collins's brilliance at taking data and using basic accurate and real metaphors to clarify our understanding.[29]

Working on my dissertation also allowed me to continue to read and research everything I could about two open inquiries: the types of peak experiences I had while coaching, and ways to improve my willpower.

Admittedly, during this time I also spent too much time at the Café de Flor on Boulevard Saint-Germain, trying to channel the existentialist Jean Paul Sartre, to see if I could finally get "it." The "it" for me was the secret to self-discipline and willpower. I thought I would find the keys to willpower, and therefore success, in the same café, maybe even the same table, at which Sartre contemplated and wrote his classic work, *Being and Nothingness.*

I believed that by "getting it" in an instant – getting that life is empty and meaningless – I would be transformed. Thereafter, I could freely give my word and honor it, accomplishing whatever I chose.

Mine was not the only midlife crisis that passed through the Café de Flor. There, and at a handful of other student cafés in Saint-Germain-des-Prés, I met exceptional people from all over the world who also found themselves in Paris with questions of their own.

I thought I truly understood that gaining additional knowledge was not the path to enlightenment. I was resigned to the sad fact that it always seemed to boil down to self-discipline and willpower.

What did not connect for me was the importance of doing one thing really well, like Collins's hedgehog. Nor did I make the connections that the flywheel effect emerges from persistent practice of doing something really well. Even though my doctoral research relied on Collins's book, I was so focused on the next breakthrough, and experiencing a transformation, that I missed those important, common-sense metaphors.

Metaphors play an important part in making meaning, and in the next chapter we will examine how metaphors also are the context.

CHAPTER 5 — NATURE'S SYSTEMS AS CONTEXT

In high school physics classes, I learned that to understand difficult concepts and ideas I needed to get outside of my head, by working with someone else or working with my hands with real models. Equations and words on a page, or even photos, were ineffective for me to get an understanding.

A flimsy model of the solar system, made from Styrofoam balls and recycled coat hangers, hung from the ceiling of my high school physics classroom. When, as a teenager, I wasn't trying to act detached and cool, I found it extraordinary to gain perspective, to clearly "see" the system in which we lived, this solar system. Only when I attained this larger systems perspective were the very basic concepts – like gravity and centripetal acceleration – knowable for me. In hindsight, I can see that the larger solar system perspective was in effect the context.

This handmade solar system hanging from the classroom ceiling also introduced me to the basic concept of the system: the fundamental idea that generally things didn't "just happen" in isolation, but are natural and predictable results within a system.

The system provided the basic cause and effect, which I, like so many others, sought and appreciated. For example, if I were to move my attention out of my head, and do something to interact with the model of the solar system, I could physically see a new perspective (one could also do this in a virtual reality simulator). If I stood in just the right spot, I would get a much deeper understanding of why the sun appeared to rise in the morning and why the moon seemed to travel across our sky. By understanding the underlying system, I came to see, I could avoid all sorts of unnecessary and magical stories.

Learning by interacting, doing, and redoing, was essential for me. Whether it was physics or interpersonal relationships (I struggled with both), I needed to get out of my head and interact with someone or the real physical world to understand the framework or the context. Listening to a lecture, watching a video, or reading a book did not always work. Very often, I thought I was slow; I certainly thought this was more difficult for me, easier for others.

Seeing the framework, or structural context, was just as essential for my understanding of the current state of coaching when I wrote this book.

From Geocentric to Heliocentric

When you are looking up at a model of the solar system, you are looking at a *system*. For our discussion here, we can identify three different systems which, over many years, have helped us to understand the role of gravity and how all planets (and objects) behave in the system.

Although these systems may be familiar to you, please allow me a brief review to make the case for the idea that, over time, our concept of the influence and behavior of gravity has changed, shifting from something that existed inside of an object like the earth, to outside the object, to outside the earth.[1]

In rough terms, starting with the Greeks, around 400 BCE, the earth was thought to be a sphere at the center of the universe.[2] This was truly a self-centered system, referred to as geocentric, in which celestial bodies like the sun, stars, and moon moved, not by the force of gravity, but by a life force bestowed upon them by the gods, and known as *vis viva*.

Twenty-five hundred years later, Isaac Newton, studying the ancient Greeks, wrote a famous notebook entry: "Amicus Plato amicus Aristoteles magis amica veritas" (Plato is my friend, Aristotle is my friend, truth is a greater friend.)[3] In other words, Newton liked these two Greek guys, but their idea of the geocentric system was wrong, and the time had come to make a system upgrade.

So, Newton, along with his predecessors Copernicus, Galileo, and Kepler,[4] changed the earth-centered system to one in which the sun was now at the center, which is why it is called the solar system. The earth was now one of the bodies, like the moon, which traveled of its own power.

However, even Sir Isaac Newton thought the reason the moon travelled around the earth and the earth around the sun, was because of the unique and magical life force *vis viva*, contained inside the planets (or objects). This theory held that the gravitational attraction of one planet on another somehow resulted from an agent inside the bodies: a "point source." Newton, like his contemporaries, bristled at the idea of something existing in the space between objects.[5] He called that an "Absurdity," and wrote:

> It is inconceivable that inanimate Matter should, without the Mediation of something else, which is not material, operate upon, and affect other matter without mutual Contact…That Gravity should be innate, inherent and essential to Matter, so that one body may act upon another at a distance thro' a Vacuum, without the

Mediation of any thing else, by and through which their Action and Force may be conveyed from one to another, is to me so great an Absurdity that I believe no Man who has in philosophical Matters a competent Faculty of thinking can ever fall into it. Gravity must be caused by an Agent acting constantly according to certain laws; but whether this Agent be material or immaterial, I have left to the Consideration of my readers.[6]

—Isaac Newton, Letters to Bentley, 1692–3

Then, two hundred and seventy years after Newton, a self-taught Briton, Michael Faraday, with the assistance and mathematical skills of his apprentice James Clerk Maxwell, developed the concept of fields. Faraday's insight changed the workings of the sun-centered system for the third time.

In Newton's system, the forces of gravity existed inside the planets; gravity was somehow located at a point source. But Faraday demonstrated the forces that caused the behavior to exist outside the object or body, in something he called a field. Faraday, after a seven-year apprenticeship as a bookbinder, changed the concept of gravitational attraction from a Newtonian point source to a gravitation field that existed between the bodies.

From Inside to Outside Our Own Heads

As we've seen, our view of the planetary system changed, from the ancient Greek view, to Newtonian, and then to field theory, as we migrated from being at the center of the universe to simply being another planet in the universe.

The system we humans use to understand and locate our consciousness or self, and therefore our personal place in the universe, has also changed over time. In this section, I draw a parallel to the migration of our perception of the "self," from inside our heads to a field outside our heads.

Again, we begin with the Greeks. Prior to Descartes, the Scholastic-Aristotelian philosophy prevailed. A methodical criticism of knowledge based on hypothetical doctrine, Aristotelian philosophy relied on the knowledge acquired through our senses and the exercise of reason. In the Aristotelian model, the moon and the heavenly bodies, such as the sun, the stars, and the planets, were made of a substance, called quintessence. They were perfect spheres, and all moved in perfect circular orbits, driven by "intelligent movers" – the gods, not gravity. The Aristotelian concept of gravity explained why lightweight bodies rise away from the center of the earth and heavy bodies move naturally toward it with a speed related to their weight.

Then, the seventeenth-century French philosopher, mathematician, and scientist René Descartes changed the way we saw ourselves. His intention was to introduce a new way of understanding the most foundational questions of cause and effect. He wanted to apply the new mechanistic approach, which was just beginning to become popular.

Descartes concluded that humans, like all living creatures, are substance. Substance, in turn, is made up of a body, which is matter, and a soul, which is form. In Descartes' system, multiple souls controlled things like reproduction, movement, and perception.

Descartes' was a system of duality, separating body from mind. Our consciousness existed in the mind, located inside of our skulls, in our pineal gland, which lies between the two hemispheres of the brain. Although physically contained within it, the mind was separate from our body. In the *Treatise of Man*, Descartes wrote:

> My view is that this gland is the principal seat of the soul, and the place in which all our thoughts are formed.[7]

After Descartes, the third system or framework for our consciousness and perception is the embodied system, in which the mind departs the pineal gland, and is thought to be embodied throughout our entire body, including our head. The field and study of embodied cognition is a relatively young science; however, it began with some of the same twentieth-century philosophers who also formulated ontology and phenomenology: Martin Heidegger, Maurice Merleau-Ponty, and John Dewey. Also, George Lakoff was a central figure in the development of embodied cognition, and, as we will see in later chapters, he has been an important contributor to ideas in metaphors, linguistics, and perception.

In this system, widely accepted and influenced by eminent scientists like American Rhodes Scholar John Searle, consciousness and perception are also considered to be embodied. In a 2013 TED Talk, "Our Shared Condition: Consciousness," Searle proposed that consciousness and perception are embodied "biological phenomena, like photosynthesis or mitosis..." that happen in the body, just like digestion.[8]

Next, we'll see what happened in the migration of consciousness and perception theory, and why it's important to coaching.

The System Outside Our Head

A few blocks from Paul Bakery, near the post office, was a small and less touristy café on Rue Buci, called Café Jade. There was nothing particularly special about it, except it was the first café I considered my own. I felt as though the waiters knew me, even if in fact I was probably just another tourist. At Café Jade, I believed I had become the "guy watching the tourists walk by" – as I had dreamt, when I sat at home alone after surgery. But if I was that guy, there was nothing magical about the experience and this too was becoming not "it."

At Café Jade, I eagerly opened the books I'd ordered from Amazon and picked up at the post office. It was there I first sat down with an amazing book called *Perceptions in Actions*, by a young American philosopher, Alva Noë. His clear and practical perspective on perception and consciousness rang true for me.

Noë's ideas use a simple metaphor to explain how we experience perception and consciousness. He says perception and consciousness are more like climbing a tree than digesting a meal or watching a movie in your head. In other words, perception and consciousness are things in which we participate, not things that happen inside us. We do them; they're not done to us.

> [I]nstead of having to ground ourselves by sheer cognition – constructing a representation of the point in space, in our minds [...] we take advantage of the fact that we have more immediate links to the world because we are in the world ... we have the sorts of bodily skills to exploit the linkages.[9]

Noë's interpretation made sense, because it seemed that when I was doing, and interacting with the physical world, I was more conscious, or conscious in a different and more focused way. I understood more deeply, like when I was interacting with the Styrofoam solar system hanging from the ceiling of my classroom. Noë says that "perception is something we enact or achieve, in motion, as a way of being part of a larger process."[10] This fit my experiences of learning by doing, outside of my head.

For me, by contrast, the linguistic representation and the concept of a mental model only was logical and compelling, but it did not accurately mirror the way my mind worked. The mental models I created were more like brief snapshots than movies. Left alone, the consciousness inside my own head was unfocused, and my mind darted from thought to thought, image to image. I had discussions and arguments with myself, and much of the time I was in a kind of automatic mode, with little control over what popped into my thoughts. However, my consciousness and perception were distinct when I interacted with someone or something outside of my head, particularly when I was coaching or being coached.

Noë's work validated my experience when he suggested that perception and consciousness do not exist only inside our heads. He offers that they exist at the intersection of our embodied mind and the real physical world. Noë's elegant idea is captured in part by the following:

> The idea that we could think that the brain is not only part of the story, but the whole story, is, well, it is unfounded… We have no better reason to think that mental lives happen in our brains than we do that speech happens in our mouths.[11]

This was the first clear interpretation I had encountered that acknowledged there's more to performance and accomplishment than what's inside our heads. After many years of my growing resignation about the impossibility of self-help, I was fascinated that Noë was looking beyond willpower, relationship to word, and the world of mental models and stories. In 2009, Noë went on to articulate this point more clearly in his book, *Out of Our Heads*.

I began to make sense of this notion of consciousness outside myself when I looked at the concept of lift. My understanding of lift also seems to fit Noë's model, in that lift does not exist inside the airplane wing, any more than consciousness or perception exists in my head. Lift also does not simply exist in a place – like the City of Paris, or Café de Flor – that I would have to geographically relocate to before I could find it. Instead, as Noë suggests happens with perception, lift emerges and exists at the intersection of the wing and the atmosphere – or the intersection of the coach and client.

Perhaps my conscious experience – including my willpower – could be influenced and even managed from the outside. Perhaps performance and accomplishment were more than just willpower and language.

The Mechanics of Rational Memory

Twenty years ago, when I was first involved in coaching, it crossed over a chasm it should not have – the psychological chasm. Looking back, the primary reason I left coaching, vowing never to return to it, was because it intruded into sensitive aspects of my life, and the lives of others, that just did not feel right nor helpful. In those years, coaches, including me, trained only through the LGAT public programs. With no clinical psychological training, we newly fledged coaches tried to address the clients' issues. As we'd been trained, we all used a quick-fix, one-method-fits-all approach that we'd learned in a few weekends during which we had been the clients whose issues were investigated by the LGAT trainers.

One of the inarguable tenets of coaching taught in the seminars was that people behave in rational and logical ways. The idea was that people made decisions consistent with how the world occurs to them through stories. I recall the ubiquitous Tony Robbins infomercials that explained people behaved logically based on pain or pleasure – but in every case, we made decisions and took action logically and rationally. The trick to many of the early motivational programs was to change these internal memories, or "change the tape" that was playing in our heads. The LGAT programs used the same logic but came at the solution in a unique way: they often used a metaphor of transformation, and bypassed the logic system, creating an easier, faster solution – more like pure magic.

In addition, they borrowed and simplified some of the then-current organizational learning theory developed by Harvard's Chris Argyris and Donald Schon in their work with single- and double-loop learning.[12]

The essence of the model was a simplified Argyris single loop: "Something happened," and then we created an interpretation – or made up a story – about what happened. That intact *story* was then stored in a file in our mind. Our story or file then shaped the way we thought. In future experiences when something happened, our story was retrieved and either confirmed – reinforcing the story – or rejected.

In the 1970s, the metaphor most commonly incorporated in this technology was that of a simple manila file folder, also called a record or tape, and later, a computer file.

With this model, transformation was accomplished when we could identify our own limiting beliefs as a file. By identifying or distinguishing those files or beliefs which limited our performance, we could choose another belief; thereby being "transformed" and freed from their limiting influence. We would now be free to think in new ways and not simply repeat our past patterns. Just as we were frequently reminded in the seminars, "The definition of insanity is doing the same thing over and over again, expecting a new result."[13]

After all, in coaching and managing, are we not just reacting based on our "story" and our files? Don't we all make up stories and live in those stories from the past? Is that not how we make sense of the world? Whether our stories are true or one hundred percent accurate, some say is not the point; it is our beliefs that influence our performance and outcomes. These beliefs are the reason we do not accomplish our dreams; these beliefs come from our past – our stories.

> My life has been full of terrible misfortunes most of which never happened.
>
> —Michel de Montaigne, sixteenth-century
> French philosopher and essayist

Relying on our stories is natural, but, in the extraordinarily complex world of the brain, we now know our stories are murky and not neatly tucked in one location of the brain. The century-old concept that our memories are stored intact and in files has been debunked by real science both clinically and from brain imaging.

> Memories don't sit in one place, waiting patiently to be retrieved; they drift through the mind, more like clouds or vapor than something we can put our hands around.[14]
>
> —Elizabeth Loftus and Katherine Ketcham

The "files" metaphor is categorized as a conceptual metaphor or a cognitive metaphor, because it communicates a concept used to understand a system or process. This metaphor and the concept of the intact file is still offered by well-intentioned, but perhaps over-zealous, LGAT seminar-trained coaches, to "transform" their clients' limiting beliefs. Many coaches strongly believe the metaphor has helped their clients, and in fact – perhaps because of the placebo effect or the Hawthorne effect[15] – it has objectively improved results in some cases. However, in the past half century this same metaphor has caused more than just ineffective coaching; it has unfortunately caused enormous damage.

In their bestselling self-help book, *The Courage to Heal*, first published in 1988 and now in its fourth edition, authors Ellen Bass and Laura Davis (neither one a trained therapist, counselor, psychologist, or physician) perpetuate this cognitive metaphor of a file: a buried or repressed intact memory. The authors endorse a free-association writing exercise – widely used in LGAT seminars in the 1970s – that helps "survivors" identify their repressed memories.

Bass and Davis say, "If you were abused as a child, you are probably experiencing long-term effects that interfere with your day-to-day functioning,"[16] and "...by going back and writing about what happened, you also re-experience feeling and are able to grieve. You excavate the sites in which you've buried memory and pain, dread and fury."[17]

Even more promising is the authors' broad claim that this exercise is specifically for you if you feel you "can't get motivated..., [or you] feel different from other people... and you have a hard time identifying your own needs [or just] feeling good."[18] The conclusion for their reader to draw is simple: if any of those things are true, you may have been suppressing your own experience of abuse in memory files that have remained intact since you were a child.

It is self-evident that stories are the way we understand the chaos and cacophony through which we trudge every day. As we'll see later in LIFT, we are all wired to find fast and familiar stories to help guide us and provide comfort.

This powerful metaphor of the repressed memory of childhood abuse can be so compelling and effective because it provides a logical and emotionally seductive explanation, or excuse, for someone's current lackluster results in life. Needless to say, genuine, complex, and intense emotions are inexorably linked to cases of abuse. Each case is highly charged and multifaceted; and most certainly requires an experienced mental healthcare professional, not a coach whose training consists of a few weekend seminars.

So, getting back to cognitive metaphors, a bestselling author and psychologist provides a different metaphor to more accurately describe how memories are retained and retrieved. In her 1994 book, *The Myth of Repressed Memory*, Elizabeth Loftus asks the reader to consider another view:

> Think of the mind as a bowl filled with clear water. Now imagine each memory as a teaspoon of milk stirred into the water. Every adult mind holds thousands of these murky memories...Who among us would dare to disentangle the water from the milk?[19]

> —Elizabeth Loftus and Katherine Ketcham

A recognized leader with thirty-five years' experience in her specialty of repressed memories, Loftus conducted research which demonstrates that memories behave as though they are interspersed like milk in water, not at all like separately retrievable files. This metaphor made sense to me when I considered how just a spoonful of harmful bacteria can affect the entire system of clean water into which it is poured – altering each individual spoonful of the resultant fluid.

One group trying to undo some of the damage caused by the notion of "intact" repressed memories (or files) is The Innocence Project. Founded in 1991, it is an organization working to overturn wrongful convictions, primarily through DNA testing. Their website claims that, "eyewitness misidentification is the single greatest cause of wrongful convictions nationwide, playing a role in more than seventy-five percent of convictions overturned through DNA testing. While eyewitness testimony can be persuasive evidence before a judge or jury, thirty years of strong social science research has proven that eyewitness identification is often unreliable."[20]

Further, "Research shows that the human mind is not like a tape recorder; we neither record events exactly as we see them, nor recall them like a tape that has been rewound."[21]

Even though the "files" or "records" metaphor has been debunked, many of the current coaching literature and foundational methodologies continue to use this same concept: there's an "intact" file of your story with its associated limiting beliefs. The methodology promotes identifying the limiting belief; once you identify and distinguish it, you can choose another belief or "complete the past," and move beyond it.

The methodology promotes "getting to know your story," to see how this easily available familiar story inhibits us from learning something new. My concern is that, by "knowing" your unique story, you didn't have to consider other causes of your behavior. Those coaches who consider themselves very transformed claim to know their own limiting files cold. The easy answer may satisfy the confirmation bias, and blind them from asking a more difficult question. As we'll see later in the book, our cognitive biases will easily grab these more accessible "easy" answers, preventing us from learning anything deeper.[22]

The apparently irrefutable logic of the stories–files approach explains that people behave as the result of a story they tell themselves. But the research of psychologists Daniel Kahneman and Amos Tversky shows that this is not quite right.[23] In decades of research, they demonstrated that people actually make systematic errors based on simple biases or heuristics, which are included in what they call the mechanics of our cognitive systems, or the "cognitive machinery."

It turns out that people do in fact behave in predictable ways, but the predictable behavior is a result of the mechanics of our error-prone cognitive systems, not just the result of their stories or files. As well, corroborating evidence comes from a completely different area of psychology, addressing the adaptive unconscious. Timothy Wilson, a psychologist from the University of Virginia, has shown that "people construct stories to explain their feelings [and actions], and these stories were often incorrect...In other words they construct a story about how they feel that is based on reasons that are not entirely trustworthy. The story has a ring of truth to people, but because they have used faulty information (reasons that happen to be on their mind), it often misrepresents how they really feel."[24]

There is something very seductive and natural about believing these stories, and if your performance – or the performance of your client – is acceptable, and you are happy and have heathy relationships, there is no need not to believe them.

But if you or your clients are not performing as you'd like, excavating these stories may be largely ineffective in understanding or influencing behavior, performance, and results. As it relates to "real" observable objective behavior and performance, understanding our cognitive machinery – with the common biases and heuristics that typically trip us up – is a more relevant line of inquiry. The Craft of Expert Coaching requires a working knowledge of, and a competency with, our cognitive machinery.

Even the current business coaching books and practices seem to hold two basic assumptions about human behavior and performance. The first is that people in business are rational, and their thinking and memory are sound. By extension this is taken to mean they behave logically or, as it's often put, their behavior is consistent with the stories they have, or how the world occurs to them. In fact, some mainstream coaching methods engage in these stories as the sole way to help the client identify their issues and make progress.

The second assumption is that our emotions, and primarily our fears, explain most of our irrational behavior, poor decisions, and limiting beliefs.[25]

With respect to the first assumption, most coaching literature has a section or chapters focused on "active listening." Many of these chapters make this point, which is taken from such a text:

> We then say that listening is linguistic, it lives in language. Listening is active interpretation, active internal story telling to myself. Listening is definitely not passively receiving objective information, but instead has everything to do with building a story, building a narrative...[26]
>
> —W. Chalmers Brothers

Active listening includes identifying one or two key beliefs and self-assessments which the coach believes hold the client back or limit their actions. A "great" active-listening coach was said to be able to "nail" the issue or limiting belief holding back the client in a one-hour session. These so-called brilliant coaches coincidentally found that most clients fell into one of a relatively few categories, for example, a victim, a fraud, or someone who is not good enough. Within the hour they could convince the client of this unique limiting belief and suggest they, as a leadership coach, just happen to be particularly good at addressing this very issue.

A better approach, which draws from one of the practices of the Craft of Expert Coaching, is to listen for what may have tripped the client up; it may be buried in a story or a decision, itself the result of the client's cognitive machinery. Assessments, like the ones mentioned in the previous chapter, identify the client's natural strengths and weaknesses. These will be reliable points of reference which can help to determine where and why the client may be stuck.

To clarify this point, let me tell you about a CEO whom I coach. With this case study, I hope to demonstrate that using validated assessments helps to remove the seduction of familiar stories. This CEO and his team were preparing to sell a company they had grown over the past fifteen years. After the initial excitement, they got down to the hard work of the due diligence, the process in which teams of accountants and consultants show up and start digging through the company's records. Even though he knew he and his team had not broken any laws or even any accounting rules, the CEO was really struggling and was literally losing sleep. He became uncharacteristically negative and suspicious, and felt the due diligence team had bad intentions and possibly ulterior motives Then, some trusted colleagues told him that his recent behavior was negatively influencing his team and possibly the deal itself. My client didn't like the assertion, but he was self-aware enough to know something was off.

So he contacted me. After a fairly brief discussion, I had him do a basic Hogan Development Survey assessment. This assessment, with which I am very familiar, is particularly useful because it identifies the behaviors that are highly likely to be expressed under stressful conditions. The results clearly indicated his natural state under stress was to be very skeptical, likely to perceive that others have "bad ulterior motives,"[27] and was "prone to negativity."

Initially he was resistant, claiming he was not a skeptical guy, and that he prided himself in taking smart risks; after all, he had built a multimillion dollar software tech company in Silicon Valley. He may have been aware of his positive traits, perhaps even a little optimistic, but he was largely unaware of how he behaved under stress. With coaching and time to think it through, however, he accepted that he had this propensity to be negative and suspicious. While he didn't like it and wanted to rid himself of it, he understood this was part of his nature and he had better learn to deal with it. Nothing about the process was instantaneous or easy, but with work and practice he became a stronger, more resilient CEO. (And the deal went through.)

Self-diagnosis in an age of immediate information can be dangerous in any field; because of this, it is now more important than ever to use validated instruments and well-trained Expert Coaches. That's why using data to focus on progress is one of the four practices of the Craft of Expert Coaching.

Next, we'll look more closely at how a good story that temporarily makes us feel good can skew our beliefs, while good data can teach us important life lessons and even save the day.

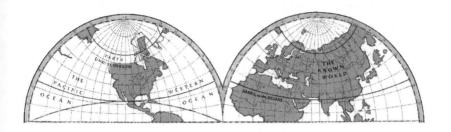

CHAPTER 6 — DATA, NOT DRAMA

The Good Story Trap

We'll always be working with stories, since they are the way we put together and make sense of our experiences. The coach's job is to listen to the clients' stories, and then, with skill and craft, discern which stories have real power, and which may be driven by an unrelated cognitive bias. In this section, we look at the cognitive biases that are a natural part of the way we make meaning.

The trap in listening to a story is believing it always provides the accurate cause and effect; the story may sound good, but the "reasons" for the client's behavior or experience may not even be conscious.

For example, suppose there is a massive failure and recall of cell phones from one manufacturer. Thousands and thousands of phones have burst into flames, causing damage. This is all over the news, and it's hardly possible to be unaware of it on an average day. On one of those average days, you're coaching an executive who complains of feeling stuck in a career rut.

After some conversation, you ask a good coaching question.

You: "Why do you say you are stuck; what is your evidence or what is the reason you have for this belief?"

Executive: "Well, I was just passed over for a promotion."

You: "Why do you think you were passed over?"

Executive: "I was passed over because I am too careful. I'm a perfectionist and I don't like to take risks, because I don't want to make mistakes. ... Just look what just happened in the news with the cell phones. If you take risks, you are likely to make big mistakes."

The conclusion that he or she will fail because of a big mistake was easily accessible because it was in the news. We'll explore this example of cognitive bias later. For now, consider the possibility that the executive's underlying reasons for not being promoted might be unrelated to the cell phone news item.

As a coach, it would be easy to chase after the belief underlying the conclusion that the client is too careful, or perfectionistic. This line of questioning may reveal the client doesn't feel good enough, or is not worthy, or is a failure, etc. and therefore does not take risks – and you as a coach may feel you have done a great thing excavating an underlying belief like "I'm not worth it," or "I'm not good enough." But these are sentiments we all feel to some degree, and probing and clever questioning can elicit them from almost everyone. The real reason your client was not promoted may have nothing to do with ideas of risk, or not feeling good enough. A well-designed and executed 360 survey or Hogan assessment, and targeted interviews with the client's boss and peers, will yield more useful results.

One compelling line of research shows that when a newsworthy disaster is easily available in a person's memory, they will use it – and make it fit their story. Large-scale disasters and failures (like the cell phones) are well documented by the insurance business, which is financially motivated to understand risk behavior. Researchers studying California's earthquake insurance activity noticed that more people purchase policies after an earthquake. They change their story about the future, and their beliefs in the likelihood of such disasters. Then after a time, as memories fade, fewer and fewer people continue with coverage – the dynamics of memory help to explain the recurrent cycles of disaster, concern, and growing complacency that are familiar to students of large-scale emergencies.[1]

Jerome Bruner was a twentieth-century American cognitive psychologist known for his work on the stories we use to make sense of our lives. He categorizes two different ways in which we come to know something and make sense of events: (1) paradigmatic and (2) narrative modes of thought. The paradigmatic mode looks outside of ourselves at the external world of nature, its laws and principles, and represents a more classical empiricist way of understanding and knowing.

Bruner goes on to describe the other mode of knowing, a narrative mode in which we learn from stories.

> The narrative mode leads instead to good stories, gripping drama, believable (though not necessarily "true") historical accounts. It deals in human or human-like intention and action and the vicissitudes and consequences that mark their course. It strives to put its timeless miracles into the particulars of experience, and to locate the experience in time and place.[2]

Bruner explains that both ways are useful; one is not better or worse than the other. But, as Bruner describes, these narrative stories may sound good, and may even have emotion attached to them; unless you as the coach understand the finer details of the business (context), you may miss the important points. Because we're always interpreting and learning in some context, business, or field, I contend that it's important for a coach to have an expertise in that specific context in which they are coaching. The practice of leadership may look very different in a manufacturing environment, for example, compared to a biotech or an advertising company.

Motorcycle shop owner, University of Virginia fellow, and author of *Shop Class as Soulcraft* and *The World Beyond Your Head*, Matthew Crawford supports this point when he says:

> When we become competent in some field of practice [a context], our perception is disciplined by that practice; we become attuned to pertinent features of a situation that would be invisible to a bystander.[3]

In other words, we learn abstractions like collaboration, alignment, and leadership in a specific field.

LIFT takes the position that without an expertise in the context, a coach can be easily misled by basic cognitive errors and iconic stories. ~~This includes compelling story of the four-minute mile.~~

The Myth of the Four-Minute Mile: Identifying Cause & Effect

To demonstrate the traps of a good story and the pervasive influence of our cognitive machinery, we'll review one of coaching's most-recited stories: Roger Bannister and the four-minute mile. This story is a great example of a "breakthrough" or "transformational" narrative. It's one of the most misleading uses of cause and effect cited in leadership and transformational literature.

If you google four-minute mile – breakthrough thinking – coaching – limiting beliefs – you are likely to get over a million hits. In many of the results you'll find companies – generally coaching, self-help, and "transformational" consulting companies. They reference the four-minute mile as irrefutable evidence of the power of "limiting beliefs." They connect the idea that our limiting beliefs, our conversations and stories, are the keys to attaining breakthrough human performance. Let's take a closer look at another version of the something-for-nothing urge, which relies on the notion of a limiting belief.

We'll analyze the four-minute mile through the lens of cause and effect.

The Cause. As the iconic story goes, up until 1954, people believed the four-minute mark for running a mile was humanly impossible to break. Some business coaches and consultants referred to Greek folklore, invoking the amusing training method of having the runners chased by lions or bulls to motivate them to run faster. These stories were all designed to build the case that since at least the time of the Greeks, man had been unable to break this barrier. The cause was clear: our limiting beliefs, thoughts, and stories were the barriers.

The Effect. According to this story, when Roger Bannister broke the four-minute mile time barrier, he concurrently broke the mental limiting belief for all athletes. The proof of this claim is that just a few weeks later, the record was broken again. And then again. As the story goes, when Bannister broke the record, a flood of people broke the same record. The following is a typical rendition:

> The most incredible part of this story, isn't Bannister's four-minute mile, but what happened to the other runners when Bannister ran his four-minute mile. Remember, the mile record had stood at slightly over four minutes for nearly nine years, but the year after Bannister broke the four-minute mile, other runners broke through their mental barrier, leading to 37 runners breaking the four-minute mile.[4]

In Figure 6.0 the published results are plotted graphically, and tell a different story.

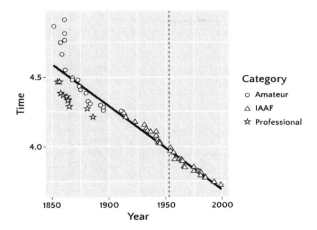

Figure 6.0[5] Chronology of men's four-minute mile race times.

In the myth, the supposed cause and effect were clear: The cause was the change in the story (which included the limiting belief), and the result was like magic, a transformation! The record was broken twice in a matter of months. It was as though it took nothing other than a thought. It really seemed like a demonstration of something for nothing.

How could this be a coincidence? The record stood for thousands of years. Then, Bam! Bannister breaks it, and others follow within weeks.

As search results demonstrate, the coaching and transformation industries rely heavily on this anecdote. In their words, *something became possible*, and by virtue of this possibility, average people were able to do above-average things.

The plotted data show what really happened. In simple terms, breaking the four-minute mile had no more or less importance than, say, breaking the 4.1-minute mile or the 3.9-minute mile. As can be seen from the graph, runners' performance progressed in the same way over time. There was no "breakthrough." A breakthrough graph, by contrast, would have resembled the water–to–vapor transformation diagram in Chapter One.

But the myth exposes one of the peskiest cognitive errors to which we all fall victim, an aspect of our cognitive machinery that deals with statistics. The four-minute mile example clearly illustrates the Law of Small Numbers, as identified by Daniel Kahneman. Many of us know that the results of large samples are more precise than those from a small sample size. But "even sophisticated researchers have a poor intuition and a wobbly understanding of sample effects."[6]

A simple way to understand this elusive error is to consider the weather in your region. Let's say you have two or three consecutive days that are below freezing in the middle of summer (a time during which it is typically much warmer). Using the Law of Small Numbers you could make the case that there has been a breakthrough in the weather! Further, you could conclude that because of this breakthrough, we'll have below-freezing temperatures in the middle of summer forever. The sample size is critical; looking at only a small number of days may lead someone to conclude that something significant, like a "breakthrough," has happened. But if you look at a larger sample size of, say, ten years, you will see that the temperature generally follows a trend. While days may fall outside the trend, over time, the weather continues to follow the larger trend.

In the four-minute mile, the error caused by the small sample size is more easily dispelled by looking at a graph of what is called a regression, which simply looks at the relationships among (or compares) the data points in a sample.

Think about how easy it is to predict or project a future based on only a few events. We say things like, "I will never trust them again!" or, "This brand is always made with good quality." We easily project into the future, and it will be either very good or very bad. This happens in the stock market and in Las Vegas all the time: "I'm on a roll..."

Running as Craft

But why is the four-minute mile such a powerful story? Chances are if you mention the four-minute mile to group of people, thirty to forty percent of the group will have some knowledge of it, and the urban myth surrounding it. What if you discuss an equally extraordinary feat in track and field like that of American long-jumper Bob Beamon in the 1968 Olympics? In an event often won by fractions of an inch, Beamon crushed the world record by six inches! Also, his record of twenty-nine feet two and a half inches held for almost twenty-three years. In that same gathering of people, it's likely that only small portion of the group would know of this record, or any number of other extraordinary world records.

The story of the four-minute mile is still so powerful today is because it plays into our cognitive machinery and trips several of the basic human biases. One cannot be faulted for retelling this story (even embellishing it as I once did), because it was in the name of inspiration. But, as I found out, to serious runners, the idea that a single mental barrier alone would enable a runner to produce a breakthrough result is silly or downright offensive. If you explain to a master athlete or craftsman that such a "breakthrough" in performance was the result of a "file" or a limiting belief, they would dismiss you as simply ignorant of what it takes to become a master. While clearly an aspect of mastery requires intensive mental training, becoming a master also requires a focus on and dedication to the "doing" – the physical training. Transformation often promotes the idea that to become a master one should "be" a master. But without a crafts-like focus, hard work, and deliberate practice "doing," the "being" is useless; worse still, looking for the transformation without any "doing" may crush your spirit and confidence.

Serious runners run for time, but they also run for the satisfaction and experience of practicing their craft. The "doing" of the craft, doing something well for its own sake, provides the reward.

In 1977, *Running Times* (now *Runners World*) published Roger Robinson's account of the breaking of the four-minute mile record, not surprisingly titled, "Four-Minute Everest: The Story and the Myth, An epic narration of the historic first sub-four mile."[7] The author called it a myth, because those who know the nature of serious runners know the real story, which differs significantly from the myth that surrounds it.

Robinson provides real data to demonstrate that a number of world-class runners were trending toward the record, and that Bannister's new record was broken shortly thereafter was actually predictable.

A brief historical account can be found in Appendix A and is plotted in Figure 6.0. The data demonstrate a slow, steady, and hard-fought progress which, over time, predictably improved.

The point of this section is to reveal the power of a narrative, and the ease with which we can create a "great" story that makes us feel good, but does not serve anyone. Without an expertise in running, which includes an understanding of what it really takes to be a competitive runner, a coach may succumb to the seduction of the something-for-nothing urge. An important aspect of another practice is a working knowledge of basic statistics. The point is, our cognitive machinery makes us prone to errors. When we jump to a conclusion, or make a long-term definitive decision based on a very small amount of data, we succumb to an aspect of human nature which is easily correctable. As coaches, we need to understand the facts and learn to analyze the data.[8]

Perhaps the more valuable lesson from Bannister's record is that human collaboration works. Some say it was Bannister's use of two runners as pacemakers that led to his success. Chris Brasher and Chris Chataway set the pace for Bannister, essentially driving his behavior from outside of his head. Also, at about the same time, Australian John Landy started making real progress when he worked with an Expert Coach, the Czechoslovak runner and three-time

Olympic gold medalist Emil Zátopek. Together they developed an innovative interval training process, which helped Landy become the first person to break Bannister's new record.

His pacers influenced Bannister's behavior and performance from the outside in. Research for years has demonstrated that cues and primers which exist outside of us in the environment (like the magnetic field) influence our behavior and performance. We'll investigate this further in Chapter Seven.

The Cognitive Machinery

To introduce the cognitive machinery as described by Kahneman and Tversky, we'll unpack the four-minute-mile myth from the perspective of the innate human biases, or the cognitive machinery.

In 1954, if you followed the world of track and field and the craft of running, you knew that a number of world-class athletes believed they could break the record and were making real progress. It was not as though people in the sport were walking around with a fixed belief that it could not be broken. Bannister knew Landy was close, so Bannister stepped up his training and decided to run when he did.[9] The times of these world-class runners had fallen over the past several years, (with an interruption because of the war), as can be seen from Appendix A, and many believed it was merely a matter of time.

Confirmation bias is our tendency to seek out, interpret, and recall information in a way that confirms our preexisting beliefs or hypotheses, while giving disproportionately less consideration to alternative possibilities. It's known as one of the "systematic biases" because it is so predictable that people will change their behavior under its influence.

It's valuable to note that the confirmation bias can be seen on both sides of the four-minute mile record. Before the record was broken, there were those who liked the story that this barrier was "natural," permanent, or perhaps God-given, based on our anatomy. These people sought and found evidence to confirm their story of a physical, and perhaps an anatomical limitation. We can observe the same type of confirmation-bias stories prior to many other firsts, like the first manned airplane flight, or the first woman to graduate from MIT. The bias is compelling; it is easy to believe.

Before the record was broken, the four-minute mile had a mystique. The mile was a familiar, iconic distance and it was something everyone could imagine and relate to. Breaking something into four quarters was common, whether it was a nation's currency, or race tracks designed to be four laps to a mile. The notion of one lap per minute also made the concept accessible and easy to understand and recall. This idea of easy recall introduces another important part of Kahneman's cognitive machinery called the **availability bias**.

The availability bias makes thinking easy and offers a mental shortcut, a reliance on examples that come to mind quickly, as illustrated with the earthquake insurance example at the beginning of this chapter. The availability bias answers an easier question than the one actually posed.

The four-minute-mile myth is also aided by what Kahneman and his associate Paul Slovic call the **affect heuristic**. The affect heuristic is an automatic bias that makes decisions and judgments based solely on our emotions. If we like it, or it makes us feel good, we decide in its favor.

Bannister's record came as the British were recovering from a devastating war in which they had been almost defenseless against the German Blitz. Bannister survived the Blitz and endured the food shortages. In the 1950s, as part of a battered generation, he had become a medical student and was a symbol to the British of renewed progress and hope for the future. This narrative was also shared all over the world, a relatively new capability made possible by the expansion of broadcast media like radio and TV.

Bannister a tall, young, handsome, and successful medical student, looked the part. Another cognitive bias relies upon physical attractiveness, and demonstrates that people are more likely to believe, and believe in, those who are more physically attractive.[10]

All these feel-good factors supported the affect heuristic, and made Bannister's story that much more emotional and pleasing – forming another reason it is used with such frequency. He was the hero who broke the limiting belief. Those who broke the record after Bannister owed him the thanks, or so the story went.

Appendix A shows the times of the four-minute mile to demonstrate two important parts of the cognitive machinery. One is the Law of Small Numbers, or the hazard of hasty generalization. Consider the nine years before the four-minute mile was broken: On July 17, 1945, the Swedish runner Gunder Hägg ran a 4:01.04 mile, and on May 6, 1954, Bannister ran a 3:59.40 mile – an improvement on the previous record of 1.64 seconds.

But on June 21, 1954, just 46 days after Bannister's run, John Landy ran the mile in 3:28, improving Bannister's record by 66/100ths of a second. With only these two data points, it could be predicted that since it took nine years to improve by 1.64 seconds (Bannister's record), simple arithmetic would tell us it would continue to take the equivalent of 18.2/100ths of a second per year. But in only 46 days, Landy's time improved by 64/100ths. That comes to 5.08 seconds per year!

Twenty-eight times faster!

A-ha! A breakthrough!!

Not really. But the popular "breakthrough" story contended that the time it took to improve the speed had increased much faster after Bannister broke the record – and therefore in the future, this reasoning suggested, we could expect much faster times. The curve should have become steeper, or become a step function (like what happens when water droplets become water vapor).

That didn't happen. The line in the graph remained straight; there was no breakthrough, no change in performance.

There are even some reasonable explanations as to why it took nine years after Hägg's 1945 record. Many of the competing runners came from nations focused less on sports and more on rebuilding and recovering during the early post-war years following 1945.

In any case, the Law of Small Numbers might suggest this nine-year gap seems significant. But over a longer period of time, as can be seen in Appendix A and B, the trend is predictable and consistent. There was no breakthrough and no step function.

Experienced runners (masters) and coaches understand well another key finding by Kahneman, called the **planning fallacy**, in which we underestimate how complex and lengthy a task or project will be. Carelessly interpreting the meaning of the four-minute mile can lead someone way off base or worse. The planning fallacy often includes the **optimism bias**, which shows the cognitive machinery is overly confident in our abilities. We underestimate the difficulty or complexity, and are therefore consistently poor at planning. Plenty of research now demonstrates that we automatically tend to see the rosy scenario for ourselves and our abilities,[11] and, without intervention, we can get ourselves in trouble by being too optimistic. The credit card and health club industries rely on this predictable optimism bias.

Kahneman's example for optimism bias is familiar to many of us: home renovations. A 2002 study of kitchen renovations found that on average families had optimistically planned for a job cost of $18,658, and in fact ended up paying on average more than double that.[12] It's not difficult to imagine how a contractor with an understanding of such errors might capitalize on this bias for the benefit of the contractor, not the customer.

Unfortunately, the optimism bias has been misused in coaching for decades. The unscrupulous transformational coach or leadership coach uses it to encourage the client to make a big commitment, to "throw their hat over the wall." These coaches know the client will likely need more coaching to address what has been, up until that time, unattainable. In the planning stages, it feels so good just to consider the possibilities that the planning is almost an accomplishment in itself. An effective Expert Coach knows to keep an eye on the planning fallacy and optimism bias so the client addresses real issues of the budget and resources required.

Where this is particularly evident, and often damaging, is when a client wants to change jobs or even make a career change. Yes, breakthroughs are possible, but at what cost?

The cognitive machinery which we use – or which uses us – to make decisions and operate in life leaves us susceptible to errors. The good news is that these errors are now clearly delineated in good research and literature. As we've discussed, another practice of the Craft of Expert Coaching includes an understanding of our human biases and heuristics. A methodical approach that looks for and addresses bias errors is necessary to help clients identify the actual cause and effect relationships with which they are struggling. We'll address this in more detail later.

Perhaps the biggest drivers of our behavior lie in the environment, not inside our heads. When Bannister broke the record that day, he employed two runner friends as pacers, whose proximity kept his first laps under one minute each. Intuiting that the environment influences our behavior, his pacers kept him out of his head, enabling him to beat the record during the final lap.

Then again, maybe what's in our heads enables us to be influenced by our environment, and maybe our social networks and our environment deserve more attention in our coaching relationships. As Matthew Lieberman says, "The self is more a superhighway for social influence than it is the impenetrable private fortress we believe it to be."[13]

In the next chapter, on the unconscious, we begin to see there is in fact more to our behavior, decisions, and actions (or inaction) than just our conscious stories, memories, values, and habits. We will also learn more about how the world outside ourselves influences our behavior and perception.

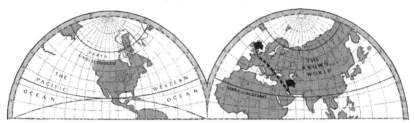

CHAPTER 7 — CONSCIOUSNESS: SWEEPING UP NATURE

The grass in Paris became a little less green after I'd lived there for a few years as a student. While I didn't regret for a moment my decision to move there, I was beginning to realize that each of my moves was the result of a version of the something-for-nothing urge. The something was the "greener grass" and the alluring idea that simply by moving to a new city or country, I could find purpose and satisfaction; from this new geography, I would be able to honor my word and accomplish my dreams – plus, after all, it's Paris!

It worked for me until it didn't, as usual.

Even after several fresh starts, when the moves did not actually provide the greener grass, I was still susceptible.

The urge was too great, and, once again, I bought into the story that *this time* it would be different and I would be happy, successful, and satisfied. In 2005, Dubai, the "City of Gold"[1] was "The" city, and I found an opportunity I thought was too good to pass up. I moved to Dubai with what was to be the largest heating, ventilation, and air conditioning (HVAC) company in the world. I joined McQuay just as it was being acquired by Daikin Industries of Japan.

The first two years in Dubai were challenging. I was working with a group of people mostly from the Middle East and, increasingly, Japan. My Western management tactics, like weekly meetings, were actively resisted. In fact, weekly meetings were so poorly attended I stopped having them. I was not managing or trying to lead a team. I was completely ineffective communicating over the phone or with emails. Email, text, phone calls, or even Skype (before it was outlawed in Dubai) simply allowed too much room for misinterpretation and miscommunications.

Out of necessity, I began having more face-to-face, one-on-one discussions, and, to my surprise, they turned out to be effective and satisfying. Although it was a last resort, I found I was most successful, and certainly happiest, when we met one-on-one several times per week, even for brief meetings. Each team member seemed genuinely interested in my experiences, good and bad, in the HVAC business. They warmed up when I shared about real wins and losses or just told a story on myself. As a manager–coach with experience and expertise in their field, I found it valuable to talk through various approaches and to recommend different tactics and methods to help them improve their performance, based on my years in the industry. These regular in-person discussions built and cemented relationships, greatly reduced turnover, and increased sales.

English was creatively used, since for all of the group members English was their second or third language. The stories they recounted about new sales opportunities, and the barriers and issues they faced, were highly complex and convoluted, typically spilling over into multiple languages. Trying to fully sort out the details and nuances of these stories proved useless. What worked instead was to spend enough time with someone to "know" how they were doing. Were they engaged, and making process in a good direction, or were they were disengaged and frustrated, or, worse, resigned to mediocrity? This discernment is somehow a natural human ability which experienced managers develop. This natural ability to "sense" and "know" how someone is feeling is a key aspect of the Craft of Expert Coaching and is part of the practices outlined in the final chapter. While we also tracked results closely, tracking is always a lagging indicator: by the time the results are in, it's often too late to intervene.

After a few months, I got to know the team members individually, and what emerged was trust. I came away from coaching sessions feeling the "lift" and in fact most of the time it seemed we were both feeling more positive and motivated.

My value as an Expert Coach was not because I understood the content of the team members' stories. It was because I was immersed in the environment and spent enough time with them to "know" how they were doing. I knew the industry and how the business operated in the Middle East, so I could help them avoid the subtle, something-for-nothing rabbit holes along their way.

What I didn't realize at the time was that when we sit across from someone and engage in a conversation, we are taking in millions of pieces of information every second. As mentioned earlier, psychologist Timothy D. Wilson, in his book *Strangers to Ourselves*, writes that the "human mind can take in eleven million pieces of information at any given moment, based on a count of the receptor cells of each sense organan... ."[2]

What science now knows is that not only do we sweep up this data, but our "adaptive unconscious" is actually learning from this unconsciously captured information. This was demonstrated experimentally fifty years ago by psychologist Arthur Reber at the University of British Columbia. His research showed that people could reliably learn a pattern in a complex string of numbers – totally unconsciously. They knew the pattern, but they didn't know how they knew it. This may validate experiences most of us have had, when we are certain that something will happen, even though we're not sure how we know.

We've all heard that communication is largely nonverbal. This idea is attributed to UCLA Psychologist Albert Mehrabian, the author of *Silent Messages*. His now-famous 7-38-55 rule says that seven percent of any communication involving feelings and attitudes is conveyed through language and words, thirty-eight percent through paralanguage like (voice) volume and timing, and fifty-five percent through nonverbal gestures, postures, expressions, and micro expressions.[3]

Micro expressions are involuntary, fleeting facial expressions or gestures. They are triggered unconsciously, and are thought to be the most accurate reflection of the actual experience, feelings, or thoughts.[4] Paul Ekman, an American psychologist, did extensive research and published important findings on micro expressions. His work inspired a television show, *Lie to Me*, which ran from 2009–2011. The show featured psychologist Dr. Cal Lightman (played by Tim Roth), who was brought in to help solve difficult criminal cases by detecting suspects' lies using his amazing abilities to recognize and interpret micro expressions.

Ekman found that about 0.25 percent of the population has an amazing natural ability to spot deception based on a subject's micro expressions. More importantly, with training and experience, almost all of us can learn to detect deception with accuracy. Ekman makes the point that we are always telegraphing deception both consciously and unconsciously through our micro expressions.[5]

However, when we look back to the unconscious pattern-recognition experiment with psychologist Arthur Reber, we can see our capabilities go beyond understanding Ekman's micro expressions and Mehrabian's non-verbal communication. This is also demonstrated in Captain Sullenberger's extraordinary performance; we humans are remarkable and can somehow tap into and use knowledge we have captured unconsciously. Sully, "knew" he needed to land on the Hudson. He didn't run the numbers and then decide, nor did he roll the dice. He knew. Although one may say it's experience, it's more

than that (as we will see later in the book). In fact, we can capture
visual information (for example) at speeds far beyond the capabilities with which we can sense them consciously. The research on
the adaptive unconscious demonstrates that we actually learn much
more than we are conscious of, and with enough time and *deliberate
practice* in a particular field with that skill or craft, we can use this
knowledge in real time.

The Adaptive Unconscious

The unconscious is not a single system, but a group of modules
– sometimes referred to as agents or processes – that gather data,
learn, and process. Wilson uses the following example to clarify:

> We have a nonconscious language processor that enables
> us to learn and use language with ease, but this mental
> module is relatively independent of our ability to recog-
> nize faces quickly and efficiently and our ability to form
> quick evaluations of whether environmental events are
> good or bad.[6]

In the same way, we can step back and "see" the parts that make
up a system, like that solar system model in my high school physics
room. By clearly identifying and understanding the parts of the
unconscious, we can (metaphorically) step back and see our unconscious mind as just a part of another larger system of the mind.
In the 1980s, MIT's Marvin Minsky introduced a very effective metaphor for the mind and the unconscious. He refers to it
as a society, with random, chaotic, and complex interconnections.
The society of mind is a great metaphor because it steps outside
the neatly organized mechanical models of the mind into the
more messy, complicated reality. Minsky was a pioneer in artificial

intelligence, and he begins his book, *The Society of Mind*, with the question:

> How can intelligence emerge from non-intelligence? To answer that we'll show you that you can build a mind from many little parts, each mindless by itself.[7]

In Minsky's society of mind, "each mental agent by itself can only do some simple thing that needs no mind or thought at all."[8] That simple "thing" may be to signal a complex process like the fight-or-flight response system as in the case of USAir Flight 1549, or it may simply be to catch a pen that's about to roll off the desk. No thinking required – we gather information consciously and unconsciously, and then react.

This helps to explain why context, or "domain knowledge," is so important in coaching. This knowledge is gathered over time, in the context of a craft or a business, and is an important part of what it means be a professional and a master.

For the Craft of Expert Coaching, it's also important to see that the adaptive unconscious has a big influence on the behavior of the people we coach, and on ourselves as coaches. As a coach, you may feel or know that something's not quite right with a client's actions in a given situation, and you may be unable to articulate it or distinguish it in words – but you know it.

Take the case of expert tennis coach Vic Braden. Braden was an average touring pro who became an extraordinary coach. After playing professionally in his twenties, he returned to UCLA where he got a master's degree in psychology, and then founded one of the first tennis colleges with tennis great Jack Kramer. Braden went on to coach and train coaches for the next fifty years. Malcolm Gladwell writes about Braden's amazing ability to "know" when someone was going to double fault[9] in a tennis match. As Gladwell describes, Braden said it almost drove him crazy, because he didn't know how or why he knew, but his accuracy was nearly one hundred percent.[10]

Much of an apprentice's learning is implicit[11] this way, as the body is sweeping up those eleven million pieces of information every second. By simple repetition and routine, our body unconsciously will "learn" to behave in a deliberate way. Muscle memory can develop in this way, as a subset of the apprentice's learned behavior.

This is how Sully was able to ignore the urge to panic. With enough deliberate practice, he was able to overcome that part of the consciousness that wanted to give in to fight-or-flight responses. As Sully's behavior demonstrated, the metis gained as a master includes the ability to distance yourself from the basic urges of fight or flight, although the urges do not go away.

Most interesting and relevant with respect to coaching and Expert Coaching, is that, according to Professor Wilson, our unconscious is responsible for a lot of our judgments, feelings, and motives. Contrary to some current thinking, the unconscious is responsible not just for the "automated" perfunctory jobs but "plays a major role in all facets of our life."[12]

The Mechanics of the Adaptive Unconscious

Research by psychologist Timothy Wilson and by neuroscientist A. David Redish at the University of Minnesota independently indicates that a number of unconscious processes are working in the background all the time. The processes function together without your knowing it, like when you acted to avoid hitting the dog that ran in front of the car you were driving. Before you were consciously aware, you made a number of fast decisions and precise actions. Some say these are merely knee-jerk reactions or "survival instinct," but it's been shown that the more experience and skill the driver has, the better these unconscious reactions become. A new driver might panic and freeze or might duck their head. But for most of us with some experience behind the wheel, we suppress the urge to duck or brace and hit the brake. To us, it's simple...

As Redish and others have described, each unconscious process, or "module," is effective at making decisions under different conditions and in response to different stimuli. While we won't spend too much time here on these details, there is some agreement about four of these modules (also called action-selection processes).

The easiest to understand is called the **reflexive module** which is hardwired into your body. This module bypasses the brain and makes you act directly, for example, when you react to a loud noise – or a flock of birds in your peripheral vision, as Sully encountered.

The next module, called the **Pavlovian module**, is easy to understand if you have a basic understanding of Pavlov's classical conditioning. As you may recall, Russian physiologist Ivan Pavlov (1849–1936) developed classical conditioning theory, which includes three elements: (1) the unconditioned stimulus – food is presented to a dog; (2) the unconditioned response – the dog salivates, and then (3) a conditioning stimulus – the bell is rung. With Pavlovian learning or conditioning, "the unconditioned response shifts in time from the unconditioned stimulus to the conditioning stimulus."[13] Essentially, the dog reacts to the bell as if it were the food.

The human adaptive unconscious also responds according to the Pavlovian system, so that an environmental cue (stimulus), like the smell of freshly baked bread, will predict an outcome and therefore influence behavior. The cues in the environment, outside of ourselves and our stories, have a powerful effect. We behave in predictable ways, and often are unaware that – or why – we do. Advertising agencies and casinos are examples of companies that exploit this aspect of cognitive science. Taking advantage of the predictability of this module, they get us to buy their client's products or go to their casinos. Later in the book we will see how this predictable response to environmental cues can be used, ethically, in coaching.

The third module is the **procedural system**, a system we know and rely on for automated tasks. This module learns a process, like driving to work, or writing our name. Once it is learned and stored, it is set, and, with enough practice, when called upon it reproduces the process. The weakness of this system is its inflexibility. The techniques in James Duhigg's bestselling book, *The Power of Habits*, rely primarily on the procedural system. Which is why, for some of us, reading Duhigg's book did not really make much difference to our lives, because we were just focusing on this one unconscious system or module only. The procedural system requires time and repetition to burn in the ability to suppress or override competing systems. If that work is not done, the procedural system alone won't be effective. It wasn't for me.

The fourth module of unconscious processing is the **deliberative system**. This system can think through scenarios. It manipulates data and is capable of seeking out resources and input from others. The deliberative system is taxing, and for many of us, even considering the use of this system requires planning. If you are a morning person or an evening person, you know when your own deliberative system, also called the goal-directed learning system, is at its best.

If those are the unconscious modules, where does consciousness come from? Opinions differ. In the Global Workspace Theory model, consciousness has been described metaphorically as the spotlight on a stage, made up of all the brain's sensory inputs, modules, and networks.[14] Redish suggests that our consciousness may merely be a feature of the operations for each of the four modules or unconscious systems.[15] Consciousness is only a feature? That is a tricky, elusive concept.

The science of consciousness and unconsciousness is complex, and this book does not attempt to address it other than to acknowledge the extraordinary importance of understanding the influence of the unconscious on behavior. An overview of the modules of the unconscious also helps us understand why self-help and self-coaching are all but impossible.

Self Help — Which Self?

In self-help, we entertain an unspoken assumption that there is a fair fight to be fought; a single obstacle to be overcome. We imagine a bad self — maybe the devil — on one shoulder and a good self, an angel, on the other. But science tells us we are way off. Rather than operating with only one conscious self, it is now believed the spotlight of consciousness illuminates only those modules with the most demanding urges and needs. Each module behaves based on its own interest.

It may be a little hard at first to accept that we have different decision-making modules within us that can be construed as separate "selves" with distinct wants. Each system or module wants what it wants, for a different but no less valid reason.

This helps to explain why, even after I knew intellectually that the geographic solution was not going to bring me to greener grass, I still had a powerful urge to move on. It also helps to explain why I failed year after year to keep New Year's resolutions. Because at the time I made the resolution, I was confident I could cut back on overeating or drinking — when I made the resolution, the module with the urge to eat or drink too much was not active (or it was satisfied, because I had eaten or had a drink). But, later, the module with the urge to eat or drink was once again demanding "more."

At least for me, because this all went on in my own head and with no help from the outside, I was defenseless for years, blaming it all on my own weak willpower. Later, I understood that when I broke my New Year's resolution, and ate or drank too much, at that specific time and in that specific context, I was influenced by a different system module which was ready to justify the action. It took deliberate practice and working with a coach for me to overcome these persistent urges for a prolonged period of time.

An Expert Coach as Part of Your Environment

Expert Coaching can provide the most effective way to "get outside" your own head. Working with an Expert Coach is a powerful way to learn and develop rituals and routines, which require getting outside of your own thoughts. This is why organizations like Weight Watchers and the twelve-step programs (like Narcotics Anonymous or Alcoholic Anonymous[16]) are effective at changing short- and longer-term behavior, for many people (not all).

The power in these methods to a large degree involves the inclusion of support outside yourself: from the group or community, as well as from an individual supportive sponsor. In both cases, Weight Watchers and the twelve-step programs, a sponsor – essentially an Expert Coach – is someone who has been there and authentically *knows* the context. Because of their unique experience as someone struggling with an addiction, sponsors *know* the tricks and can see the red flags and pitfalls the new member may encounter. Sponsors also act as role models for new members, demonstrating and authentically living the skills, practices, and techniques for losing weight or stopping an addiction. The sponsor or Expert Coach helps the client "get out of their own head," addressing the very real urges as they arise, and helping them to *work the program* of recovery which includes routines, rituals, and practices.

Expert Coaches or sponsors in these proven programs, which help millions of people overcome life-threatening challenges, do not influence their clients with language alone or promises of something-for-nothing transformations.

Like these sponsors, a true master or Expert Coach knows what it takes to succeed, but somehow, our popular culture does not want to believe it. Next, we'll look at one hugely successful example of the something-for-nothing phenomenon.

CHAPTER 8 — ALCHEMY

Metaphors & Magic

Venice was THE entrepôt city in the thirteenth century, much like modern-day Dubai, where traders from all over the world met and exchanged goods. In fact, journal entries from the sixteenth century show that the two cities actually traded pearls and gold. "Venice, like Dubai, lacked natural resources, but grew ostentatiously wealthy and studded with palaces and cutting-edge architectural icons."[1] Venice was described as "the most dazzling city in the world."[2]

The mirror image of modern-day Dubai, Venice was surrounded by powerful religious fundamentalists in the papacy who frowned upon Venice's trade with the Muslim world. Today, Dubai is often criticized for its trade with and accommodation of non-Muslims.

In October 2005, when my Emirates Air flight landed in Dubai, the early morning temperature was 110°F – cooling off after another record-breaking scorcher of a summer. Shortly after arriving and getting settled into a long-term hotel–apartment in the old part of Dubai, near the Gold Souk, I was off to the Mall of the Emirates to take a walk in cool air and get some supplies. This mall, now the second largest in Dubai, is two and a half million square feet of glimmering marble and over six hundred trendy shops. There is an indoor snow park and a ski hill with four chairlifts, a unique attraction and destination for expats and their families. The opulence and ostentatious wealth in the mall had its desired effect, and I felt as though I was finally on my way to real wealth and fulfillment, pulled by the urge of something for nothing. Now, as I look back, I'm also reminded of Shakespeare's knowledge of human nature in his famous proverb, "all that glitters is not gold,"[3] in a play set in Venice, the Dubai of the thirteenth century.

The Virgin Atlantic store, on the second floor, had a large book and magazine section, and that day two six-foot-high floor-mounted signs flanked the entrance. These signs resembled the faded parchment and wax seal of *The Da Vinci Code*, coincidentally the number one movie in Dubai at that time. But this sign was advertising something called *The Secret*.

While I was attracted to the packaging, even more seductive to me was the book's claim. It used "Principles of the Universe" and "Physics" to reveal secrets of the universe which could bring me, and anyone who learned them, this secret great wealth. I wanted to know the secret! The faux parchment paper and wax seal theme seemed to be everywhere, so there must be something to it. Even the number-one movie had the same look.

A very simple explanation of this secret is given by the author in the preface. During a difficult period in her life, she had stumbled upon a hundred-year-old book called *The Secret to Getting Rich*, by Wallace Wattles. In Wattles's book, the author found that some great men of science and philosophy like Sir Isaac Newton, Albert Einstein, Thomas Edison, and even Plato knew of this secret. The more she researched the secret, the author claimed, she became like a magnet, attracting more and more of history's greats. She claimed she was on the right path because they all knew this secret too.

This led to the revelation which is central to the book, a law she claims is a fundamental law of the universe. The "law of attraction" has been around since the late eighteenth century and emerged from the New Thought movement.[4] *The Secret's* author quotes from the work of James Allen, one of the founders of the self-help movement, with his 1901 book, *From Poverty to Power.*[5]

The Secret book relies on anecdotes, stories, and explanations from twenty-four men and women, "teachers" from many walks of life who all share a New-Age feel, and claim to be practitioners of the central idea of *The Secret*: Ask the universe, and you shall receive. These twenty-four include healers, authors, leadership coaches, motivational speakers, metaphysicians, moneymaking experts, chiropractors, psychologists specializing in mind potential, non-aligned trans-religious leaders, Feng Shui masters, an MD, and stock traders.

I had already bought the book when I realized it was strange that a book which referenced the laws of the universe and a fundamental law of physics included no physics and no physicists. None. But the seductive claim was that, by knowing the law of attraction, you will "come to know how you can have, be or do anything you want. You will come to know who you really are, you will come to know the true magnificence that awaits you."[6]

The book is essentially a collection of brief quotes reinforcing the claim that you can have whatever you desire just by thinking about it. In case you had any doubts, "*It always works; it works every time, with every person.*"[7]

There's no shortage of people selling books claiming to have the secret formula or guaranteed how-to method, but the difference here was the scale, and the massive appeal. The book and the movie became phenomenal successes, staying on *The New York Times* best seller list for 146 weeks and cumulatively selling more than $300 million.

This is important to the Craft of Expert Coaching for at least two reasons. First, *The Secret* illustrates the power of a simple metaphor that has crept into common usage and into coaching, particularly in North America. In the next chapter, we'll investigate more about the power and peril of metaphors. Second, the book and movie demonstrate the power and consistency of the biases that make up the cognitive machinery, as introduced in the previous chapter.

The Secret uses the metaphor of a television station transmission tower, broadcasting a signal via a frequency that your television transforms into pictures on the screen. Chiropractor Joe Vitale explains;

> Your thoughts are sending out that magnetic signal…You are a human transmission tower and you are more powerful than any television tower created on earth. You are the most powerful transmission tower in the universe. Your transmissions create your life and create the world. The frequency you transmit reaches beyond cities, beyond countries, beyond the world. It reverberates throughout the entire Universe. And you are transmitting that frequency with your thoughts![8]

Now, it is not my intention here merely to focus on scientifically debunking this metaphor, *MythBusters*-style, as more qualified engineers and physicists have thoroughly done this in the past decade. Instead, I'll focus on some of the very basic and obvious fabrications as they relate to the metaphor and to coaching.

The concept that we are like TV transmitters and that our brains are a source of electromagnetic energy is not completely inaccurate. Our brains do produce an electric current, and if there is an electric current, there will be electromagnetic energy around the flowing current. This much is high school physics. But there are serious issues if we attempt to explain *The Secret*'s metaphor using real science. Here's a taste.

According to the most up-to-date equipment and measurement procedures, the electromagnetic energy that comes from a typical human brain is 0.000,000,000,000,001 tesla (or 10^{-15} tesla).[9]

Now, we also know the earth has electromagnetic energy, because when we use a compass, the compass needle reacts to this energy, pointing to the North Pole. By comparison, the electromagnetic energy of the earth is ten orders of magnitude greater than the energy we humans produce. That is ten million times greater! Not only would our signals get overpowered by those from the earth, the energy we produce is so small it is in fact unable to travel outside of our heads, which is why we need to use electrodes to even detect it.

There's more. Even if the wave energy were to get outside of our heads, its strength is governed by a rule called the inverse square law, which makes the human transmitter metaphor in *The Secret* even more nonsensical.[10]

A part of the cognitive machinery that psychologist Timothy Wilson calls the "psychological immune system"[11] looks for ways to make us feel good. Since we think we know and trust how a real TV tower works, our "fast thinking" and slightly lazy cognitive system automatically apply the metaphor. With no legitimate available comparison or reason to refute the metaphor, we believe it; after all it feels good. Then, because we understand the metaphor, the story gains credibility, and the metaphor you understand and trust is the link that helps tie together a good story. You're not alone. Millions of people fell for it. Including me.

To any electrical engineer or scientist who works in this field, there simply is no factual basis, anywhere, for this metaphor. The human transmission tower metaphor is not physically possible using electromagnetic signals.

As a kind of diversionary tactic, or red herring, quantum physics is also used to explain this "law of nature." Invoking the subject of quantum physics may sound like an intelligent answer, but it is just another tactic our cognitive machinery uses to find an easy answer that just makes us feel good. Even a brilliant physicist of the twentieth century like Richard Feynman will acknowledge what they know and what they don't know[12] about quantum physics. Feynman is a good example because of his often-repeated story in which he said he tried to prepare a freshman lecture on an aspect of quantum physics, and was unable to, leading him to acknowledge, "I couldn't do it. I couldn't reduce it to the freshman level. That means we don't really understand it."[13]

It's accurate to say quantum physics is widely used and understood today, but only under certain conditions. For one example, quantum mechanics works at the subatomic level. But even the top physicists today, like Leonard Susskind,[14] will acknowledge that, outside the subatomic world of quantum physics, they know little of how quantum mechanics relates to larger non-subatomic structures which are well explained by classical Newtonian mechanics. The other condition in which quantum mechanics works is when particles travel at or close to the speed of light; again, not applicable in the scale in which we live.

But clearly the TV tower metaphor of *The Secret* caught on. The metaphor became the "proof" of the possibility – and propelled its success, but why? In the next section, we'll examine the power of a simple mechanical metaphor to transfer an idea or process to a wide audience. Even if people acknowledge that the science may be wrong, the metaphor is still compelling and can replace real, deeper thinking, by providing an easier way to arrive at a conclusion, particularly if the conclusion makes you feel good. We'll also see that the TV tower metaphor supports another compelling idea: the "something for nothing" urge, a fundamental human desire.

The Secret: You Can Have Something for Nothing

Years after being swept up by the phenomenon of *The Secret*, we can see clearly the human urge and compulsion to believe in and want this something-for-nothing offer. When that offer is combined with a familiar mechanical metaphor like a TV transmission tower, we will automatically create a story to make meaning from the events happening around us.

The law of attraction, and the "clearing" use simple metaphors to weave compelling ideas into a narrative, a story. There are several explanations for why people believe them, but based on what we've introduced in this book, we'll look at a few key mechanisms.

The first mechanism is the **psychological immune system**. The adaptive unconscious is not governed by "accuracy or accessibility alone." As Wilson says, "…our judgment and interpretations are often guided by…the desire to view the world in a way that gives us the most pleasure." The feel-good stories of rags to riches also press the psychological immune system buttons.

Now when that story is laced with brief positive accounts and credible endorsements to support the claim, our **confirmation bias** will also, automatically and without conscious thought, find evidence to support the something-for-nothing story.

The frequency and repetition of the message and style of *The Secret* also play nicely into the **availability cascade**,[15] a self-reinforcing process in which a collective belief (the feel-good criterion) becomes more plausible through repetition. What could feel better than believing your dreams will come true just by thinking about them?

The packaging and marketing of *The Secret* targets the cognitive machinery, also engaging the availability bias. The tremendous success of *The Da Vinci Code* book and movie helped to set up the availability, by making these faux parchment and wax seal images easy to remember.

We are all familiar with, and subject to, the compounding effect of the confirmation bias used by the self-help industry, specifically in their use of **celebrity endorsements**. As those 1990s-era ubiquitous Tony Robbins infomercials demonstrated, celebrity sells.

While it was easy to do, refuting the science did little to dissuade many people. As we look back at the adaptive unconscious and our cognitive machinery, we can begin to understand why this message was and is so compelling.

In the same way the four-minute-mile myth created a "likeable" story, so too did *The Secret*. This time it used a familiar metaphor, and it addressed the six key principles of a memorable story, as introduced by Chip and Dan Heath in their bestselling book, *Made to Stick: Why Some Ideas Survive and Others Die.*[16]

The Heaths outline six principles which form the acronym SUCCES – and help to explain why the story told by *The Secret* "sticks" in our memories.

- **Simple**. The TV tower metaphor is simple, easy to relate to and understand – physically oriented vertically in the same way we are oriented.

- **Unexpected**. It is unexpected, in a good way; we learn we have such a capability. We get something for nothing.

- **Concrete**. The metaphor relies on something real and concrete. TV towers are visible and can (could) be seen all the time, along the roadside.

- **Credentialed**. Many of the 24 "teachers" have a PhD or use the title of Doctor.

- **Emotional**. The metaphor and idea appeal to the "greatness" in the human spirit, generally an emotionally charged issue.

- **Story**. A good metaphor enables a process or a cause and effect, from which we can build upon a favorite age-old story of rags to riches.

Is the "How-To" Necessary?

From the Expert Coaching perspective, we see another seductive concept in *The Secret*. This concept, which has also crept into transformational consulting and coaching, essentially says, don't worry about the "how to do it," don't worry about a plan, or market research, or data analytics. Just commit to it, and throw your hat over the wall.

> The Universe will start to rearrange itself to make it happen for you.[17]
>
> —Dr. Joe Vitale

The sentiment is incredibly appealing, because, as we saw with the planning fallacy in Kahneman's research, we are generally overly optimistic. We systematically undervalue what it will take, in dollars and time, to complete the job. In the same way, we undervalue what it will take to make our dreams come true.

For those authentically interested in developing their lives and careers, this line of thinking is not only dangerous, it flies in the face of solid experimental data and objective evidence that experience, deliberate practice, and expertise matter. A master craftsman would certainly not agree that the way to extraordinary results in their craft is by simply committing to something extraordinary, instead of committing to putting in the practice and work to achieve it.

Although it's astonishing how many normal people get conned, we now have a better understanding of how our minds work and how the cognitive machinery can be tricked in the short term. As coaches, it is our job to look out for the instances where the cognitive bias can lead a client to bad decisions and easy answers.

Used appropriately, the BHAG, (Big Hairy Audacious Goal) which Jim Collins introduced, is a valuable longer-term motivation and a way to align a team around a common goal. As Collins explains in several books and articles, some important assumptions come into play with the BHAG. One essential aspect of developing a strategy in the first place is to only pursue those activities or business opportunities in which you are or can be the best in your field or market. So before a BHAG is set, the underlying skills and competencies of your field need to be in place.

Another claim from *The Secret*, also captured in the *est*–Forum "clearing" metaphor, is perhaps the most thoughtless and potentially damaging – the notion that "the law of attraction does not care whether you perceive something to be good or bad, or whether you want it or not. It's responding to your thoughts…"[18]

So, this so-called law says whatever you think about you attract, which is absurd, and insensitive to the brutal history of groups of people including Syrians, Jews, Iraqis, Native Americans, and African Americans. The message of *The Secret* is simply nonsense and unacceptable.

In our fast-paced day-to-day lives, anyone serious about achieving a result does not rely on this so-called law. Imagine your dentist or accountant suggesting they ask the universe for the outcome you want, rather than doing what they were trained to do. When we understand the basic physical cause and effect of a situation – or the mechanics of a situation – we are less likely to believe we need magical solutions.

The Power of Celebrity & the Availability Bias

Celebrities like Jim Carrey are held out as examples of the something-for-nothing power of *The Secret*. One of the most popular YouTube segments is an interview with Jim Carrey in 1997 where he describes his visualization techniques. In his story, he tells how, years ago, he wrote himself a check for ten million dollars post-dated three years into the future. Carrey would regularly go up to Mulholland Drive and visualize "having good things come to him."[19] As the story goes, the universe delivered, since, as he states in the interview, three years later he was paid $10M to star in the movie, *Dumb and Dumber*.

What does not make it into the headlines or inspirational YouTube videos is the factual account of the fifteen-plus years of focused dedication Carrey devoted to his craft before winning any real acclaim. As is well documented, his family was homeless for a brief period, and lived in a van. There were no music lessons or summer camps in Carrey's life. At sixteen, he quit school and worked full time to help support the family. He was still too young to drive, so Carrey's father drove him to comedy clubs where he – and occasionally his father – would do a set. When other kids his age were playing baseball or hockey, Jim Carrey was on stage, his adaptive unconscious sweeping up information and learning. He had started apprenticing as a comic.

Richard Sennett describes the craftsman process in the medieval guild in his book, *The Craftsman.*

> In the medieval guild, male authority was incarnate in the three-tiered hierarchy of masters, journeymen and apprentices. Contracts specified the length of an apprenticeship, usually seven years, and the cost, usually borne by the young person's parent. The stages of progress in a guild were marked out first by the apprentice's presentation of the chef d'oeuvre at the end of his seven years, a work that demonstrated the elemental skills the apprentice had imbibed. If successful, now a journeyman, the craftsman would work another five to ten years until he could demonstrate, in a chef d'oeuvre élevé, that he was worthy to take the master's place.[20]

Jim Carrey's apprenticeship started at age fifteen, doing stand-up in church basements, and progressed to comedy clubs, random TV sketch comedy spots, and finally a break in Los Angeles in 1984. At 22 years old, Carrey got the lead role in a network comedy called *The Duck Factory* that was cancelled after thirteen episodes. For another ten years, as a journeyman, he did several small movie parts, sketch comedy on TV's *In Living Color*, and perhaps most importantly, was taken under the wing of an Expert Coach, and master stand-up comedian. Rodney Dangerfield signed Carrey to open his show in Las Vegas, and then toured with Carrey for two years in the late 80s. In 1994, at 32 years old, Jim Carrey had completed the seventeen-year development period of an apprentice and a journeyman. Within a timeframe similar to the medieval pattern Sennett describes, Carrey had done the work to become a master craftsman. In other words, when he wrote the check dated three years into the future, Carrey had already put in more than his 10,000 hours.

In 1994 he starred in *Ace Ventura Pet Detective*, *The Mask*, and *Dumb and Dumber* – three number one movies in one year – a *chef d'oeuvre élevé* or master work. Rather than submitting his work to a master, Carrey obtained his master status when moviegoers voted with their wallets. That year millions of people couldn't help but answer at least one question with "Aallllrighty, then!," "Take care, now...," or "Bye-bye, then!" The studio heads ran the numbers, and a star was born.

CHAPTER 9 — METAPHORS, MANAGEMENT & MISCHIEF

The earth's surface is like the floor of a massive ocean some three hundred miles deep. This is not the fanciful plot of an underwater apocalyptic zombie movie but part of the curriculum for first-year mechanical engineering students. To introduce the subject called Fluids, professors use the water metaphor when they talk about our atmosphere. The "atmosphere is like water" metaphor provides a complete picture or system, where water surrounds – and therefore influences – everything in it.

Just as our atmosphere surrounds and influences us on earth, when we talk about a specific industry or craft as "the context," we mean its situation and setting, which, like our atmosphere, surrounds and influences the behavior of everything in it. The context is based on what actually exists, and we sweep it up both consciously and unconsciously.

Centuries earlier, Leonardo da Vinci, who was obsessed with flight, appreciated the significance of this water metaphor in a new science he pioneered, called fluid dynamics. His research, sketches, and observations about fluid flow and flight are found throughout his notebooks. In 1505–1506, in the *Codice sul volo degli uccelli*

(Codex on the Flight of Birds), he wrote; "[O]bserve the swimming of fish and you will understand the science of flight."[1] Leonardo came to "know" that flight, and therefore lift, were possible because of the nature of fluids.

More broadly, da Vinci looked to nature as a way to understand how things actually worked.

> Nature is the source of all true knowledge. She has her own logic, her own laws, she has no effect without cause nor invention without necessity.[2]

What the Hell Is Water?

David Foster Wallace was not the first, but is perhaps the most influential contemporary American novelist to use the same water metaphor as Leonardo. In a commencement speech he delivered in 2005 to the graduating class at Kenyon College in Ohio, Wallace retold what he called the requisite fable:

> Two young fish swim along and happen to meet an older fish swimming the other way. The older fish nods to the two younger fish and says, "Morning boys, how's the water?" And the two young fish swim on for a bit, and then eventually one looks over at the other and goes: "What the hell is water?"[3]

Wallace used the metaphor of water as the context for themes he wrote about extensively in his many books and particularly in his acclaimed tour de force, the novel *Infinite Jest*.

Wallace's writing, particularly in *Infinite Jest*, speaks to the stories we swim in, and notes that much of what we "tend to be automatically certain of is, it turns out, totally wrong and deluded."[4]

His writing exposes the influence of social media, and how we are blithely unaware that our attention is being hijacked, through TV and our devices, by resource-rich groups and corporations which control them and us. The book tackles some complex current issues like mental illness, addiction, and the pervasive influence of the entertainment and news oligopolies. With plenty of characters, the intricate plot revolves around a kind of video game or "cassette" called *Infinite Jest,*[5] which takes control of your mind and forces you to watch it until your death.

From a coaching perspective, it's valuable to see the degree to which what is happening outside of our heads influences what we think and how we behave.

Wallace also addresses one of the central points of this book, an issue which deeply affects American baby boomers: our blatant materialism coupled with our demand for self-actualization.

At the heart of my decision to work in the Middle East immediately after graduating from engineering school was the belief that the most important thing to me at this point in my life was to be or become someone that mattered, someone rich. What mattered was not skill, training, fellowship, or mastery; it was how I thought I would feel, and what my life would be, if I were rich. While I'm not blaming MTV or Hollywood, those media deliver a single powerful message above all others: that this life is about me, my happiness, my personal power, and my self-actualization – which are measured by much stuff I can buy. This message played out on the big screen, with the character Gordon Gekko's "Greed is Good" soliloquy in the 1987 movie, *Wall Street.*

> The point is, ladies and gentlemen, that greed for lack of a better word is good.
>
> Greed is right.

Greed works.

Greed clarifies, cuts through, and captures the essence of the evolutionary spirit.

Greed, in all of its forms – greed for life, for money, for love, knowledge – has marked the upward surge of mankind.

And greed – you mark my words – will not only save Teldar Paper, but that other malfunctioning corporation called the USA.[6]

The leadership industry is a high-level facilitator of this same narrative. Its job is to create an organization of self-anointed leaders. Leadership practitioners are quick to point out, however, that leadership does not mean you must lead by example, or demonstrate your commitment and dedication to doing something well. Instead it means being the best you can be, demonstrating your genius, your greatness, and your superior alpha-transformed self. In this everyone-is-a-leader culture, we're all striving to elbow out anyone standing in the way between us and the fulfilled life promised to us. Then again, if the explosion of personal development, personal power, and leadership training was effective, would the job satisfaction and employee engagement surveys look as dismal as they do?

No wonder we buy into flimsy metaphors like the human TV transmitter: these metaphors invoke stories with happy endings, just like the movies. And like a good religion, the metaphors also offer some hope, and the belief that the shitty life I have, sitting in traffic for hours, and then eating drive-through crap (knowing it is crap), will somehow be OK if I just ask the Universe for something better. These metaphors help to create stories that deliver a good feeling, at least for a while; and seem to be the only possible path to the "good life" as seen on TV, or in a Tony Robbins testimonial.

In this chapter, we look more deeply into metaphors, both as the larger systems, like our atmosphere, and as the building blocks we use to make meaning in any context. While we may have little control over the physical environments in which we work, we can gain some control over the ways we distinguish and understand the influence of metaphors.

Metaphors in Coaching

As we have seen, our behaviors are heavily influenced both by our innate automated way of thinking and by our biases. We've also seen how behavior is affected by our multiple unconscious modules, which are sweeping the environment all the time, gathering information. In addition to these automated influences, we will now look at another potent influence on behavior: the use of metaphors in our thoughts and language.

George Lakoff, mentioned earlier for his work on the theory of embodied cognition, is also one of the leading scholars in the field of metaphors. He builds a strong case that metaphors are powerful instruments for change, and for the transfer of complex concepts.

"Metaphors are more than a device of poetic imagination and the rhetorical flourish… they govern our everyday functioning…our conceptual structures."[7]

Metaphors surround us and shape the way we form and use concepts, mathematics, and language. Author and psychologist Steven Pinker puts it this way:

"Metaphor is so widespread in language that it's hard to find expressions for abstract ideas that are not metaphorical."[8]

The first three sentences of Lakoff's book, *Metaphors We Live By*, a central text in the field written with long-time collaborator Mark Johnson, read:

The mind is inherently embodied. Thought is mostly unconscious. Abstract concepts are largely metaphorical.[9]

—George Lakoff and Mark Johnson

We've addressed the idea that our thoughts are mostly unconscious, and, in this chapter, we'll dig into the idea that abstract concepts are largely metaphorical. What resonates for me is Lakoff's idea that our thoughts do not come with words. Now, you could say that the only reason I can use this metaphor is because of language, but Lakoff and Michael Reddy argue that this is not so. Cognitive linguist Michael Reddy, a contemporary of Lakoff's, elevated the conceptual metaphor, acknowledging that "the locus of metaphor is thought, not just language."[10] Reddy described the metaphor as an indispensable part of our way of conceptualizing the world, and that our everyday behavior reflects our metaphorical understanding of experience.

The point of this discussion is not to identify a right and wrong, but to demonstrate the power and usefulness of metaphor. In any case, many experts agree that we already think with metaphorical concepts. Hopefully this chapter will provide more options for learning and doing, and then teaching and contributing, using the power of metaphor.

Gerald Zaltman, a professor emeritus from the Harvard Business School, identifies three levels of metaphor: **surface metaphors** that we consciously select and use in our everyday speech; **metaphorical themes**, which are metaphorical concepts just below the surface and not completely unconscious ("time is money" is an example); and **deep metaphors** which are below consciousness.[11]

These deep metaphors influence our perception, and therefore drive behavior. According to Zaltman, deep metaphors "... are enduring ways of perceiving things, making sense of what we encounter, and guiding subsequent actions. Put differently, deep metaphors are the product of an ever-evolving partnership between brain, body and society."[12]

Zaltman and Penn State professor Jerry Olson run a market research firm, Olson Zaltman Associates, and have developed a survey method called the Zaltman Metaphor Elicitation Technique (ZMET) to reveal deep metaphors within an organization. Their research helps companies understand what is driving purchasing behavior by identifying, through their interview and survey methods, the deep metaphors of target consumers. In the book *Marketing Metaphoria,* Zaltman details how they assisted Proctor & Gamble to understand how consumers perceived a new product, Febreze, through their deep metaphors. They then used this awareness to create the messaging and to select the most effective metaphors for the marketing and advertising strategy. This process proved to be effective, resulting in the best product launch in P & G history.[13]

Deep metaphors operate at a subconscious level, and influence the way we perceive and make meaning. Through their research, after over twelve-thousand interviews in thirty countries, Olson Zaltman have identified seven primary deep metaphors. These seven were common to all industry segments in all countries. The seven primary deep metaphors are balance, transformation, journey, connection, resource, control, and container. A brief summary of each follows.

Balance is one of the earliest deep metaphors we develop and is naturally manifested from our embodied cognition; meaning we just know when we "feel" balanced in mind and body, a psychological balance; feeling safe and secure yet free, or balancing family and work life.

Transformation includes significant natural events like the birth of a child, or the maturation of a girl to a woman or a boy to a man. Transformation is a real process, directed by nature.

The **Journey** metaphor is deeply personal and involves a marking of important events as well as significant periods of time. It is perhaps the most widely examined deep metaphor[14] and may involve individuals or groups of people. Many relate to this metaphor as the framework for their "story." Zaltman says that "our interactions with consumers can prove more successful when we take the time to focus on the themes that a particular journey holds."[15]

Connection is a very deep visceral experience, critical to our very survival. Our ability to connect and collaborate gives us options and outcomes not available to us as individuals. The consumption of products or services may offer an opportunity to be connected to a larger group, like the invitation to "The Pepsi Generation." Some products or services may also enable a stronger personal connection with our inner self.

Resource metaphors are associated with our conscious and unconscious need to achieve goals and acquire things. These deep metaphors affect how consumers believe they are seen or judged by others.

Control is a deep metaphor involving a desired state in a person's life and career – the ability to control our time, earning power, and, ultimately, our destiny. The lack of control, or the experience of feeling dominated, is a powerful motivator associated with this deep metaphor. Doing something well is rooted in the control metaphor, as we have control of an instrument or tool. Control is also metaphorically connected to emotional stability, as in maintaining control or losing control.

Container metaphors use a more fundamental metaphorical structure. Our language is packed (sorry!) with container metaphors that greatly influence our thoughts and behaviors. We think of ourselves as containers with an inside and an outside, and because of this we also project this orientation onto objects and things; we consider they too have an inside and outside. As containers, we automatically think in terms of the following:

• We are filled with emotions like love, fear, anger, and rage.

- We are filled with experiences. I have had enough frustration (I am full).

- We are full of substances too: He is full of crap, or energy, or rage, etc.

- We are full of qualities like wisdom, knowledge, experience, hustle, and metis.

- As a container, each of us is a separate entity which can be "in" or "out" of the crowd, in or out of favor. We can be up against it, and we can be stretched and worn out.

- As separate containers, we share the space and we need our space.

- As separate containers, we can also be physically oriented above or below, in front of or behind.

We dig deeper into metaphors, with examples that are useful in coaching, in Appendix C.

The Power of Metaphor

Jim Collins, author of some of the bestselling business books of all time, masterfully uses metaphors. His work can be described as research- and data-driven, but the way he communicates ideas and concepts is often through clever, simple metaphors.[16]

Remarkably, even twenty-five years after his landmark book, *Good to Great,* was launched, while people may have forgotten much of the book, they very often are still able to recall the fox and hedgehog metaphor and its subtleties as they relate to business and strategy.

MIT professor Peter Senge in his bestselling book, *The Fifth Discipline: The Art & Practice of The Learning Organization,* introduces systems thinking with an excellent, complex metaphor drawn from nature:

> A cloud masses, the sky darkens and leaves twist upwards, we know intuitively it will rain. We also know that after the rain the runoff will be into groundwater miles away and the sky will grow clear by tomorrow. All these events are distant in time and space and yet they are all connected within the same pattern. Each has an influence on the rest, an influence that is usually hidden from view. You can only understand the system of a rainstorm by contemplating the whole and not any individual parts of it.[17]

Because we are part of the system, it is difficult to separate ourselves, or appreciate we are "in" the system – like "what the hell is water?"

Again, quoting Senge:

> [W]e tend to focus on snapshots of isolated parts of the system and wonder why our deepest problems never seem to get solved. Systems thinking is a conceptual framework of knowledge and tools that has been developed over the past fifty years, to make the full patterns clearer, and to help us see how to change them effectively.[18]

Short-term or snapshot thinking will create inaccurate cause-and-effect relationships, and produce what Senge calls "the delusion of experience." It is delusional because the experience is gained by looking at only a small part of a larger system, and seeing a cause-and-effect relationship where none exists. We examined this in the four-minute-mile myth and in the Law of Small Numbers. Looking at a snapshot metaphor, another important bias is demonstrated. The acronym Kahneman uses for this bias is WYSIATI – What You See Is All There Is. This bias is a version of the Law of Small Numbers. It considers only what it currently sees and then makes up the "best possible story that incorporates ideas currently activated…This is commonly known as 'jumping to a conclusion.'"[19]

Why Study Metaphors?

Why spend all this time studying and listing metaphors? Because a coach benefits from a working awareness of metaphors and an appreciation and understanding of their power to influence our behavior and the stories that we tell. In other words, an awareness of metaphors will provide another diagnostic tool for the coach. An Expert Coach offers more to a client than just asking good questions. Experts learn to do things using metaphors, and when a coach shares a metaphor, far more real knowledge and metis is transferred than if the coach uses abstract and generalized language. To gain metis, coaches will find, the study of metaphors is extremely valuable.

Metis is possible only when deep knowledge has been gained from actually doing the craft or business. Metis enables us to access the unconscious and to tap into the deep metaphors used in the craft or business.

"The fact is, the interpretation of a situation is inseparable from the analogies [and metaphors] … it invokes."[20] In other words, we understand, learn, and recall using metaphors.

The top-performing executive with a lot of experience in a specific field will have a distinct understanding of the metaphors in an organization, including the wider systems perspective, and thereby wield an advantage over someone who does not. Masters and experts have created and adopted metaphors based on their experience in the craft. Lakoff supports this point, saying,

> In actuality we feel that no metaphor can ever be comprehended or even adequately represented independent of its experiential basis.[21]

Therefore, to offer a metaphor effectively, the coach needs to have actually used the metaphor effectively in a specific context.

Sculptors, musicians, jewelers, and even surgeons use a hammer. A carpenter knows how to use a hammer to frame a house, but would not be an effective coach in the other fields or contexts in which a hammer is used. This is not to say that a master carpenter would not be able to shed new light on how to use a hammer. The point is a carpenter may not the most effective hammering coach for an orthopedic surgeon.

Next, as we begin Part Two, on craft, we look at the metaphor of lift in the craft of coaching.

CRAFT

PART TWO

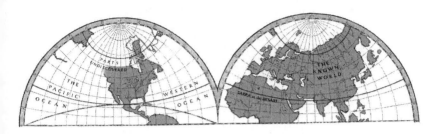

CHAPTER 10 — THE CRAFT OF COACHING WITH LIFT

Dubai was soaring in 2005, even if my spirits were not. When I'd lived in Saudi in the 80s, the Middle East was comparatively peaceful. In 2005, the same could not be said, and I admit I was a little concerned. But remarkably, in a region with so much conflict and despotic rule, Dubai was not only peaceful and orderly, it was thriving. This, too, resembled the Venice of the thirteenth century, which was described as "a strong superbly ordered republic, possessed of a constitution that had almost effortlessly weathered every political storm."[1]

The pace of new construction in the United Arab Emirates was ramping up. Spectacular mega-projects like the world's tallest building, the Burj Dubai (now called the Burj Khalifa); the artificial archipelago of islands shaped like a giant map of the world, and Dubai Land – a cross between Disneyworld and Las Vegas – were all well underway. Selling air conditioning in Dubai seemed too good to be true. Perhaps my ship had come in. Maybe this would be it.

Everyone was hustling to get in on the next big project. The airport was packed. Sheikh Zayed Road, the eight-lane (both ways) main drag, was gridlocked most of the day, and busy late into the night. In 2005, cars and SUVs were randomly parked anywhere there was space – even on sidewalks and esplanades. Lobbies of office buildings were literally packed. People huddled around the entrances, waiting in 120°F temperatures for the chance to get inside and onto the overcrowded elevators. The grocery stores had huge lines, the many bars and discos were shoulder to shoulder, and even Gold's Gym was so full you had to wait in a line of four or five people to get on a piece of equipment. The entire city was standing room only, and for good reason. The construction and air conditioning businesses were booming. We were bidding on massive projects, unheard of on this scale anywhere in the world until now.

In a large North American city, like Chicago, there may be two or three office towers and another two or three large scale renovation projects bidding in a year, with the total cooling requirements for large water chillers of 40,000 tons. By comparison, in Dubai in 2006 we were actively bidding on over 800,000 tons. Dubai looked like one large, dusty construction project. The flat horizon was obscured by construction cranes and towering buildings in various stages of completion.

H.H. Sheikh Mohammed bin Rashid Al Maktoum, the Vice President, Prime Minister, and ruler of Dubai, issued a directive to use EMPOWER's chilled water for all large buildings. EMPOWER, my customer and the governmental water utility, sells chilled water in much the same way other cities sell electricity and natural gas. Its district cooling system[2] runs massive water pipes into each building. EMPOWER was led by a young, charismatic, and extremely smart native of Dubai. This young man brilliantly executed the Prime Minister's vision, and is largely responsible for the growth of district cooling in the region, which has driven down energy usage and carbon emissions in the Emirate.

It's a clever system. It frees up rentable space, and removes unsightly equipment and noise on or around the building. According to the United Nations Environment program (UNEP), district cooling can be more than twice as efficient[3] as traditional decentralized air-conditioning methods.[4]

With this massive scale of activity and opportunity, it did not take me long to get swept up in the frenetic pace of the city. Within weeks I found myself once again in a familiar routine, buried in work. I was living more and more inside my head. This kept me fully occupied, anxious, and increasingly isolated from others, who, I believed, didn't understand the issues I had, and couldn't relate.

The twelve-hour time difference with the United States meant that I was often on conference calls late into the night and regularly got calls at two or three in the morning, which made sleep even more challenging. Mornings, in particular, were becoming increasingly difficult. My critical self-talk was waking me up into a state of worry and anxiety. It was as though I would automatically scan my mind, looking for something to worry about – often, something from the past or something that might happen in the future. I had the gnawing feeling of being stuck. I was running out of time.

Maybe it was because I was closing in on fifty, but I started thinking more and more about what I had and had not accomplished, and where I was going. I was concerned about how I was perceived by my family and friends. Had I wasted my life in search of some heroic story? Would I be seen as a failure because my life didn't look like an infomercial testimonial? In the busy but certain world inside my head, this was all a result of my apparent lack of willpower and self-discipline.

Again and again, I believed the grass somewhere was going to be greener, but I seemed to keep ending up in the sand.

Each time I moved to a new city or country, I believed I would see the world in a new way, "transform," and ultimately "be" the person I dreamt of being.

The move to Dubai was jarring. The change of scenery wasn't working its magic. I was just looking for a way to feel better, to beat back anxious uncomfortable feelings. It was during this difficult time, mostly out of desperation, that I found the value and effectiveness of the thing I call lift.

From Leadership to Craftsmanship

At the heart of my concerns was an assumption that there was a "right" way in which my life should go. I had a picture of myself as an adult, and an expectation about who I should be and what I "should" have. A baby boomer, I was part of a generation of men and women who experienced unprecedented economic growth and technological advancements enabling more free time ("me time") and disposable income than previous generations.

My focus was on me, my personal power, my feelings, myself, and my-everything.

As a baby boomer, I had grown up more influenced by television than the previous generations. David Foster Wallace, a member of gen X, captured it well with another water metaphor in a 1996 televised interview with Charlie Rose.

> [A]t least the generation I think of myself as part of right now, was raised on television, which means that, at least I was raised to think of television as my main artistic snorkel to the universe. ...[5]

Illustratively, I watched this interview on YouTube, the next generation of TV. The American dream of the self-made leading man was loudly and widely depicted most nights of the week on hit TV programs like *Dallas*, *Dynasty*, and *Hart to Hart*. Among the top movies as we baby boomers were coming of age were *Wall Street* and *Rocky*. Each of these programs exemplified the self-made man, inspiring young men and women all over the world and reinforcing the promise of a purer form of self-interest in the USA. It was this same ideal I followed, and had most recently chased back to the Middle East; where I believed this self-created ideal was still possible – and just around the corner.

The American dream, as it was force-fed, essentially meant doing it on your own, demonstrating self-actualization, getting what you wanted, and being the best even if it meant being an asshole. It seemed everyone wanted to be a brash, crude self-made man like Donald Trump. In fact, people lined up week after week to be his apprentice on the new TV show, which was a big hit in Dubai at the time.

I didn't realize I had moved into the distinct stage in life that Erik Erikson called the generative-stagnation stage. Erikson, a brilliant German-born American psychologist and psychoanalyst, actually started out to be an artist but was drawn into psychology because of his interest in children's development. I gravitated to Erikson's work because he applied a logical systems approach and a familiar metaphor to look at the way we changed and developed over a lifetime.

He looked at the human life cycle in the same way Peter Senge looks, metaphorically, at the life cycle of a rainstorm, as we saw in the previous chapter. Erikson's approach looked at our entire life cycle and identified distinct elements which drove different thoughts and therefore behaviors at our various ages and stages of life.

With his wife Joan, also a psychologist, he presented a model of psychosocial development that defined eight stages in a normal life. At each stage, we experience a personal psychosocial crisis – more commonly called "an identity crisis" – which we must confront. Erikson's model uses two words representing the opposite poles of each stage, both of which must be addressed and reconciled before moving on to the next phase of maturity. The two-pole metaphor provides a visual, of the earth, for example, with a north and south pole. It allows you to see that it is not an either/or choice; but rather we are managing the range between the poles.

For example, in the early adult stage of life, from twenty to thirty-nine years of age, we confront questions of intimacy and isolation. Successfully transiting this stage involves confronting and reconciling questions like: Can I trust someone and myself in a loving, trusting intimate relationship? Can I live in a committed long-term relationship and, if necessary, live and function alone? Erikson explains that when we successfully reconcile and resolve each crisis, we grow psychologically, developing a healthy personality.

When we move to the generative-stagnation stage from forty to sixty-five years of age, the stage in which I found myself, we take stock of our lives and question whether our lives have made a difference. Up until that time, I could justify myself and my loner behavior as it seemed to be aligned with the idea of chasing after the goal of becoming a self-made man.

While I have become skeptical of behavioral theories that lump people into a few general categories which presumably remain unchanged over long periods of time; Erikson's theory seemed to me flexible enough to allow for a more realistic account of the constantly changing moods that I experience. This model allows for both a short and a more long-term view of an entire lifetime, which addressed many of the questions and concerns now relevant for me.

As we will see, one of the more important new findings in psychology is the idea that we do continue to change the way we learn and think after the age of twenty-five. American psychologist Bob Kagan, in independent research, has concluded that adults do grow and evolve in the ways we think and make meaning over time. This is not merely explained by added experience; instead, the structure of our brain changes, and we progress through more complex ways of thinking. This may be why the one-method-fits-all approach to leadership coaching and managing is not producing good results.

So, in the "generative" stage of Erikson's model, we move forward, learn, and generate new meaning and purpose. The opposite pole is "stagnation" – feeling as though you have no purpose or hope for a better future. Stagnation arises from feeling dissatisfied and stuck in our lives, resulting in feelings of regret and failure, and, ultimately, isolation and depression. I most certainly moved in and out of stagnation, alone. It was terrifying.

I woke up one morning into what I can only describe as a raging state of anxiety, which would not subside. My thoughts were racing, my heart was pounding, and I was getting more and more desperate. How can I go to work? Will this go away? I tried to distract myself, watching TV and trying to meditate, but neither of these provided any sustained relief. Alcohol had always calmed my typical lower-level anxiety, so I waited until opening time at the Ramada Inn bar, and walked the few blocks. After two fast glasses of wine the anxiety subsided… I was going to be OK. I drank a few more glasses of wine just to be sure I'd fall asleep, and went home and to bed.

At 3:00 a.m., I woke up with a start. The anxiety was back, but this time angrier and even more aggressive. My first reaction was to fight it – to find something to do that would beat back these feelings. I went outside for a run, to exercise them away. At this time of the morning, the normally blistering hot chaotic streets of Bur Dubai were eerily quiet, and cool, but I recall feeling as though I was surrounded by danger and being hunted. I started to run but my heart was beating so hard I couldn't keep going. My attention dominated by the struggle to fight back the anxiety, all I could do was slowly walk.

I recall thinking this was it. I was not going to recover from this. The flood gates opened, the river banks began to collapse and even more anxiety flooded my chest, making me dizzy and stopping me dead in my tracks. I knew something really bad would happen.

I was going to lose my job, become the object of ridicule from my colleagues as the "guy who went crazy." I was truly screwed. No way I would be the lone hero of my story, and, worse, I would be an unemployed guy with mental issues. What the hell was I going to do?

One day, shortly after that episode, I was literally yanked out of the anxiety, albeit for just a few moments. I was at the office in Qatar, sipping on the only thing I felt I could eat or drink, a cold 7-Up. I had set up in the conference room when one of the engineers transferred from the Dubai office, a Northern Indian whom I'll call Norman, barged in and began to rant about what he felt was a real injustice. I was startled, but was instantly pulled into his story...in fact I knew this story: a project manager was threatening to withhold payment, was issuing a change order, and was making demands.

I recall instinctively jumping into a discussion with Norman, trying to understand the important facts and the real forces at play. We then engaged in a conversation in which I asked him to consider that perhaps he was stuck in a confirmation bias – maybe this change order would not be like others, and maybe the guy was not trying to get something for nothing. Then together we sorted fact from fiction (story) and tried to look at the situation from the perspective of the customer, and the forces he might be reacting to.

It was in this conversation with Norman that I was able to see it: if I could just get the attention off me, and stop fighting against the anxiety, I was released from it. In fact, I felt a lift.

Like we defined early on, lift results from action, from doing something. A wing or a propeller does not have lift somewhere magically inside; it emerges when the plane is in motion. When I retreated from the conversation with Norman, and went back into my head, I could feel the anxiety again replace this feeling of lift.

It may sound simple and even magical, but this very real process was the secret to managing my anxiety. But it was one I had to work at and practice. I literally had to force myself into a conversation, to dive into the conversation, and care more about helping someone else than feeling anxious and sorry for myself.

Now what was interesting to me, again, was the work of Erikson, in the life-cycle phases he describes. If I could get outside of it and see it like the model of the solar system in high school, I could see that I was simply in one phase of life in which contribution is more a part of our human nature. It's hard to explain, other than to say I "knew" that this was the right thing for me to do. It was as though I was just following human nature, living according to nature as the Greek Stoics would say.

Erikson explains that most of the boomers now are on the continuum between generation and stagnation, moving back and forth as we react to the challenges and victories life presents. It's a time in our lives when we begin to combine our own needs for self-fulfillment with the welfare of a larger social group, satisfying a need to contribute in ways that will survive our death.

In fact, not doing so seems to only magnify feelings of stagnation, isolation, and depression.

Why Lift?

My move into the Dubai office was not at all appreciated by one faction of the existing staff.

In the 1970s and 80s, the United Arab Emirates, of which Dubai is one part, had been a sleepy, second-tier market. Despite the subsurface potential, it was isolated, and not yet oil-rich. Because of their proximity and time zone, European countries like Greece and Italy often managed these regions for large American corporations. McQuay was no exception, with several product lines managed directly from Italy. However, like many large American companies, our company grew by acquisition, which resulted in product line duplication. Some of the chiller (large air conditioning unit) product lines were also made in Italy, which created some internal competition at McQuay between the US and Italian products. My arrival annoyed the Italian management because they believed I would steer business away from their products. They were right, but not simply because the chillers were made in the USA. It was because the American products used a different technology, centrifugal compression, which allowed for much larger compressors than the European-made Archimedes screw-type compressors.

Because of this, my reception at the office was less than warm. The office was run by a tight-knit clique from Southern India, closely allied with the Italian management, and they tried to shut me out.

Several Indian engineers within the office knew the centrifugal products were better suited to the district cooling applications, but, not surprisingly, they were not supported or promoted, and were performing poorly in Dubai. This group also did not feel welcome in the Dubai office, primarily because they were from Northern India. Many were on the verge of leaving the company. The most experienced and talented Northern Indian engineer was ready to quit, but had just moved his wife and family from India and simply didn't want to move them back again. So, in what they may have thought was a crafty move, the Italian management sent the Northern Indian team to Doha, Qatar – at the time, a much smaller, sleepier market than Dubai – in an effort to get them out of their hair. Maybe, the Italians hoped, the exiled Northern Indians would voluntarily leave the organization.

Even then, oil and gas made Qatar the richest country per capita in the world with an average income of almost $90,000 per person per year.

Qatar became a British protectorate in 1916 and not just coincidentally oil – lots of high quality oil – was found five years later. The British benevolently granted a 75-year oil concession to Qatar Petroleum Company.

In 2005, Qatar was ruled by the Emir, H.H. Sheikh Hamad bin Khalifa bin Hamad bin Abdullah bin Jassim bin Mohammed Al Thani, a member of the ruling Al Thani family. With a population of only two and half million, there were nearly three times as many expatriates as nationals in Qatar. Many of the visitors were employed in oil and gas businesses, and in the growing construction and tourism industries.

I enjoyed traveling to Doha, and developed a great relationship with Norman and his team. After a long hot week, the team would go to the Ramada Hotel and enjoy the Hindustani music. The Ramada, like many American hotels in the region, was tightly controlled by heavily armed security forces. Fully armed security staff patrolled the fortified access gates, and Humvees complete with large caliber machine guns surrounded the hotel. Indoors, past the metal detectors, the dining room looked like the set of an early James Bond movie. The eclectic group of locals and expatriates, with the sitar-playing band from India, was straight out of central casting, absent the voluptuous Bond girl. We relaxed on bench-style seats with plenty of pillows, surrounding large, low tables. Each table was separated by decoratively carved wooden panels. The tables, which seated six to eight, surrounded a central elevated stage where the musicians performed. A sweet smell from the hookah pipes overtook the pervasive cigarette smoke. The music was rhythmic and haunting, creating an exotic, surreal environment.

We'd hang out, drink whiskey, and talk for hours. Norman and his team were starting to make real progress. However, they needed assistance just getting simple things done with the engineering departments back in the United States. They'd often get stuck simply because they didn't know who to talk to, or how to handle a routine issue. Often, they just needed a lift, which took little time. Like many young engineers in India, Norman and his colleagues grew up dreaming of working for a big American firm, and were keen to learn, but also quite intimidated. The previous management treated these Indian as colonials and had not encouraged them to visited our US plants and engineering centers in Virginia and Minnesota. Even Norman, the top producer in the region, hadn't personally met the engineers who had helped him select and design systems worth millions and millions of dollars to our company.

The Indian engineers knew their names and spoke with true deference about these American men and women, but little did they know they were newly graduated engineers, most of whom had never travelled out of the United States. They too were too self-conscious to build a relationship with these more seasoned mid-career international sales engineers in the Middle East. The American engineers were whizzes with the equipment selections and optimization using the latest CFD (computational fluid dynamics) programs. What they didn't know was how to select the equipment, originally designed for American climates, to operate in this very different environment, and outsmart the competition in the bid.

The engineers in Qatar benefited from Norman's years of experience, as he had developed sophisticated ways of modifying the selections for the extreme weather conditions. But I knew if he developed more in-depth relationships with the US design engineers, we could do amazing things.

This is where we started working together. Doha was just starting to grow, slowly spinning the flywheel and jealously watching as Dubai, its aggressive and rich neighbor, gained fame and fortune. Qatar had a few spectacular projects underway, like the National Library and the Pearl artificial islands, and construction was picking up. But then something unprecedented happened. Qatar won the bid to host the 2022 World Cup. This was a huge win for Qatar and the entire region. After the announcement, all hell broke loose and the pace of construction in Doha skyrocketed. It was insane, and I was pulled into meetings in which we discussed designing the first outdoor fully air-conditioned football (soccer) stadiums with cool air seeping up through the field. The lavish, extravagant, and daring architecture of its neighbors was now coming to Qatar.

My role as the Expert Coach was to support the progress of the team. This included frequent brief one-on-one meetings – the key was to help them get unstuck and make progress. Making progress always included helping individuals become free from negative thoughts and perceptions, as well as more practical and mundane issues like getting emails or phone calls returned. This type of coaching is a good match for the Progress Principle which we'll discuss in detail later.

I began to experience the same kind of lift as I had enjoyed twenty years before. The feeling was just as remarkable. I lost track of time and somehow always knew what to say and how to say it. There was no pretense or manipulation going on. I was pulled outside of my own head and self-centered criticism. My energy level increased, and my mood and disposition improved.

What I didn't realize is that I was satisfying my need to reach out, to support, and to guide the next generation, just as Erikson's research had described. It recaptured the extraordinary feeling that lured me into LGAT-style coaching back in the 80s. The Maya Angelou quotation once again rang true for me. I might forget the content of our coaching discussion but I would recall how I felt. Now, I felt good.

Later when I read the work of psychologist Matthew Lieberman, author of *Social: Why Our Brains Are Wired to Connect,* I better understood my feelings of coherence. It just felt right. It felt as though I was doing the right thing. Lieberman explains why:

> We both feel good in a discussion like this where we are both the generator and receiver of positive feeling. It's because we mammalians are wired to connect with and care for others. When we do, our bodies reward us with both oxytocin and natural opioid-based pleasure processes.[6]

Lieberman cites research showing how our brains developed because of the evolutionary advantages of being social. Our large neocortex is a better design for operating in large social settings and groups of people. However, when we are one-on-one, our brain naturally initiates an internal network, which comes on a like a reflex, and prompts understanding, empathy, consideration, and collaboration. We automatically and reflexively use this neural network to help us become more empathetic and to harmonize with others.[7]

In my twenties and thirties, I simply did not seem to trust or understand the importance of these feelings. The messages of consumerism and self-importance from social media, including TV, were more compelling. Now in my forties, I found that the more I invested in coaching and advising someone, the better I felt. I also noticed that the feeling would last longer than it had before. The simple version was: I needed to get myself to do, to act, and not rely on my longer term vision of who I could be.

Becoming aware that we think differently as we go through the different stages in life has proven extremely valuable for my personal health and stability. It provides a way for me to gain a perspective, to locate myself, as I did with the solar system model back in physics class. If I am stressing out over feelings about the direction of my life, or assessing my successes and failures, I can pause and appreciate that this is just part of a natural stage in the system or process of life.

Importantly, I now know that if I take the actions to get outside my own head and to engage in a coaching discussion, I will have a good chance of getting to a better place while experiencing the lift of contributing to another. It is very much like exercise, because it is only by Doing that we experience the benefits. It's not just the change in perspective. By actually doing something and contributing to someone, the body produces chemicals that support the good feelings.

Helpfully, the very design of the craftsman process accounts for this desire to contribute and take action. Just as Sully progressed through the <u>craft</u> process of being a pilot, and was passing on the metis he gained as an airline captain, many of us will have the opportunity to transfer the metis we have gained in our respective fields. The knowledge and the metis you have developed in your field, profession, or business are of value to someone moving up and developing in their career.

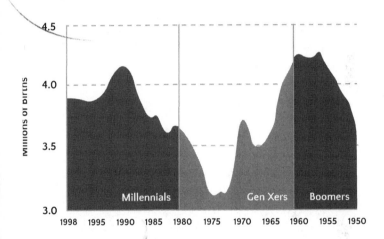

Figure 10.0 The working US population in three demographic groups

This transfer of metis will be a big job because the next cohort, gen X, is a much smaller group than the boomers: We are handing over control and management of our hospitals, industries, schools, and government to a smaller group who will be servicing massive numbers of consumers and customers, including both the aging baby boomers and the rising millennials, who recently overtook the boomers in total population for the United States.[8]

The Craft Is the Context

LIFT builds the case for developing senior managers and executives into Expert Coaches inside their organizations.

Embedded in the Expert Coaching model is the idea that your particular business, profession, or niche IS the context. It was under the influence of this context that your leadership, management, and relationship skills first developed.

You gained metis in this specific context. This may seem self-evident, but many current coaching methods rely on abstract all-purpose interpretations of *transformation*, leadership, and speech acts. These generic qualities of leadership are promoted over skill development and craftsmanship. This is certainly not a new or original idea; Aristotle points out, "Lack of experience diminishes our power of taking a comprehensive view of admitted facts," and favors "those who dwell in an intimate association with nature and its phenomena." He contrasts them with "those whom devotion to abstract discussions has rendered unobservant of facts," because they "are too ready to dogmatize on the basis of a few observations."[9]

More recently, Matthew Crawford depicts the importance of the skill development process in his book, *The World Beyond Your Head.*

> When we are engaged in a skilled practice, the world shows up for us as reality of its own independent of self … external objects provide an attachment point for the mind; they pull us out of ourselves.[10]

Research from the early twentieth century supports this idea that our behavior is not driven by character traits that apply from one context to another.[11] Rather, we behave as we do because we learn from experience in the context. Athletes or musicians may be effective leaders on the field or in the studio, but what they know

*Ccopective, collaberative & (Co
Competchorve*

about how to lead and be effective does not necessarily transfer to leadership in other organizations.

HR professionals go to great lengths to recruit top-performing executives. Industry experience is a key criterion by which new hires are evaluated. But this same focus is often not applied in coaching, and particularly in the "transformational" coaching business where experience and skill in a business or industry is discounted or not considered relevant. In the craftsman model, leadership is distributed among the guild members. In this context, there is "just enough leadership,"[12] as Professor Henry Mintzberg explains. Leadership in a workshop is not the "heroic" leadership model, or the everyone-is-a-leader model we inherited from the twentieth century.

Adopting a craftsman model means moving away from the individual to the community in an organization. We humans are social animals, as David Brooks writes, and we evolved with, and because of, our extraordinary capabilities to collaborate in a community. "The human race is not impressive because towering geniuses produce individual masterpieces. The human race is impressive because groups of people create mental scaffolds that guide future thought. No individual could build a modern airplane, but modern companies contain institutional knowledge that allows groups to design and build them."[13] Psychologist Daniel Goleman, author of *Emotional Intelligence*, has called this "social intelligence."[14] Metis is valuable because it includes both the content – the institutional knowledge – and the skills to develop our collective human potential using the natural strengths of cooperation and collaboration.

By contrast, the individualist everyone-is-a-leader culture has promoted the superstar CEO with obscene compensation plans, driving a wedge in the culture rather than building or serving the community.

We can focus instead on cultivating a community and a culture where those with the most industry and business metis become the Expert Coaches. These senior employees are given the responsibility for shepherding in the next generation. Fortunately for us, because of the demographics, there will be plenty of senior managers from which to select the most qualified and the best fits. Senior management and the operating teams move closer together in the craftsman culture, retaining and integrating these senior leaders as Expert Coaches. It may not be simply fashion, or coincidence, which has attracted the millennials to a more collaborative way of working. They seem to intuitively know that we don't need more heroic self-centered leadership, we need more collaboration and community.

Being an Adult is the
adoption of responsibility.

An adolescent has nascent potential
to transition towards adulthood,
however they can remain of this
state of arrival indefinitely.

To (Qn) ? How to we facilitate
a gradual progression towards,
rather that entropy

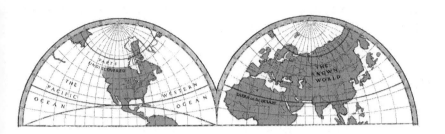

CHAPTER 11 — YOU ARE HERE: WHAT THE HELL IS WATER?

If I could just get myself moving, doing, and out with others, I had a very good chance of getting outside the self-criticism. Lift was affording me a new perspective; while in coaching discussions, it felt as though I was free from the daily chokehold of stress and anxiety, and outside of the dark metaphorical container. Lift brought me up and created distance between me and those foggy, heavy feelings. This perspective is much like what Ron Heifetz describes in his book, *The Practice of Adaptive Leadership,* when you move off the dance floor and onto the balcony where the dance floor can be observed from a different perspective.[1]

My new perspective allowed some critical thinking and the time and space to piece together how I got to this point. I wanted to find the spot on the map that says, "You Are Here." It was like the model of the solar system in high school physics – when I could get outside of it and see it from a larger perspective, I could then see where I was. As with a big framed map in an airport, if I knew where I was – "You Are Here" – then I knew how to get where I wanted to go.

In this chapter, we try to get outside the tangle of issues today and understand from a larger perspective the historic factors that have influenced how we baby boomers got to this point, with record levels of depression, anxiety, and suicide – and how to overcome and move on to success and even to serenity.

At this point in the book, you might say I'm steering the argument toward an antiquated, melancholy image of a "craftsman," nostalgic for the craft culture; a way to sway you and win support for what is, in the end, an impossible fantasy. Or you might say I'm using craftsmanship as an easy, oversimplified answer to a complex issue; to make us feel good, taking advantage of the psychological immune system introduced in Chapter Six.

However, the argument for craft runs deep, and it speaks to longstanding concerns. The nineteenth-century French sociologist, Émile Durkheim, was also interested in the question we're now addressing: why the rate of suicide was so high in such modern and prosperous countries (at the time) as France, the UK, and Denmark.

Durkheim, well known as the "sociologist of anomie," essentially looked at suicide as a result of what happened outside your head. He wrote about the negative effects individualism has on the social structure, the family unit, and also on the individual's sense of self, and as a member of a family, guild, or community.

As the old saying goes, when the student is ready to learn, the teacher will appear. In my case, the teacher was literally right there beside me. Long before I was ready to learn, back in the 80s when I was in Saudi, shuttling back and forth to our plant in Épinal, France, I would have had plenty of time to learn about Épinal's famous son, Émile Durkheim, and even to read some of the work that earned him the honorific, "the father of sociology." Then, when I began working on this book several years ago, learning about the work of Émile Durkheim took on a very different tone for me. The time was right; I was ready. His findings revealed an aspect of our human nature, which I too was now experiencing, and which may be common to us all: The societies in which we live and work (outside of our heads) have an enormous influence on our feelings and behavior.

I observed three significant social factors that seemed to dominate the news and the bestseller lists. The confluence of these factors led me to appreciate the utility and elegance of the craftsman model.

The first of these factors is the **decline of social capital** in the boomer generation. There is compelling evidence that, as a generation, the baby boomers have retreated from participating and collaborating in their communities. One perspective is offered in a 2000 book, *Bowling Alone: The Collapse and Revival of American Community*, by Robert Putnam, an award-winning and highly respected academic, and Dean of the Kennedy School at Harvard. His research shows a significant migration away from social (civic) connections, and a decline in "social capital" during the baby boom years. He defines social capital as the grease which allows for communities to advance smoothly – the collective participation, collaboration, and reciprocity that result in a community of trust.[2] These same qualities are also present in the craftsman culture.

Putnam's research focuses on neighborhoods and communities, including community activities like bowling leagues. However, Putnam makes the important point that more people are bowling today than in the 1960s. It's not that we have traded our bowling shoes for a virtual-reality bowling game, which can be played on the couch. The point is, we have nearly stopped bowling – or doing much else – in communities. And this path has led to social isolation, which is neither healthy nor productive.

I am under no illusion, nor do I believe businesses will return to a "craftsman culture" as in olden days. However, as you may know if you have children who are millennials and gen X, they lean toward a more collaborative craft-type working style and not the lone self-centered hero style followed by boomers. In *Millennials Rising*, a best-selling 2000 book by Professors Neil Howe and

William Strauss, the authors validate the point: "Millennials aren't doing this alone as entrepreneurial loners. Instead... they're banding together, in their own clubs and classes online..."[3]

Millennials, and to a lesser extent gen-Xers, are gathering in workshop-style shared "co-working" spaces. From 2010 to 2016, the number of co-working spaces saw a nearly twenty-four percent growth rate, and Emergent Research predicts a forty-one percent increase between 2016 and 2020.[4] These spaces are not simply for startups with limited budgets; they are used by some of the largest and most influential companies, including Google and Facebook.

This category of working space as a deliberate choice is relatively new and is now favored and appreciated by many young companies in all industries. What is interesting for the discussion about craftsmanship is that this concept mirrors the workshops of craftsmen in Renaissance Italy.

If Venice was the Dubai of the thirteenth century, then Florence was the Silicon Valley of the fifteenth century, where the co-working spaces were called "bottegas."[5] Florentine workshops were communities of science, craftsmanship, and innovation, where creativity, practice, passions, and partnership could intertwine. In these bottegas, a master craftsman or artist would strive to create the next generation of masters to carry on the craft and the culture. These shops were a central part of the community in which apprentices and journeymen worked shoulder to shoulder, learning and honing their craft and their character. Apprentices, journeymen, and the masters were interdependent, yet free and flexible. It was in these shops that new artistic forms came to life, with artists competing among themselves but also collaborating.[6] During the Renaissance, the knowledge transfer in these bottegas gave young people a brighter, more secure future.

The craftsman model provided the context which helped to attract and develop some of the greatest names in art, philosophy, and science. Leonardo da Vinci spent at least a decade logging his

10,000-plus hours as an apprentice at a Florentine bottega, run by Andrea del Verrocchio.[7]

> A good artist but a better businessman, Verrocchio surely spotted the burgeoning genius in the young artist from an "illegitimate" family, but he nonetheless insisted Leonardo start on the bottom rung like everyone else, sweeping floors and cleaning chicken cages. (The eggs were used to make tempera paint before the advent of oil.) Gradually, Verrocchio gave his charge greater responsibility, even permitting him to paint portions of his own artwork.[8]
>
> —Eric Weiner

Leonardo provides a good example of a craftsman. He could have left the workshop after a decade and found higher paying work elsewhere, but he stayed another two or three years until he was twenty-six. He did so to continue to advance his art, and to work with a true mentor. Michelangelo was also found and trained in a similar fashion.

There is almost no mention of mentors or mentorship in this book, yet some may think that Expert Coaching is merely a form of mentoring. The difference is stark. The label "mentor" has been almost irreparably damaged from misuse, so to avoid the confirmation bias, I choose not to use the term in this book. At the heart of my concern is the notion of a mentor as a detached, generally "nice," disconnected generalist who offers kind words of wisdom and vague, inarguable advice, generally out of the actual context. Mentoring today often does not require a commitment to an ongoing relationship as central to the mentor's role.

Later, we'll dig deeper into the Craft of Expert Coaching, and will address this critical point in more detail. The Expert Coach, Verrocchio, (whom some might call a mentor) is the central reason da Vinci stayed at the bottega long after his apprenticeship. He stayed because of his relationship with Verrocchio, his coach. "[Leonardo] could have found work elsewhere, but he clearly valued the experience he acquired in the dusty, chaotic workshop. Too often, modern-day mentoring programs, public or private, are lip-service. They must instead, as during Leonardo's time, entail meaningful, long-term relationships between mentors and their mentees."[9]

An entirely new way of thinking emerged in these craftsman communities of the Renaissance, one which valued science and the arts and their usefulness to humankind in the present, not a way of thinking solely focused on the religious dogma or mystical afterlife.

The influence and the widespread use of new technologies, and specifically the movable-type printing press, dramatically increased the speed of knowledge transfer and collaboration on new ideas. Innovation and wealth emanated from Florence, and as with the Silicon Valley of today, mathematics also played a central role. In Florence, mathematics made great advances and was used in a wide variety of the arts; the geometrization of space in visual perspective developed during this period. Also, sculpture first appeared in the round, not just as relief decorations on cathedrals. The artists and craftsmen of the Renaissance played a significant role in new concepts of space and form, in ways that literally changed how we saw and related to the world.

The second factor that led me to recognize the value today of the craftsman culture was the **obsolescence of "leadership."** This was not entirely a surprise to me. As a former executive and as a consultant and coach, I found compelling the growing body of literature and good data that cast dark shadows on the lone, self-centered, everyone-is-a-leader culture. By almost any relevant measure, whether it's a financial or a job satisfaction metric, the data are clear and demonstrate that a focus on leadership in its current form is not working.[10]

Far from it. A growing group of academics who have been writing about it for years are now raising red flags and shooting off flares trying to get our attention. As discussed earlier in the book, many business professors are calling into question our almost singular focus on leadership training and leadership coaching, questioning its efficacy. McGill professor Henry Mintzberg puts it this way:

> The more we obsess about leadership, the less of it we seem to get. In fact, the more we claim to develop leadership in courses and programs... the more we get hubris. That is because leadership is earned, not anointed. Moreover, by putting leadership on a pedestal separated from management, we turn a social process into a personal one. No matter how much lip service is paid to the leader empowering the group, leadership still focuses on the individual: whenever we promote leadership, we demote others, as followers. Slighted, too, is the sense of community that is important for cooperative effort in all organizations. What we should be promoting instead of leadership alone are communities of actors who get on with things naturally, leadership together with management being an intrinsic part of that.[11]

It's not just that the leadership focus is not producing improved job satisfaction or business results; but baby boomers, and to some extent the gen-Xers, are more depressed and anxious than any previously recorded generations.[12] The fact is, our work lives are not contributing to our well-being. In 2015, Anne Case and Angus Deaton, Princeton economists, published the following research findings:

> [A]lthough mortality is declining for virtually every other demographic group in every developed country, it has been rising for middle-aged white Americans since the early nineteen-nineties.[13]

The increase, they claim, is due almost exclusively to what they call "deaths of despair" – suicides, drug and alcohol poisoning, and chronic liver disease.

While one cannot make a direct causal relationship, the raw data alone tell part of the story. "The suicide rate is rising sharply for males aged 45 to 64 (from 20.8 to 29.7 deaths per 100,000 between 1999 and 2014) [43%] and females... (from 6.0 to 9.8 deaths per 100,000 between 1999 and 2014) [63%] among all age groups by gender."[14] Many of those men and women were skilled professionals (with and without college education) and leaders/masters in their communities, schools, government, industry, and healthcare. So, if you live in a community of 100,000, nearly thirty men in this age group will take their own lives this year. In that same community, seven women in their early sixties will commit suicide. Although their suicide number is still relatively low compared with men, it is up by more than sixty percent in the last decade.[15]

The third factor supporting the Craft model can be deduced by simply looking at the **demographics**: about seventy-six million baby boomers are beginning to retire, handing control over to the fifty-five million gen-Xers – metaphorically resembling what Sully did at takeoff when he said to second-in-command Skiles, "It's your airplane."

Plenty of good data demonstrate that there will be significant demand for highly skilled and "human touch" types of jobs – the jobs held by masters, experts, and skilled, experienced managers. The Employment Policy Foundation estimates that eighty percent of the impending and inevitable labor shortage will involve a scarcity of complex skills like problem solving, judgment, listening, relationship building, collaboration, and management.[16]

In the next section, we'll look at how we got to our current predicament from a longer term historic view. We'll also consider why these disturbing trends occur primarily in the United States.

Co-opting Enlightenment

Coming of age in the 70s and 80s, I thought enlightenment was something that emerged from the Far East – through religion or mystical tradition. But then, as a frustrated hockey player – and, worse, an engineer – I did not care much for philosophy. I associated enlightenment with the turn to spirituality the Beatles made when they adopted an Indian guru and Yoko Ono joined the band.

But as I came to learn, the Enlightenment was very much a Western creation that had a profound influence on the United States, and to some extent on Canada as well. Although the exact timeframe for the Enlightenment is contested, it happened in seventeenth- and eighteenth-century Europe. The name Enlightenment is itself a metaphor, about bringing light after the Dark Ages. Darren Staloff's book *Hamilton, Adams, Jefferson: The Politics of Enlightenment and The American Founding,* explains clearly the importance of the Enlightenment on the culture of the United States.

> The United States of America was forged in the crucible of the Enlightenment; no other nation bears its imprint as deeply. Our ideals of liberty and equality, the ringing "self-evident truths" of the Declaration of Independence, and the measured tones of the Constitution and the Federalist [Papers] all echo the language of the Enlightenment and express its most profound convictions about the political life and natural rights of mankind.[17]

So, if I wanted to understand how we baby boomers got to "Here," I needed to better understand the Enlightenment.

The Enlightenment was called by some the age of mechanistic philosophy.[18] Mechanistic philosophers re-oriented the former geocentric system, endorsed by the church, in which the earth was literally at the center of the universe. The mechanistic teaching of

Descartes in the sixteenth century led to the great advances in physics and astronomy in the seventeenth century by Kepler, Galileo, Copernicus, and Newton.

Courageous and brilliant men and women in Europe fought against far more than simply the structure and configuration of the planets. They were up against what the church and community leaders believed to be a "natural order" as described by God and written about in the Bible, and therefore beyond question. In addition, the church applied the persuasive reconsideration policy of torture.

Between the fifteenth and eighteenth centuries, amazing new technologies in communication (the printing press), transportation and navigation (the sextant), and astronomy (the telescope), accelerated our unique human ability to collaborate and gain knowledge. This started a period of extraordinary scientific advancement, as Sir Isaac Newton acknowledged when he developed his laws of mechanics, "standing on the shoulders" of previous generations in science and philosophy.

Newton's laws of motion changed the way we thought about our place in the universe and the behavior or motion of the planets – including the earth. This behavior could now be determined, predicted, and proven using empirical science and mathematics, not magical stories, miracles, or mysticism.

How Gravity Influences
Behavior from the Outside

As we saw in Chapter Five, three successive astronomical systems informed our perspective about the way we saw our place in the universe. Here's a brief recap of that three-step process.

First, the ancient Greeks proposed that we on earth were quite literally at the center of the universe. According to Aristotle, this was obvious, because we did not move. His logic was that if the earth did rotate or revolve, and a stone were thrown vertically up in the air, it would land at some distance away from where it was thrown because, while the stone was in the air the earth would have moved under it. In addition, it was believed the force that moved the planets and stars was something called *vis viva*. This force, separate, unique, and "inside" each of these planets, was given by the Gods.

The next step, in the centuries of the Enlightenment, brought a change in perspective. The earth was not at the center, but, like other planets, part of an expanded system called the solar system. However, according to Sir Isaac Newton, the separate and unique forces that made the earth and all the other planets move were still to be found *inside the planets*, bequeathed by a Christian God.

The third step, in the nineteenth and twentieth centuries, came about as we expanded our knowledge of electromagnetic forces. Englishman Michael Faraday proved through experimentation that electromagnetic forces existed *outside* an object − in a field that surrounded it.

We came to understand that a force could act on an object, from a field surrounding the object. So, based on this new knowledge of forces being exerted by fields, scientists proposed that the force of gravity did not exist inside an object or a planet. Instead, gravity existed in a field surrounding the object or planet.

This was a very big deal, validating a concept even Newton had dismissed.

How Context Influences Our Behavior from the Outside

In the same way that the forces of gravity and electromagnetism influence the physical behavior of objects from the outside, our mental behavior is influenced from the outside as well. Our unconscious sweeps up information and influences our behavior. In the Craft of Expert Coaching we address the powerful influence of the unconscious, which is not entirely virtuous, as it is subject to the biases and errors built into our cognitive machinery. Therefore, because of these systematic errors and biases, our unconscious needs supervision from the outside, and ideally from an Expert Coach who is equipped to guide us past our blind spots.

For these reasons, as we will see in more detail, the context in which someone works has a far bigger impact on their behavior and performance than is currently recognized. We are sweeping up all this information from our surroundings – our context – all the time, and, from this information, our unconscious learns, and influences our behavior.

One of the most challenging behavioral issues many people can relate to – or simply struggle with – is losing weight. But solid evidence demonstrates that our behavior, even with a difficult issue like weight control, is far more predictable – and thus potentially solvable – than previously believed.

New research shows that one of the most effective ways to deal with weight management does not take place inside your head. In his book *Mindless Eating: Why We Eat More Than We Think*, Brian Wansink, a professor and director of the Cornell University Food and Brand Lab, demonstrates that our environment – not our mindsets, willpower, or exercise programs – exerts a powerful and predictable influence. This is great news for the Craft of Expert Coaching. As Wansink explains, "It's easier to change our environment than our mind."[19]

In the "popcorn bucket" study – perhaps the most well known recent diet experiment – Wansink and a group of his graduate students tested the long-held belief that "how much they eat is mainly determined by how hungry they are, how much they like the food, and what mood they're in."[20] They conducted an experiment at a suburban movie theater near Chicago. "Every person who bought a ticket – even though many of them had just eaten lunch – were given a [free] soft drink and either a medium-sized bucket or a large-sized bucket [of popcorn]."They were told the food and drink were free and "we hoped they were willing to answer a few concession stand-related questions after the movie." Wansink threw in another variable: unbeknownst to the moviegoers and even the assisting grad students, the popcorn was stale – it had been popped five days earlier. After the movie, when the audience members were surveyed, those with the large-sized buckets were asked if they felt they had eaten more popcorn simply based on the size of the bucket. Most people said they had not, and many said, "Things like that don't trick me," or "I'm pretty good at knowing when I'm full."[21]

Regardless, as in the four-minute-mile example, the data told another story. Those given the larger buckets ate fifty-three percent more popcorn: twenty-one more handfuls than those with the smaller buckets.

In his book, Wansink describes another more elaborate experiment they did at a restaurant in North Dakota. Not just any restaurant, this was a fine-dining lab sponsored by the Department of Food Science and Human Nutrition at the University of Illinois at Urbana–Champaign. This time, changes were made to more than just the size of the bucket or plate. The restaurant was divided in half by an imaginary line, but without any physical cues in the environment.

In the research experiments, diners on each side of the restaurant were treated exactly the same: same decor, same wait staff, and the same food and drink. On one side, though, a clear effort was made to indicate a higher level of quality, using targeted visual cues: the menus were in French, and the wine was from California (according to the label on the bottle). The other side of the restaurant served the same food and the same wine but the menus were in English and the wine label said it was from North Dakota. All the wine labels had in fact been removed from the bottles and replaced with either a label indicating a California wine or a North Dakota wine, both from fictional wineries.

At the end of the meal, diners were asked to take a survey. Meanwhile behind the scenes, the food that diners left on their plates was weighed and logged, and the amount of wine consumed at each table was tallied.

Those sitting on the "fine" side of the restaurant ate more food, stayed at the restaurant for a longer time, drank more wine, and gave higher marks on the survey. The results were clear: The behavior of individuals had been influenced by the environment and the context.

How does this research relate to coaching and Expert Coaching? It reminds us that there's more to behavior change than what is going on inside someone's head. In follow-up interviews after the meal, diners were debriefed on the research methods, and the changes that were made by the researcher. Interestingly, when the diners were asked if they felt they had been influenced by the label on the wine bottle, for example, nearly all of them said, "No I wasn't."[22]

Wansink's research supports the notion, as we discussed earlier, that the stories we tell others and ourselves are often inaccurate and do not reflect what in fact happened. Because we are unaware of the influence of our unconscious, we simply don't know why we did, or did not, do something; we make up a story to validate our actions.[23] The story we tell may, for example, support a familiar belief about ourselves like, "my willpower is very weak when it comes to food," which may not be accurate, nor be the cause of our behavior.

Additional research in Massachusetts studied our behavior with food from a different perspective. This time a person's eating behavior was examined, not with inanimate objects in the environment like menus or wine labels, but with real people in the places and networks where they spent their time. In their book, *Connected: The Surprising Power of Our Social Networks and How They Shape Our Lives—How Your Friends' Friends' Friends Affect Everything You Feel,*

Think, and Do, the authors reveal their decade-long research that essentially supports the subtitle of the book. Nicholas Christakis, a physician and social science researcher at Harvard, and James Fowler, a social scientist at the University of California at San Diego, used data from a well-known epidemiology study started in 1948 in Framingham, Massachusetts.

Designed to study the determinants of cardiovascular disease, the Framingham Heart Study has yielded good results and helped physicians and scientists learn a lot about cardiovascular issues. In a turn of good fortune, Christakis and Fowler found that the Framingham researchers had collected detailed information over a long period of time, and kept hand-written notes on topics relevant to their food research. The Framingham researchers updated the subjects' body weight and other key physical measures every two years when they came in for testing. From this data, Christakis and Fowler "painstakingly were able to reconstruct social networks of all the subjects. Ultimately, they were able to map more than fifty thousand ties."[24] With this data, they were able to create a network of 12,067 subjects, tracking the weight of each of the subjects over almost forty years. They also could track how individuals moved – and how their body weight changed – within their networks.

They wanted to explore causation, to see if they could prove that someone's body weight would change as the result of a relationship with another person. What they found was not surprising, given the subtitle of the book. Said another way, "One person could actually cause weight gain in another, in a kind of social contagion."[25]

To make a long story shorter, this research is fascinating and, for the purpose of this book, these "social contagion" findings again demonstrate that human behavior is influenced by more than just what goes on inside of our head. Weight loss, according to this study, can't just be about willpower – it's about who you spend your time with, too.

How Metaphors Influence the Context

At several points in LIFT, we've looked at the fundamental idea that our conceptual understanding is largely metaphorical.[26] The use of metaphors is an effective way of transmitting a message, like the flawed TV tower metaphor used in *The Secret*. It was effective in spite of its flaw, because metaphors help us complete a story or concept (particularly one we like), regardless of its basis in science or other reality.

Our own solar system has been used as a metaphor as well. I make the case that early Enlightenment philosophers, whether consciously or unconsciously, used the metaphorical concept of a solar system and gravity to make sense of man's individual or personal perception and consciousness.

Enlightenment philosophies – of Immanuel Kant in particular – supported the idea that our consciousness, and therefore our will and willpower, existed inside of us as individuals. This was the origin of the lone heroic individual model.

Just as nineteenth-century scientists moved the force of gravity from inside an object to a field outside, contemporary philosophers like Alva Noë have moved the location of perception and consciousness from inside our heads to outside. Based on this new model of perception, our behavior is no longer the result of what's inside our heads, any more than gravity was the result of what was inside the earth.

It's now clear that forces which influence behavior emerge from the context in which we live, from our environment, and from the people with whom we associate. (Just reflect on the research with the popcorn buckets, wine labels, and overweight friends.)

This perspective removes the notion that willpower and self-discipline are the sole drivers of behavior. As I came to understand this idea of context, which includes the environment and other people, my own quest for answers began to make more sense. Context was revealing itself as the key to understanding my behavior.

My next questions were:

- If the context influenced the way we thought and behaved, what was the context in which we, as baby boomers, were raised in the twentieth century?

- From which side of the experimental restaurant did we dine?

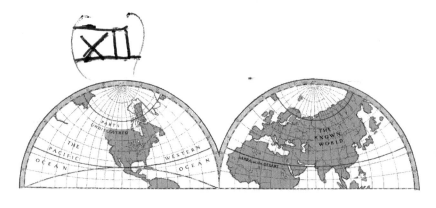

CHAPTER 12 — COLLABORATION AS CRAFT

In this chapter we will consider the factors outside of our heads which have influenced American coaches and managers. But, to avoid being tripped up by the Law of Small Numbers, we will use a larger sample size, over a longer period of time. By looking at the American business environment or context from a longer term historical perspective, we'll better understand how and why we've ended up the way we have.

By the seventeenth century, Europe was swept up in a fast-moving river of change. New ideas and concepts in sciences, religion, and human rights were colliding, churning, and gaining momentum. France was on the brink of a revolution, and within a century America would follow with a revolution of its own.

French and British colonies in North America were growing rapidly, establishing and building communities. People were flocking to the New World, enticed by hyperbole to a land of plenty that offered easy gold and silver, and a better life.

In 1620, Francis Bacon, the Englishman known as the father of the scientific method, said it was all "gold, silver, and temporal profit" driving the colonization project, not "the propagation of the Christian faith."[1]

Later, in the eighteenth century, these new ideas about equality and individual rights articulated during the Enlightenment inspired and influenced the founders of what were to become the United States. The men and women who led the fight for independence understood very well the importance of these new philosophies. They were willing to give their own lives to ensure that future generations in America would live with the freedom and equality on which the revolution was based. They fought one of the most important battles in history, championing human rights and the freedom to pursue life, liberty, and happiness. It would be a new order of the ages – *Novus ordo seclorum* – as expressed on the Great Seal of the United States (and, since 1935, on the one-dollar bill, just below the pyramid).

The founders fought for a true republic – of the people, by the people, and for the people. As we must with the ancient Greeks, we note the tacit exceptions made as to the rights of women, Native Americans, and enslaved people in the British colonies and later the United States.

There is little dispute about the influence of Enlightenment philosophy on the American fight for freedom. Englishmen John Locke (1632–1704), and Thomas Hobbes (1588–1679) before him, played prominent roles, as did the German philosopher Immanuel Kant (1724–1804).

Kant's influence on the new American politics is expressed in the freedoms granted in the Constitution.[2] And it was Kant who laid the foundation for the lone heroic leader model in America, to which we'll return.

Kant's philosophies articulated the fundamental idea of individual freedoms and equality. But Kant went further to make the case that it was morally and ethically right to *make it on your own*, to transition into maturity and let go of the need for the guidance (or nonage[3]) of others. Kant's writing was very personal and practical, as expressed below in his 1784 essay, "What is Enlightenment?"

> Laziness and cowardice are the reasons why so great a portion of mankind, after nature has long since discharged them from external direction (naturaliter maiorennes [those who come of age by virtue of nature]), nevertheless remains under lifelong tutelage, and why it is so easy for others to set themselves up as their guardians. It is so easy not to be of age. If I have a book that understands for me, a pastor who has a conscience for me, a physician who decides my diet, and so forth, I need not trouble myself. I need not think, if I can only pay – others will easily undertake the irksome work for me. That the step to competence is held to be very dangerous by the far greater portion of mankind (and by the entire fair sex) – quite apart from its being arduous is seen to by those guardians who have so kindly assumed superintendence over them...[4]

Kant's essay, or parts of it, must have been studied by the best and brightest of the late eighteenth century, like those wildly ambitious young men who proposed the founding of a new nation.

These vital concepts used in the Declaration of Independence and the Constitution molded the American culture and are echoed today in the American dream. This dream is still an immensely attractive and relevant force and is exemplified by the lone heroic leaders in business, sports, and entertainment. The American dream did not then, nor does it now, necessarily include being part of a collaborative community. Representative icons were the lone self-made men like Henry Ford and John D. Rockefeller. It was the Marlboro Man, not the Marlboro Community.

The philosophical ideas of Kant, Locke, and Hobbs were mixed with religious beliefs to form a foundation for the new nation, but the founders interpreted the ideas in a way that created a hard edge, against which our values and beliefs were cast. And it was this perspective that informed the context – the water in which we swim ("what the hell is water?"). This Enlightenment–based philosophical context influenced the behavior and ultimately the culture of America, guiding us to the ideal of the lone heroic self-centered leader and turning us away from the craftsman culture.

The American Myth of the Lone Heroic Leader

Paul Revere's famous ride is an example of the type of independent spirit which forged the American consciousness. However, "Paul Revere's alarum was successful only because of networks of civic engagement in the Middlesex villages. ...Nevertheless, the myth of the rugged individual continues to strike a powerful chord in the American psyche."[5]

One twentieth century American lone heroic leader was Alfred P. Sloan, a remarkable man who made a big contribution to general management theory and, by extension, business coaching. "Silent Sloan," an engineer from MIT, became president of General Motors in 1923, only fifteen years after it was formed. Sloan revolutionized management of these large "general organizations," using what he later called "federal decentralization." He reorganized GM into separate autonomous divisions subject only to financial and policy controls from a small headquarters staff. He took GM from an industry laggard to number one in six years, with revenues of $1.5 billion, nearly quintupling its market valuation. His organizational structure has been copied and used as a template for large American organizations for decades. Sloan was by his own admission a "professional general manager" who brought a methodical engineering precision and structure to management. He was known for his generous philanthropy, but his management style was as a behind-the-scenes, silent, detached, and somewhat cold leader, thus validating the lone heroic leader confirmation biases in the United States.

Since the early twentieth century, large American companies have taken to naming their companies as "General" organizations, for example, General Electric (1889), General Dynamics (1952), General Foods (1929), General Mills (1928), and General Tire (1915). These companies were so named after they acquired a number of smaller companies and "rolled them up" into a "General" holding company. Their managers were influenced by Frederick Winslow Taylor's scientific management. Using the same logic as for the production of a widget, Taylorists sliced up management into smaller specific pieces and processes, increasingly distant from the trade–craft of building a product. Using the latest time–motion studies to efficiently design, plan, delegate, coordinate, staff, organize, and make decisions so they could attain a desirable profit-making result for an organization,[6] these general corporations were training the next generation of general managers.

After Taylor and Sloan came Peter Drucker, introduced earlier as one of the leading voices in American management. Drucker thought little of the emerging focus on leadership, and in an interview with Forbes in 2004, Drucker said:

> The only thing you can say about a leader is that a leader is somebody who has followers. The most charismatic leaders of the last century were called Hitler, Stalin, Mao and Mussolini. They were mis-leaders! Charismatic leadership by itself certainly is greatly overstated. Look, one of the most effective American presidents of the last 100 years was Harry Truman. He didn't have an ounce of charisma. Truman was as bland as a dead mackerel.[7]

Nevertheless, for some, a proficiency in leadership alone became enough. It was just the right tool to help an ambitious manager skip over rungs on the way up the corporate ladder. These large general conglomerates were growing dramatically in the post-war expansion, managing a more and more diverse portfolio of companies. The lone heroic leader played the part as written by Kant, and it made for a good story, a good fiction.

In this fiction, naturally gifted, tall white male leaders did not need experience or skill in the businesses they led. By the 1970s, leadership – alone – was enough. No longer one of the competencies of a successful businessperson, leadership stood supreme.

Leadership Coaching – LGATs Go Corporate

One reason for this excitement came along in the 1980s, when new methods and materials for personal development were transitioned into the much more lucrative world of corporate leadership development seminars.

Many of the weekend transformational seminars were structured so that participants had the experience of "coaching" others in paired sharing exercises. Key limiting beliefs, believed to be buried for years, were revealed and "transformed," in minutes. Participants found their short-term results remarkable. The seminar coaches were keen to help others when it meant digging into their pasts and miraculously diagnosing the underlying cause. The simple models allowed early coaching success, using what was believed to be a fast and accurate way to understand what was holding someone back.

Starting in the 1980s there was an explosion in new "transformation" consulting and coaching companies; their common element was that no specific business knowledge or competency was required.

However, many people ascended from these weekend seminars as righteous experts, soon called "est-holes" by their uninitiated friends and associates.

Gradually, personal accounts from the seminars emerged, and a more inclusive overview could be pieced together. Several damaging books and a TV movie severely criticized Werner Erhard.

To add to the continuing controversy was the revelation that Jack Rosenberg from Philadelphia was a complicated guy who "deserted his first wife and their four children to reinvent himself as Werner Erhard on the West Coast."[8] While he had no education beyond high school and no formal instruction in philosophy or psychology, he had begun, as we have seen, by dabbling in Mind Dynamics and Scientology.[9]

The transformation train remained in motion after Erhard left the station. In the 1990s, personal power (thanks in part to the omnipresent Tony Robbins infomercials) and leadership were attained by "breaking through" our limiting beliefs, certainly not by apprenticing and learning how to develop skills and expertise. We created new "realities," and broke old rules and barriers, which were no match for pop-nihilism and the newfound transformative power of language. Companies like WorldCom and Enron were proof of these new realities. Just like the four-minute mile, we had broken through more limiting beliefs – for a while.

A Whole New World of Possibilities

The phrase, "a whole new world of possibilities" was catching on in corporate American in the 1990s and early 2000s. It seemed every hip young corporation included this phrase somewhere in their business description and offerings. A new category of "transformation" consultants and coaches claimed it as their own. However, the unseen part of this "new world" relied on a fictional narrative that did not need business management, market research, or improved business practices – this whole new world would naturally just happen as a result of the *transformation*. Ultimately the dirty little secret came out: we'd collectively believed we could now get something for nothing.

On December 2, 2001, Enron filed for bankruptcy. With $63.4 billion in assets, theirs was the largest corporate bankruptcy in US history – until seven months later, in July 2002, when WorldCom declared bankruptcy with $107 billion in assets.

Dozens, maybe even hundreds, of academic papers and articles were published about the failures of both Enron and WorldCom. University of London Professor David Tourish outlines Enron's demise and connects it with the misuse of transformational leadership in his book, *The Dark Side of Transformational Leadership*. He exposes the objective failures of this "new world of possibilities," with its charismatic founders' personal insights which passed for leadership, and a cult-like culture of submission and conformity which passed for a strategy.[10]

It was certainly not the "transformational" methods which caused the illegal acts, but, as we discussed earlier, it was an organization climate tempted by the something for nothing urge and the desire to go along with the crowd which influenced good people to do bad things.

But it's not even as though the boomers came through these troubled times with the spoils. The boomer generation in the United States is struggling with obesity, drug addiction, depression, and suicide at increasing and unprecedented rates.

So Where Do We Go from Here?

If you are a business executive, manager, entrepreneur, consultant, or coach, chances are you're familiar with the best-selling *StrengthsFinder* book and online assessment. *StrengthsFinder 2.0* is one of the best-selling business psychology books ever, having sold over five million copies.[11] Now renamed CliftonStrengths, the assessment survey tool is based on the research of Donald Clifton, a professor of educational psychology at the University of Nebraska from the 1960s to 80s. He is known as the "father of strengths-based psychology and grandfather of the positive psychology movement."[12] The basic question at the heart of his research was, "What would happen if we studied what is right with people?" This was based on his belief in the importance of identifying and developing each person's positive attributes, and letting them contribute their particular strengths to a collaborative effort.

From the simplest perspective, it makes sense. An analogy used in the *StrengthsFinder* book provides the essence: If you bring home a report card with five As and one D, it makes sense to focus on the things you do well, and not spend time trying to improve the D, if that's not relevant to your career aspirations. According to the Gallup organization, owner of CliftonStrengths, "Our research indicates that your greatest room for overall personal improvement isn't where you're weakest, but rather where you're strongest. ... The assessment measures your natural patterns of thinking, feeling and behaving, so when you're done you'll have discovered your talents. Developed over decades spent studying millions of CliftonStrengths assessment results, these insights explain exactly *how* each of your Signature Themes makes you stand out in the world. The pinpoint accuracy will leave you inspired and empowered with a newfound self-awareness."[13]

The associated survey explains that the "online talent assessment is your way to: discover what you naturally do best, learn how to develop your greatest talents, use your customized results to live your best life."[14] Germane for us is that the message does not jump on the leadership train, and instead creates a pathway to collaboration and community.

*People want to cooperate, however,
First they want to know you care for
& understand them*

With this in mind, I propose we look for the natural strengths of *Homo sapiens*. What strengths supported our evolution? After all, we did adapt and survive. Fortunately, we've seen exceptional research and writing on human evolution. In his book, *Species: A Brief History of Humankind*, Yuval Noah Harari offers a hypothesis to account for why we, *Homo sapiens*, out-evolved other species. Harari maintains that it is our ability to create fiction and then cooperatively work in service of the fiction. The common thread running through most of Harari's work is that our strength for cooperation and collaboration has separated our human species from the rest.[5] So from a simplistic perspective, our strength as a species is in collaboration and cooperation.

Neuroscientist Matthew Lieberman comes to a similar conclusion, when he writes that we have evolved because of our ability to collaborate, and to function in a social environment.[16] He goes on to say,

> Our wiring motivates us to stay connected. It returns our attention again and again to understanding the minds of the people around us like a rubber band snapping back into place. And we have this center to our being, what we call our self, which among its many jobs serves to ensure that we harmonize with those around us by lining up our beliefs with theirs and nudging us to control our impulses for the good of the group. ... The biological depth of our sociality is important because it fleshes out a woefully incomplete theory [story] most of us have about 'who we are.'[17]

Now perhaps we can realign our idealism away from the lone heroic leaders and toward our natural propensities and strengths to collaborate and cooperate.

Quoting President Reagan, "It is easier to ride a horse in the direction that the horse wants to go."[18] We can follow that path that feels right, and experience the natural generative rewards which Erik Erikson identified – the deep satisfaction of contribution and leaving something useful and positive to our successors, the gen-Xers and millennials.

In the final chapters, we take a deep dive into the Craft of Expert Coaching and how it fits the burgeoning craftsman communities.

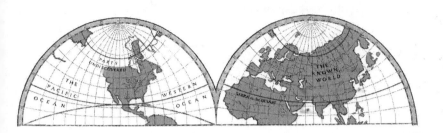

CHAPTER 13 — THE NATURE & CRAFT OF COACHING

While the Craft of Expert Coaching may seem in some ways familiar, the Expert Coaching model we introduce is distinct from the current leadership coaching model. Expert Coaching concentrates on more than leadership, with an emphasis on doing one's job well and making progress in business results. It also addresses the current need to transition to the next generation of managers and leaders.

This approach may seem familiar because it resembles the type of coaching we know from sports, highly skilled professions, and trades. Its function is to improve performance, collaboration, and satisfaction through ongoing consistent internal coaching and skill/metis training. Expert Coaching differs from leadership or transformational coaching in three distinct ways:

- Expert Coaches are trained and developed within an organization. An understanding of the "health"[1] and "climate" of an organization are important responsibilities.

- Expert Coaching inevitably requires some transfer of knowledge to the client, so coaches need to be proficient and up-to-date with new technologies, and they need to understand and appreciate the context: the culture, products, or services, and the technical distinctions within that business and industry.

- Expert Coaching focuses on collaboration, performance, and competence in business functions and is measured in terms of progress: daily progress toward longer-term organizational goals. It strives to coach a C player to a B player and a B player to an A player.

Expert Coaching is always assisting individuals to move forward, get unstuck, and become free from negative perceptions and self-assessments – creating small (and large) wins, and daily progress.

Our impending generational transition will be a challenge like nothing before, and the demographic numbers tell the story. This transition also provides us with the crucial and time-sensitive opportunity to develop in-house coaching competencies in our enterprises, training Expert Coaches from among the current senior organizational leaders, before they fully retire.

Thus, building a coaching competency into an organization is becoming more important and relevant. One reason Michael Bungay Stanier's book, *The Coaching Habit: Say Less, Ask More & Change the Way You Lead Forever*, is popular is that it addresses this real and growing need to train internal managers to coach.[2]

Such an internal coaching model parallels the craftsman culture, which I advocate in this book. It also enables the natural transfer of metis and domain knowledge, another important theme in LIFT.

Earlier in Chapter Three, we compared the role of the master craftsman to that of the Expert Coach. In this chapter, we look at the Expert Coaching process and a specific methodology.

What Really Works?

In 2010, I read a paper called "Breakthrough Ideas for 2010: What Really Motivates Workers."[3] The research and the concepts offered resonated for me as an executive. I could relate it to the flywheel metaphor, in that it promoted the idea of small wins day after day, just the kind of effort required to get a flywheel spinning. At the time, our company used outside coaches; and we found this targeted coaching took too long to manifest results. It also created disconnections and jealousies in our organization, between those who did and did not receive coaching.

The research for this paper, by Harvard Business School psychologist Teresa Amabile and independent researcher Steven Kramer, PhD, later became part of their book, *The Progress Principle.* Their findings and conclusions with respect to motivation and coaching seemed to accurately align with my thirty years of practice as a successful entrepreneur, Fortune 100 senior executive, and executive coach. More specifically, their research revealed that "ninety-five percent of leaders and employees misunderstood the source of motivation... ."[4] Most managers and leaders erroneously believed that externally imposed stretch goals or breakthrough goals produce the best results.

Two years after the article came out, Daniel Pink launched what was to become the best-selling book, *Drive*. I enjoyed this book, and almost immediately saw its relevance to coaching. But it took some time to connect the work of Daniel Pink and the research he used with the primary research of Amabile and Kramer in their book *The Progress Principle.* It then became clear they were both pointing to the same thing – which I had run up against personally in my life and as a coach.

Both books showed that externally imposed goals or targets, along with artificially imposed team alignment to the goals, just didn't work in the long run. In the best case, they ultimately boiled down to a kind of existential choice based in language, self-discipline, and willpower, which sounded like "I will do it because I gave my word." But the research proved this was not effective. Instead, it proved that "the best way to motivate people day in and day out was by facilitating progress – even small wins."[5]

The research of Pink, and of Amabile and Kramer, shared a foundation in logic and psychology; both sets of research were anchored in positive psychology. From my perspective as a coach, this could not be better news.

The positive psychology movement is completely consistent with the reason I, like many others, started coaching in the first place. It has helped coaches move away from attempting to transform (fix) dysfunctional thinking and break through so-called limiting beliefs and stories. Leading scholars in this field are Martin Seligman,[6] Carol Dweck,[7] and Teresa Amabile, co-author of *The Progress Principle.*

As Pink says, "the positive psychology movement has reoriented the study of psychology science away from its previous focus on malady and dysfunction and towards well-being and effective functioning."[8] Positive psychology is not a new version of self-help, motivation, or the power of positive thinking. While some call it the psychology of happiness, that can be misleading. The following definition seems more accurate:

> Positive psychology is the study of the conditions and processes that contribute to the flourishing or optimal functioning of people, groups, and institutions.[9]
>
> — Shelly L. Gable and Jonathan Haidt

This movement provides a bright spot on which the field of coaching can focus. It offers a positive and optimistic view of personal development as it relates to progress, satisfaction, and doing meaningful work.

This movement is more interested in moving toward human flourishing, well-being, and effective functioning [or doing.] Self-Determination Theory, a subcategory, was developed in the 1970s by Edward Deci and Richard Ryan. Their work has filled many of the perennially favorite business books, and is extensively quoted in new research. Perhaps it is so widely accepted because it matches actual experiences and results, and thereby corroborates what many of us know from experience.

Self-Determination Theory validates the idea that we have basic needs when it comes to work and productivity: (1) the need to feel competent, (2) the need to feel autonomy, and (3) the need to connect with others. The research demonstrates that when all three of these conditions are met, we are intrinsically motivated to make progress, and, as a result, are satisfied.[10]

So a big part of Expert Coaching is aimed at addressing these three needs for competency, autonomy, and connection.

Simply stated, doing good work in a craftsman-like community is healthy from a number of different psychological perspectives.

As Daniel Pink says,

> Human beings have an innate inner drive to be autonomous, self-determined, and connected to one another. And when that drive is liberated, people achieve more and live richer lives.[11]

Inner Work Life

Like many important discoveries, this thing called "inner work life" was not what the authors of *The Progress Principle* were looking for when they commenced their research. But when they studied the data, the concept found them. They defined inner work life as our real and authentic experiences and moods during the work day, not some abstract and ideal way of being, or artificial mindset, but the actual ups and downs we all experience.

Inner work life distills down to our perceptions, emotions, and motivation; using brief surveys, the researchers tapped into these throughout the day and at the end of every day.

While it may be obvious, it's important to know objectively that our inner work life is important and valuable.

> Inner work life [as defined] matters deeply to employees … and is profoundly influenced by events occurring every day at work. … Inner work life matters for companies, because no matter how brilliant a company's strategy might be, the strategy's execution depends on great performance by people inside the organization.[12]

The dynamic nature and complexity of a person's inner work life make it difficult to test for a direct causal relationship; however, the research "shows unambiguously that positive inner work life promotes good performance…people do better work when they are happy, have positive views of the organization and are motivated primarily by the work itself."[13]

If you're a manager or a coach and you work with smart, capable people, you know they're busy and don't need or have time to learn, or to "try on" one more self-help method, scorecard, or mindset. Neither do they have time to create a new habit – they probably don't want time-consuming off-site events, or team-building excursions. Very often they simply want and need a lift – some assistance – so they can make progress. This assistance may come as help addressing a negative perception, or it may entail actual content training, or networking.

With access to an in-house Expert Coach this may require just a few minutes, not an hour-long coaching discussion. An important part of making progress and improving performance is knowing that we are not alone and don't need to become lone heroic leaders.

We've had plenty of leadership training in the past few decades. I'm suggesting we also need to focus on doing good work through collaboration. We don't need any more lone heroic leaders. Our strength as humans is collaboration, so let's train in collaboration too.

What gets in the way of progress? Our perceptions of our coworkers, managers, customers, and the others with whom we work. Negative perceptions indiscriminately pop into our thoughts without warning, and can significantly affect our inner work life and impede progress. Although not explicitly stated in *The Progress Principle*, Amabile and Kramer's research demonstrates the value and importance of one-on-one coaching to nourish and to make progress.

Seasoned managers can learn – without a lot of training – to become Expert Coaches and to provide the interpersonal support and nourishment required to facilitate progress. This type of coaching is much like the "in-the-game" coaching we know from sports like basketball. It differs from some of the current coaching models which commonly use a preset appointment, sometimes weeks away, based on the psychologist or physician appointment model.

But Expert Coaches "needn't fret about trying to read the psyches of their workers, or manipulate complicated incentive schemes, to ensure that employees are motivated and happy. As long as they show basic respect and consideration, they can focus on supporting the work itself."[14]

One goal of Expert Coaching is to nourish the employee when they are stuck, or down, helping to lift them up to a positive inner work life. This type of coaching elevates one's experience. You might say it's "uplifting" for the client as well as the coach.

The Progress Principle puts it this way:

> You won't have to figure out how to x-ray the inner work
> lives of subordinates; if you facilitate their steady prog-
> ress in meaningful work, make that progress salient to
> them, and treat them well, they will experience the emo-
> tions, motivations, and perceptions necessary for great
> performance.[15]

As we've discussed in some detail in LIFT, we now know that a lot of our immediate reactions and actions are driven by our adaptive unconscious and the biases of our cognitive machinery. Older coaching methods encourage an excavation of "stories," or mislabeled limiting beliefs. However, good research has now demonstrated that we often make up "stories," not based on our distant past, but on the most available information from our close relationships and our environment. Then, believing them to be true, we base our actions upon them. As we've reviewed, we make up or adapt old stories to satisfy ourselves and to prove we know what is happening. This may be because, as research confirms, our behavior in fast-paced environments can be so automated that we cannot fully explain our actions.[16]

To make matter worse, a perhaps well-intentioned coach with limited training may buy into these stories and unknowingly collaborate in their retelling. This collaboration or interpretation may even (coincidentally) support the coach's methodology or their hammer. And as the old saw goes, if your only tool is a hammer, everything looks like a nail. While such story–collaboration may seem like good psychological intuition by the coach, and it may even ring true for the client, it ultimately provides little more than a short-term insight and offers no way to improve performance or to make progress, therefore contributing to poor results and low satisfaction scores.

When I first found the Progress Principle in 2010, I thought it was too simple and too narrowly focused, and that it did not adequately address people's capacity for development. But after some experience with it, I recognized that its simplicity is the real strength of this structure for coaching. *The Progress Principle* addresses what I have found to be the heart of the matter: the very human daily ups and downs, small and large, that pop up and slow progress, or worse. Static processes, metrics, and tracking processes are often too time-consuming and complex, or operate only after the fact. Meeting once per month and looking at data establishes a backward-looking approach that relies on the clients' memory, which, as we've discussed at length, may be inaccurate.

We've seen throughout the book that an intimate knowledge of the business or industry is required for Expert Coaches. Effective coaches authentically appreciate what it is truly like to do the job, in the environment of the person they are coaching. Part of our social nature is our ability to sense inauthenticity in others, and without industry knowledge, it is impossible to authentically appreciate a situation.

The most effective coaches have actual experience in the context they are coaching. We are coaching action, performance, and progress, not generic abstract concepts of leadership. We're coaching what to do. Aristotle had a pretty good handle on this when he said:

> Lack of experience diminishes our power of taking a comprehensive view of the admitted facts: Hence those who dwell in intimate association with nature and its phenomena are more able to lay down principles.[17]

By focusing on progress, every day, we as internal coaches are getting as close as possible to the daily experience of the client. This will reveal what really impedes our clients' progress.

There are two key elements of the Progress Principle which I have found particularly effective. The first is the tight focus – as Expert Coaches we are working with someone to address only those things which affect their performance and progress.

By contrast, starting a coaching conversation with open questions like, "What's on your mind?" may plunge you deeply into an issue or line of discussion you're unable to address. There may be times when a client has some issue front of mind which is emotionally or mentally inhibiting them from doing their job. It's not because you're insensitive that you don't want to go down this path, but because you don't have the skills and knowledge, and are untrained to handle some deeper psychological issues.

In most cases when the client or team member is stuck, down, disinterested, and despondent, they simply need assistance and support; the metaphorical lift. As the coach, it is your job to position yourself to advise, and frankly, to help them. You will be recognized as a useful resource in the organization who is there to help, not someone who thoughtlessly holds them to account, and pontificates on the importance of our relationship to our word.

The second key element is that the coach also acts as a visual cue, and, when in the environment, helps to redirect the team back on task. In much the same way that individual relationships influence eating behavior and body weight, the Expert Coach influences behavior in the organization.

Surveillance Capitalism & Social Media

In addition, new active participants in your daily life are constantly trying to elbow their way in and to claim your attention, often taking it away from you, your customers, and employers. Methods of coaching developed before social media, artificial intelligence, and big data are disadvantaged because they do not account for these new demands on our attention.

Our environment at home and at work is now wide open to the 24/7 interconnected world, under the influence of what some call *surveillance capitalism*.[18] We now need to contend with the wealthiest and most powerful companies in the world like Google, Facebook, and Amazon, which are often directly connected to you, and are doing everything possible to grab your attention as well as your data and your resources. What makes this even more disconcerting is that these companies all sell us stuff, and get paid to give our personal information to other companies that want to sell us stuff.

It's hardly a fair fight. They employ thousands of smart, ambitious people to figure out how to get to you. They also use sophisticated artificial intelligence which captures and uses your every move to learn how and when to take their best shot. So, it is important to understand how we can manage and collaborate in these new environments. As yet, there is little research on how best to manage the influence of our devices at work, so the most effective path at present is to make a game plan with an Expert Coach as to how often you will check your devices.

BE – Don't DO – HAVE

Early in my business career, I bought into a belief that through transformation I could create the kind of life I would love. The model I was introduced to twenty-five years ago is still being dragged out today and offered as "new" in some coaching books. It's called the BE > DO > HAVE model.

This model starts with a critique of our default, two-dimensional, linear, way of thinking about success. We start out believing you need to HAVE an education, or HAVE a skill (or an apprenticeship) in order to DO a job or DO the work you want to do, and only then will you BE a master or an expert. This flawed model, according to its critics, goes from left to right: HAVE > DO > BE.

The LGATs say that we've got it all wrong, and that we should instead believe in the BE > DO > HAVE model. This transformational model says that you should not focus on what you HAVE, as in having skills or experience, nor should you concentrate on what you DO, but rather on who you are BEING. So to BE a master or an expert at something you have to behave, or BE, like a master. This conceptually makes some sense in the controlled environment of a seminar, but does not work in the fast pace of the real world.

But the real mischief and magical thinking occurs in the next step, where this simple model says that by changing the way you BE, you will magically change the way you DO your work. This was the type of linguistic sleight-of-hand magic that convinced me and many others the road to mastery was not in doing, or in skill training, but in being.

When this strategy is attempted outside of the controlled environment of a seminar, it is exposed for what it really is, a kind-of existential get-rich-quick method, essentially something for nothing.

Flourishing: Doing a Good Job

Like many, I worked for years trying to lead the team and elbow my way to the top, and not trying to master the job I was doing. Mastery for me meant a kind of passive-aggressive leadership; or fast-talking inspirational abstraction of transformation. I had convinced myself that success was a result of transforming a limiting belief. Just like the people who bought the four-minute-mile story, I believed that if I transformed my beliefs, I would one day get there.

Well, that path and method failed over and over. I can now attest, from years of experience, that _mastery_ requires DOING something really well. This quote from C. Wright Mills points toward the direction for the next part of LIFT:

> The laborer with a sense of craft becomes engaged in the work in and for itself: the satisfactions of working are their own reward; the details of daily labor are connected in the worker's mind to the end product; the worker can control his or her own actions at work; skill develops within the work process; work is connected to the freedom to experiment; finally, family, community and politics are measured by the standards of inner satisfaction, coherence and experiment in craft labor.[19]

We will see later in this chapter, and as we near the end of LIFT, that lasting and real satisfaction can come from DOING your work.

Do you remember that definition of insanity that the LGATs used? A more accurate definition of insanity from my perspective is this:

> Insanity is doing the same thing over and over, knowing exactly the result you will get (and don't want) – and doing it anyway.

—BRD

When we improve the way in which we DO our work, we gain competence and confidence. When we make _progress_, and help others to make _progress_, our work is a source of deep satisfaction.

The most compelling aspect of Expert Coaching using the _Progress_ Principle is its simplicity. As we'll see, the metrics for _progress_ in coaching are clear, simple, and unchanged over extended periods.

The methodology (with the supporting research) has produced exceptional real results, while providing the important benefits of retaining happy and motivated employees – all while operating at the speed of the internet.

Meaningful Work

It took twenty years of struggle before I realized that lack of willpower and self-discipline hadn't caused my struggle. The real cause was completely natural and largely due to the cognitive machinery of being a human. It turns out the struggle is OK, and is a necessary part of the process of learning and evolving. Another important part of the process is appreciating that grit, persistence, and hard work are the important traits necessary for mastery and growth as a person, which can only be accomplished by DOING and developing skills.

My struggles and attempts to avoid further struggles were created, in part, by the lack of meaning I brought to the doing of my work. I seemed to be constantly working in one job thinking about getting to the next bigger breakthrough goal. I used this same thinking in career decisions as well, as I was always looking for the next better job, degree, or city. I had focused on "being" a success and missed the lessons gained in the "doing" of good work.

The Craft of Expert Coaching is about individual growth and productivity, not the in-depth psychologically based leadership development of a select few. Wonderful benefits reward the practice of doing something really well, as is demonstrated in the arts and sports. With an intention to do something well, the skill or competency will demand that you are mindful, present in the moment. This is the therapeutic and rejuvenating nature of concentrating on and doing a job well. Making objective progress, every day – those are the small and large things that make our work meaningful.

To encourage this, some say we need to put away our phones and stop emailing, etc., but Robert Pirsig, the author of *Zen and the Art of Motorcycle Maintenance*, makes an important point:

> Flight from and hatred of technology is self-defeating. The Buddha, the Godhead, resides quite as comfortably in the circuits of a digital computer or the gears of a cycle transmission as he does at the top of a mountain or in the petals of a flower. To think otherwise is to demean the Buddha – which is to demean oneself. ... New technology is not the problem, technology is just technology: What's wrong with technology is that it's not connected in any real way with matters of the spirit and of the heart. And so it does blind, ugly things quite by accident and gets hated for that.[20]

Fortunately, business environments are changing, according to organizational psychologists Chip Espinoza and Mick Ukleja, the authors of *Managing the Millennials*. Their research makes it abundantly clear: "Millennials want, no, need to find meaning in their work."[21] They are happiest and most productive when they work collaboratively in work they find meaningful.

It is the job of a good craftsman and Expert Coach, I argue, to demonstrate that both what you do and how you do it are meaningful. Pirsig explains:

> [T]his concept of peace of mind is introduced and made central to the act of technical work. A fusion of classic and romantic quality can take place at a basic level within a practical working context. ...To say that [skilled craftsmen] are not artists is to misunderstand the nature of art. They have patience, care and attentiveness to what they're doing, but more than this – there's a kind of inner peace of mind that isn't contrived but results from a kind

of harmony with the work in which there's no leader and no follower.[22]

This way, the quality of your work is an expression of how you want to be known, by others and by yourself.

You don't have to seek a meaningful environment by traveling around the world (and not finding it) like I did, nor do you have to change occupations, if you bring meaning into your work. And contrary to the views of some, technology is not to blame for poor job satisfaction or poor relationships with management and leadership.

Also, the craftsman community provides the social interaction that we now know is essential for productivity and a positive inner work life. In tight-knit communities, virtual and real, we can get the support we may need to turn around the issues that bring us down.

The paradox is, we are already making meaning from our work all the time – but often it is an automatic force-fed meaning, imposed through advertising by default rather than by design.

By wresting back our attention from the powerful online vendors mining us for our data, we can train our attention to the way we work, and, in doing so, bring meaning back to both the way we work and the reasons why we work.

Twenty-five-hundred years ago, the Greeks saw craftsmanship in a much broader context. "All craftsmanship is quality-driven work; Plato formulated this aim as the *arête*, the standard of excellence, implicit in any act: the aspiration for quality will drive a craftsman to improve, to get better rather than get by."[23] The progress principle may be effective because it creatively taps into the inner work life. As we will see in the next chapter, coaching in the framework of the inner work life is straightforward and can be clearly defined and objectively managed and tracked.

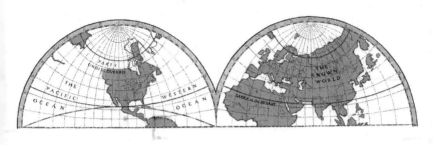

CHAPTER 14 — THE CRAFT OF EXPERT COACHING, FAST & SLOW

In this chapter, we continue to build out the structure of Expert Coaching. We'll pull together the new knowledge about human heuristics with the fast and slow ways of thinking discussed earlier, and integrate these ideas with the progress principle.

If progress is such a powerful motivator, how do we use its motivating force inside an organization? How do we as coaches and managers, from a very practical perspective, use it to motivate individuals and improve overall performance? Before we can approach those answers, it turns out the first question to ask is this: How can you tell that progress is being made?

In 1980, Richard Hackman, now of Harvard, and Greg Oldman, of Tulane, wrote an important book with respect to this question, called *Work Redesign.* The book addresses personal productivity and creativity at work as a function of what lies outside of our heads, of our environment, and of the design of the work itself. *Work Redesign* offers valuable observations that dovetail nicely with the craftsman culture as detailed in LIFT. The authors found "work should be designed so that in the act of carrying out the work, people gain knowledge about the results of their effort."

The preferable way to determine progress is "...getting feedback from the work itself;"[2] in other words, connecting your progress and results to the overall outcomes produced by the team or organization. Part of the learning process with an Expert Coach is to understand this feedback and develop metrics together, thereby highlighting progress and identifying challenges. This immediate and direct feedback is critical to understanding progress and effectiveness, particularly in large organizations.

In addition to this direct craftsman-like relationship to the work, *The Progress Principle* gives us three "key influences"[4] for managers and coaches to apply toward a good inner work life.

Key Influences

- By far the most significant influences on inner work life are the individual's sense of making progress, combined with objective measures.

- Next are the catalysts: Managing, coaching, and coordinating events that directly support the work project.

- Finally, one-on-one coaching is significant to help recover from a setback, to lift you when you are stuck or just down, and to provide the guidance and nourishing help to get back on track and make progress.

The linkage is clear: Seventy-six percent of the subjects in *The Progress Principle* research reported their best inner work days happened when they made progress.[5]

A "catalyst" here means something done by an individual or a team to support a project. In-house Expert Coaches may know the right connections and resources in the organization, and can help facilitate meetings and collaboration, which help move the project forward – creating a catalyst event.

But perhaps the most important and relevant finding of *The Progress Principle* as it relates to coaching is that the days reported as best days occurred when someone felt personally supported – the term Amabile and Kramer use is "nourished."[6] Nourishing is something that we as coaches have the privilege and opportunity to do. To be frank, most effective coaches live for this opportunity – and it's a powerful source of lift.

Of the 283 people surveyed, in twenty-six project teams in seven different companies and spanning three industries, fully eighty-three percent reported their best days happened when any one or more of these three key influences were present.[7]

"The more frequently people experience that sense of progress, the more likely they are to be creatively productive in the long run. ...A person's inner work life on a given day fuels his or her performance for the day and can even affect performance the next day."[8]

But, regardless of our intentions and good work, there will be events and people who negatively influence our inner work life. The authors propose three potent and frequent negative influences – the opposites to the three influences listed above. They are setbacks, inhibitors, and toxins:

- Setbacks are the opposite of progress.

- Inhibitors are the opposite of catalysts.

- Toxins are the opposite of nourishers.

The data from 12,000 daily diary entries showed the worst days at work happened on eighty-one percent of the days on which they had just one of the following; a setback, an inhibitor, or a toxin.[9] This research reveals what most people already know, the little things that happen can really mess up a day. And, if a day is messed up, progress is impeded, which only adds to the bad day.

There are obviously factors outside of work that affect inner work life. But the research found that "mostly, inner work life revolves around the three types of events that happen in organizations."[10] In other words, bad days at work most often arise from things that happen at work.

In the last chapter, we saw the data on inner work life and how important it is to performance and progress. In the next section, we'll look at how perceptions – oftentimes automatic – influence our inner work life, why they are inevitable, and what to do about them.

Perception Errors

If you're like me, your perceptions happen automatically. So, when I'm in a high-profile meeting with lots of people all vying for attention and influence, I don't stop and think to myself, "Hmmm… gee, I wonder if the guy who just contradicted my point is an asshole?" Instead, a System 1, fast-thinking, automatic perception pops into my mind and it most often sounds like, "What an asshole." What's more, I then don't automatically think, "OK, I'll need to put a little extra effort into this next thought and transition to my more deliberate System 2."

System 1, our fast-thinking system, doesn't do deliberation. It responds very quickly. Only if you are practiced and alert, can you pause and call on System 2 to form a more detailed answer. Primarily through the research of Daniel Kahneman and Amos Tversky, we have come to know a lot more about how we think and make decisions using these two systems.

But because we're all moving so fast, we don't usually have time to analyze our thoughts, or even consider that our thoughts need analyzing. Perceptions are formed immediately and automatically by this fast-thinking system, which is a little lazy and wants to find easy and quick answers. Because of this system, we humans have developed a competency to make decisions fast and with limited information. This competency uses heuristics, and it's clear that heuristics are error-prone. We often label these biases and heuristics as our human nature, both good and bad.

Nonetheless, since we all have perceptions that automatically pop up, we are using heuristics all the time. An understanding of how heuristics influence perception is critical to coaching and managing, because it helps us see why we repeat the same poor decisions, and why we do not produce the results we want.

Heuristics are not derived from some obscure theory or research finding, but rather are shown to influence almost all decisions under uncertainty. In other words, we use heuristics when we make choices based on limited information, in what we may think of as immediate judgments, or gut-feel guesses. The study of heuristics is now recognized as critical to understanding and predicting human behavior. It is therefore of interest to any number of powerful global interests from OPEC to NATO. The Adaptive Behavior and Cognition (ABC) Research Group at the Max Planck Institute in Berlin is among the top research institutions in the world and is currently devoting significant resources to research the basic heuristics, known as "fast-and-frugal"[11] heuristics. They are studying how and under what conditions we make decisions, and in their words, "[W]e make decisions in one of three ways, either by logic, probability, or by heuristics."[12]

Psychologists understand that we do not use pure logic or probability to make most of our day-to-day decisions. We simply don't have the time nor do we have the built-in computing power to do all the calculations. Heuristics are in fact a strength, and enable us to make pretty good decisions, quickly, and based on limited information. As the pen starts to roll off my desk, I don't have to run numbers, I just use an automatic heuristic and make a very good prediction where the pen will roll. Then I catch it.

Einstein appreciated the importance and power of heuristics, and used the term heuristic in the title of his 1905 Nobel Prize-winning article on quantum physics to indicate that even he considered his view as incomplete, even false, but of great transitory use toward a more accurate theory.[13]

Wellspring 2021

Biases & Heuristics in Coaching

At the heart of most perception errors are a group of biases that deal with statistics and probabilities. Research has unequivocally shown that, "because of their cognitive limitations, humans are unable to perform rational calculations and instead rely on error-prone heuristics."[14] While these heuristics are useful and necessary, they do lead to inaccurate perceptions and conclusions. Las Vegas is as rich as it is, in part because of these perception errors. Our System 1 way of thinking wants to find easy patterns fast, and it will do so with only limited information.

A familiarity with the commonly used and tricky heuristics or biases is valuable in coaching, so let's look at some examples, and how they may be observed in action.

Anchoring or the anchoring effect is our tendency to be influenced by something in the environment. For example, in a business negotiation, when one party throws out a number, the other party, without much thought, uses that number as an anchor for their next move, even though that number may be irrelevant and not based on logic or research.

Another example: Consider a real estate agent who has an exclusive listing on a home at $800,000. The experienced agent may first take a prospect to a less desirable home in the same neighborhood, with an asking price of over a million dollars. The anchoring effect will have the million-dollar home become the base, or anchor against which other homes are compared.[15] At $200,000 less, the agent's exclusive listing will now look like a great bargain.

Our perceptions are influenced by anchoring, and as demonstrated experimentally, the anchoring process happens without awareness. This perception error leads to poor and inaccurate decisions, sending us off in random directions, and ultimately causing setbacks. Setbacks lead to bad days and poor performance.

The **availability heuristic** is the part of our cognitive machinery which determines importance or relevance based on ease of recall. Branding takes advantage of this heuristic, which skews our perception by leading us to believe that one thing, like a brand name, is better than another simply because one is easier to recall – or is more available to us. Generic pain medication is an example. Many people, including me, pay more for the name brand Advil, than the generic brand, even though the two are identical. Sometimes the heuristic is so effective I find myself making up a story to support my choice for the Advil. I tell myself, "it's probably more thoroughly tested, etc." (even though I have no proof).

Similarly, this heuristic leads us to believe one consequence is more important than another, based on our ease of recall of the consequence. If I'm coaching someone who graduated from, say, the University of Iowa, and my ex-wife is the only other person I know that went to the same school (she didn't), then my perception of this Iowan grad will be skewed and based on the most available and easily accessible information.

Attribute substitution bias is the tendency of our System 1 way of thinking to substitute a simpler question for a difficult one. It is believed this psychological process underlies a number of our cognitive biases and perceptual illusions.[16] Stereotyping or racial profiling is a type of attribute substitution bias that alters our perception by unconsciously judging someone based on their race, age, skin color, gender, education level, etc. This bias is particularly potent in fast-paced and stressful environments. Research shows we may not think we have a stereotype bias when in fact our decisions demonstrate we do.

Optimism bias is considered by Daniel Kahneman, the author of *Thinking Fast and Slow*, to be the most persuasive of the System 1 biases. It is more commonly known simply as over-confidence. It informs our perceptions by thinking for us that we are more capable, skilled, etc. than we actually are. It leads us to believe we can do something faster, cheaper, or better than another, with no evidence or experience. This can be dangerous in the project-planning and budgeting process with inexperienced team members – and can be very disruptive to teams and individuals. It is often the reason for individual setbacks. Also, using an inaccurate metaphor or a story like the four-minute mile will take advantage of and leverage the optimism bias, creating unnecessary stress and disappointment. This bias is most dangerous if it's not addressed early, since it will negatively influence and distract from a methodical process of training and skills improvement.

The perseverance effect. In 1998, Spencer Johnson, an American physician, wrote a small, simple book called *Who Moved My Cheese?* The book spent more than 200 weeks on the *New York Times* bestseller list, and sold over twenty-six million copies. One of the central elements in the book illustrates the *perseverance effect,* sometimes called the *belief perseverance bias,* which is thinking the same way over and over, even with contradictory evidence and feedback.[17]

We all have these *cognitive rut*s; mine are often just thoughts based in fear. My experience with anxiety is an example of fear-based repetitive thoughts. Inside that cycle of anxiety, alone, there did not seem to be a way out. It was pure good fortune, and perhaps a survival instinct, which propelled me to connect with someone and coach or be coached during this time. What worked for me was doing something; the act of coaching pulled (or lifted) me out of my head, and out of the cyclical rut of the perseverance effect.

While I knew conceptually my anxiety was irrational, that knowledge did little to get me out of the cycle. I needed to get moving and do something before I was able to overcome the power of the perseverance effect.

The representative heuristic. Like most heuristics, this is a shortcut. It checks to see if a new perception matches a representative story or belief.

If you are interviewing candidates for the job of quality manager, and one candidate arrives to the interview late, wearing dirty, sloppy, casual clothing, you are unlikely to hire the candidate because they do not fit with your representation of how a quality manager should look. A good clothing salesperson may use this same heuristic when advising that "you should look the part."

Small Sample Size

One of the most damaging and tricky biases is the incorrect deduction and belief based on a **small sample size**. This bias is subtle and leads even the most experienced manager to inaccurate perceptions and decisions, particularly if they took the time to collect some data. In Chapter Six, we reviewed the myth of the four-minute mile, specifically calling out the biases used. At the heart of this myth is a powerful bias: The belief that we are seeing the entire picture. Sometimes called WYSIATI (What You See Is All There Is) the bias influences us to believe we are seeing enough data to make a valid deduction.

When we looked at the data from ten full years before and ten years after Bannister's run, we saw only a twenty-year sample size. Looking at just this sample size, or timeframe, many deduced that breaking the four-minute mark was special and significant. So, as we fiction-makers or storytellers will do, they concocted a story about limiting beliefs. This story sounded reasonable, and made us feel good, for a short time. But as any skilled statistician will tell you, more (good) data are desirable, and when more good data were included, a more accurate result was found. When we studied a larger sample size, plotted over fifty or even 150 years, it was clear that the performance remained consistent, before, during, and after Bannister's famous race. The four-minute-mile record behaved in the same way as any other point on the graph. Breaking the four-minute mile elicited exactly the same performance as breaking the 4.2-minute-mile record, and the 3.9-minute-mile record. All the data regressed toward a mean. In other words, over a longer period, the data followed a simple and predictable straight line pattern, once again proving that there was no breakthrough or magical transformation – and demonstrating the deceptive power of the Law of Small Numbers.

But even with some knowledge of the Law of Small Numbers there are still subtleties and traps. One such trap is the idea of **causation versus correlation.** In the four-minute-mile example, we could say that, over time, if we look at a large enough sample, people just naturally run faster. In other words, the cause of faster running is simply the passage of time. We'd be basing our statement on correlation, not causation, and it would clearly not be an accurate conclusion to draw.

These heuristics demonstrate an overall operating principle of our human cognitive machinery: We will search for and find cause and effect, even where they do not exist. In Chapter Eight we looked at *The Secret*, a compelling book which employed the common metaphor of a TV transmission tower. Even though the metaphor relied on inaccurate and fabricated pseudo-science, it created a story with a seemingly logical cause and effect. Most importantly, it was a something-for-nothing story that people wanted to believe in because it made them feel good... and they spent over $300 million doing just that.

What is unique to the Expert Coaching model introduced in LIFT, is the use of heuristics and biases to understand perceptions and behavior and therefore inner work life. An understanding of the powerful and subtle influence of metaphors is also essential to understanding perceptions and behaviors, and in the next section we discuss a systems metaphor which is particularly useful.

The Flywheel Effect – The Power of Small Events

As discussed in earlier chapters, metaphors are powerful ways to transfer ideas and processes. The flywheel, introduced by Jim Collins in *Good to Great*, is a well-known metaphor to describe the influence of the three forces that drive our inner work life. Essentially a flywheel is a heavy wheel that spins freely once it begins to move. When this heavy wheel is spinning, it has momentum – which is a measure of how long the wheel will continue to spin, or make progress on its own with no additional pushing.

Metaphorically, the flywheel represents the business organization, and the speed at which the wheel is spinning is the forward progress a business makes. A business with a lot of forward progress will continue to spin on its own for a long period of time without an external push. Collins describes how the "great" companies get this forward momentum through the process of many small pushes from within the organization.

"[T]he process resembled relentlessly pushing a giant heavy flywheel in one direction, turn upon turn, building momentum…"[18]

What is not always clear to the employee or the manager is that a small and sometime insignificant thing can have an overweighed response. In fact, research for *The Progress Principle* showed twenty-eight percent of small events result in "big" reactions – both positive and negative.[19]

CHAPTER 15 — DOING GREAT WORK: WORK AS CRAFT

"Go and get your things," he said. "Dreams mean work."[1]

—Paulo Coelho

The vision, determination, and hard work of the Al Maktoum family, who first settled Dubai in 1833, forged it into the world-class city it is today. H.H. Sheikh Rashid bin Saeed Al Maktoum, the father of the current ruler of Dubai, ascended to control in 1958, and began what has proven to be a series of brilliant strategic steps. He began by dredging Dubai Creek, a natural port and inland waterway from the Arabian Gulf, to allow larger vessels to dock and then load and unload the heavy industrial equipment used in the flourishing oil and gas businesses.

In 2013, his son, H.H. Sheikh Mohammed bin Rashid Al Maktoum,[2] initiated another dredging and expansion of the creek, into what is now known as the Dubai Canal Project. The extended creek is now two miles long and for the first time is connected right through as a "U'" shape, from the Gulf inland and then back out to the Gulf. This allows improved water conditions as well as more efficient shipping and transportation. Also, it created more desirable waterfront real estate, something Dubai has developed particularly well.

Again, the parallel to the dazzling Venice of the thirteenth century has not been forgotten in Dubai. Rather than gondolas though, now traditional Arabic *dhows* shuttle residents and visitors to Venice-themed restaurants and shops selling Murano glass, gold, and jewelry.

And now, in keeping with Dubai's extraordinary aspirations for the future, a new project is underway to build *The Floating Venice*, which will be permanently moored off the coast of Dubai in the archipelago of artificial islands called *The World*. The $680-million project is billed as earth's first luxury underwater vessel resort. The project developer, Kleindienst Group, a private Austrian company, is also promising to plant 400,000 square feet of coral, visible through the underwater level of the resort, where several of the twenty-four swimming pools will have glass bottoms.

To complement the experience, the adjacent islands on the artificial archipelago will sport a "Heart of Europe" theme, which will include Switzerland Island, the first fully enclosed island resort in which real snow will fall on demand.[3]

The Dubai Canal is also the home of the world's tallest building, which got an abrupt name change during the 2008 financial crisis. The Burj[4] Dubai quietly changed its name to the Burj Khalifa to acknowledge the financial assistance of H.H. Sheikh Khalifa bin Zayed Al Nahyan, President of the United Arab Emirates, and the ruler of neighboring Abu Dhabi.[5] The capital of the UAE, and Dubai's wealthy emirate-brother, Abu Dhabi lies just sixty miles south and west along the coast of the Arabian Gulf.

Although I lived in Bur Dubai,[6] the historic, original part of the city, I didn't spend much time there because of the contentious relationship with the Dubai office. When I wasn't in Qatar working with Norman and his team and dining at the Ramada, I regularly traveled from Dubai to Abu Dhabi to visit our office and customers. The drive took a couple of hours down the coast past empty desert on one side and the beautiful turquoise blue-green Gulf on the other. These trips provided a nice break from the crazy Dubai traffic, and allowed me time alone to think. Time alone had become almost sacred to me over the years and reliably elicited a comfortable exciting sense of progress, in which I could plan my next move.

But things felt different now. Both my alone time and relocation strategy which had reliably delivered results in the past – at least in the stories I told myself – no longer felt right.

Satisfaction and deep fulfillment, I believed, were found inside of me, deep inside. Who I would be, not what I did, always seemed to be just around the next corner. In this dream, I would *be* more self-assured and more satisfied in my work, just like in the Tony Robbins testimonials; I would be better in relationships, less anxious and less depressed. Essentially, I would be more the lone heroic leader. But to authentically *be* this hero, I needed to *be* in a certain job and a certain place, befitting a twenty-first-century hero.

Planning the next quest allowed me to avoid the confrontation with what I believed were the more mundane and secondary aspects of *doing* my job well, in the present. That liberating experience of preparing, once again to cast off – the anticipation and excitement of planning the next adventure – had been replaced by an anxious uncertainty. I was now confronting the fact that I might never actually be the heroic leader.

During the drives to and from Abu Dhabi, with no outside forces vying for my attention, I was left to the persistent dialogue inside my head. The discussions became so loud and intrusive I found I had to turn the radio down just to keep up.

I had come to the end of my metaphorical rope. Maybe it was because I was somehow unconsciously trying to transition to this new stage of life as described by Erik Erikson. Or perhaps I was just realizing that I didn't have many more relocations left in me.

I had tried everything I could think of alone, inside my head. I'd moved from the Left Bank in Paris to Dubai, but this was still not it. It was never just about the money for me. I had enough, more than most people, but it was what I did not have, and believed I should, that weighed heavily. I felt as though I was being pulled down by an overwhelming gravitational force and was now hanging on tight just to get by. I blamed my anxiety and depression on things inside me, like my weak willpower and self-discipline. The strategy I had used most of my adult life was used up. I was running out of rope, cities, emirates, and time.

I imagined I was like Santiago, the shepherd boy in Paulo Coelho's *The Alchemist*, as I chased my dream across the desert. But I now had to confront my reality once again: even this life in the Middle East was not "it," and I was not Santiago, nor one of the fictional leaders I dreamt of being. Worse still, I might never be one of them.

While I can't claim it was a sudden realization or lightning bolt of insight, something started to sink in. One day, on a typical trip to Abu Dhabi, I found myself driving slower and slower, finally coasting off the road into a small oasis. Sitting in that peaceful oasis, I began to realize that there was simply nowhere to go, and no one else to be. My dream – and always counting on the next thing – was almost bankrupt. I was naturally recognizing and letting go of the seductive idea of getting something for nothing by trying to *be* someone I wasn't.

Over the following weeks, I slowly loosened my grip on this idea, and slowly, the obsession loosened its grip on me. I felt a gradual release and liberation, which made way for a calming humility and honesty: I accepted who I was in the present, warts and all.

It occurred to me: Perhaps *being* and *doing* happen together; one does not cause the other, and the two are not mutually exclusive. I saw that the linear left-to-right sequential BE > DO > HAVE model was invalid, because it wrongly implied cause and effect.

"Faith ~ want works is dead

When I was focusing on *doing* a good job as a coach, I found I was simultaneously *being* the kind of person I would later come to appreciate. I wasn't *being* someone or something in the future, I was *being* myself, now.

Over time, I started to regain a healthy sense of myself; a new and genuine feeling of self-respect and self-appreciation. This was one of the dots in life which Steve Jobs referred to, when he famously said,

> You can't connect the dots looking forward; you can only connect them looking backwards.[7]

Then, in time, the next dot from my past reappeared. I realized that, by taking action and *doing* something – actually doing something I enjoyed and wanted to do well – I could create satisfaction and lift.

I was beginning to feel as though I was fulfilling a dream. Again and again, I returned to the advice of Nobel Laureate Richard Feynman:

> Don't think about what you want to be, but what you want to do. [8]

This idea of focusing on what I was *doing* in the moment felt right. The simple metaphor of lift began to help me connect to more dots in my life and career.

Recharacterizing Work

I had found work that was really uplifting. (Perhaps this is what Martin Luther was getting at five hundred years ago, when he opened up the possibility of work being an honorable pursuit. "[I]f righteousness is by faith, ... then the contemplative life of a monk and a priest is neither higher nor lower than the active life of the faithful farmer, cabinetmaker, or homemaker...suddenly all work, so far as it is morally legitimate (not evil), is sacred. Priest and farmer, nun and homemaker, theologian and laborer, all stand, in faith, before God."[9]

Until the Renaissance, work was considered undignified, degrading, and even shameful – to be done by animals or slaves. The attitude toward work was clear: work was a burden which, at best, should be avoided.

According to early church doctrine, doing good work was important, but only as an expression of gratitude to God, not as a way to gain salvation, or to improve one's status and well-being.

Then in 1517, Martin Luther introduced the idea that living a good life under God was gained through faith and not only as a calling. The very concept and definition of the word "work" changed in sixteenth-century Europe to reflect this new, inclusive viewpoint.[10]

Martin Luther also initiated what Max Weber later referred to as the Protestant work ethic in which work could now be a source of self-expression and self-fulfillment. Perhaps for the first time, people in the West could express themselves and create beauty for its own sake and for the meaning and satisfaction they derived from doing something well.

During this time, a group of philosophers, artists, and engineers in a prosperous Florence seemed to be at the epicenter of this newfound freedom to create beauty. There, masters like da Vinci, Michelangelo, and Raphael embodied the belief that by engaging in creative work and becoming more skillful at it, they could become personally fulfilled and even, for some, move closer to God. These artists of the Renaissance are still celebrated as among the greatest masters of all time. Today, people pay huge premiums for their creations, and are standing in line, right now, somewhere in the world, just to see and be in the presence of their work. The Renaissance was quite literally a rebirth of the way in which people did their work and the way in which they related to doing work.

By the end of the Renaissance, work was considered human-kind's essential activity,[11] in which our capabilities and talents were to be developed and perfected. Craft work was not something to be avoided, but a path to meaning, satisfaction, and community. In effect, we had discovered what Dr. Martin Seligman calls well-being.

In fact, this ethos was so profound that it influenced the interpretation of the essence of God. After the Renaissance, "God was recast as a cosmic craftsman and creator, referred to with new titles like Supreme Maker or Mightiest Architect."[12] Renaissance philosophers considered that doing work gave people pride and dignity. The rationale was evolving in favor of engagement and of doing great work.

Two centuries later, in 1876, Friedrich Engels, a German philosopher known for his work with Karl Marx, saw work as central to human existence. In an unfinished article, called "The Part Played by Labour in the Transition from Ape to Man," he argues that labor – or the act of making things – shapes who we are. In this thesis, extremely controversial for his time, Engels posited that labor "is the prime basic condition for all human existence, and … we have to say that labor created man himself."[13]

The idea follows from the evolutionary thinking that when we began walking unaided on two feet, we were free to use our hands to perform tasks. The progression of these tasks did more than merely aid in our early survival. As Engels proposes, it also accelerated our differentiation from other animals. It was this progress that brought men and women together under conditions where they needed to communicate and "where they had something to say to each other."[14]

So, Engels further proposed, labor created the need for communication and collaboration, and led to the need for language. Engels suggests that "with labor came speech and the stimuli under the influence of which the brain of the ape gradually changed into that of human beings. Further evolution along this path led to society."[15]

Seen this way, it was because we worked that we naturally came to be human.

Coaching & the Environment as Context

When I started working with the team in Qatar, I shed the pretense of fighting for who I was going to *be* someday. I stopped trying to present an inauthentic leadership agenda based on who I thought I, as a lone heroic leader, should *be*.

Perhaps in some way, I surrendered to a reality of who I am today. It was liberating to simply be myself at work, tell the truth, and share experiences good and not-so-good. This honest humility allowed room for the younger engineers to be themselves, and gave them an opportunity to talk about their challenges, and the progress they may or may not have been making that day or week.

Most often, it is difficult to understand why someone feels defeated or down, particularly during a busy day. It was always challenging to identify the negative perception which resulted in feeling down, but like a blind man tapping his way through a crowded room, I would reach out with simple questions and react based on what I would feel. With a good understanding of the industry, the key players, and the business environment in the region, my attention was only on helping the person get free from a negative assessment or perception. I could usually hone in on the negative perception – and help them work through it, so they could get back to making progress and spinning the flywheel.

As an Expert Coach with real industry or content expertise, you have the advantage of being able to observe and recognize a blind spot as a simple common heuristic error, often easily corrected, not some deep, dark, past-based limiting belief or unspoken commitment which would require drawn-out psychological coaching. This type of brief coaching helps the apprentice retain momentum and progress. Then slowly, like pushing the flywheel, these frequent brief discussions start to gain more momentum and move forward more easily. The progress and momentum are natural, not forced, and they symbiotically nourish and lift the entire office, leading to better results.

Good Expert Coaching requires being mindful and attentive to the mood or state of another. It requires getting out of your own head, staying focused on helping someone make progress, and trusting your instincts (and the data). By getting to know someone and spending time with them, you will be able to sense their moods, both consciously and unconsciously. It is a powerful capability we have, and not something artificial intelligence will replace anytime soon.

Science has paradoxically shown that in some human processes, the natural way produces better outcomes than those imposed in the wake of the industrial or "scientific" revolution. Childbirth is one example.

In the mid-twentieth century, children in the West were supposed to be born under bright lights in a cold hospital delivery room. Babies were whisked away from their mothers and put in isolated cribs in brightly lit rooms with other babies. The Taylor-inspired mass production process had replaced the "natural" way of having a child. But over time and with good research, open minds, and data, the medical community has returned to a more "natural" way of childbirth, which has proven to produce better outcomes for mother and child. In modern childbirth, mothers-to-be work with an Expert Coach, called a birthing coach. They develop an open, trusting relationship in which the birth is less a medical procedure and more the beautiful human experience in which an extraordinary relationship is created and a new baby lovingly welcomed.

Modern Elders

Expert Coaching in the management of a business or organization, which includes leadership, is another natural human process which has undergone radical change as a result of the industrial and scientific revolutions. And now I build the case that our places of work can and should be managed in the same way humans naturally work and live together. Like the craftsman shop, Expert Coaches become integral parts of the community as collaborators and contributors, whether that community is in person, online, or both.

As discussed earlier, the gen-X and millennial generations are somewhat naturally returning to a more collaborative way of working together. They've watched the boomers go through more divorce, more materialism, more financial failure, more depression, and more isolated, workaholic careers. Now, they too are products of their environment, and are wisely trusting their instincts and experience, moving away from the unnatural "lone heroic leader" model toward one of more collaboration. *Village*

In a more natural working environment, there exists intergenerational diversity, which enables continuity, community, and a transfer of knowledge. An organization's value is derived from its institutional knowledge, systems, and the culture in which it operates. The transfer of this knowledge and the continuity of the culture are possible with an intergenerational workforce.

The natural role and duty of the senior members of the organization – the elders – is to share their metis, to prepare the next generation with perhaps the most valuable knowledge that can be transferred. The ancient Greeks understood this and held metis dear. More recently, it was his metis that informed the decisions Sully made that fateful day. Sully's metis, like ours, developed consciously and unconsciously in the context of work accomplished over the years. It naturally enabled him to make better decisions in a complex and ambiguous situation, ultimately doing what no artificial intelligence could do.

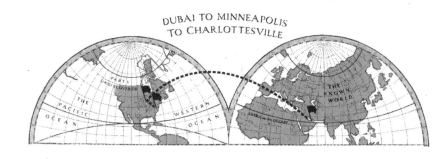

CHAPTER 16 — THE NATURE & SCIENCE OF LIFT

Leaving the Middle East this time was different. I wasn't fleeing, or chasing, and I knew I would soon be back. I appreciated these proud and ambitious people, and realized their culture and customs were part of the context I had come to "know."

Because of Daikin's reorganization, I'd been asked to move back to the US headquarters in Minneapolis – in January! The existing American management team was methodically being replaced, yet the Japanese managers made the best of a difficult situation, and were thoughtful and professional.

In stark contrast with the American team was the Japanese managers' depth of knowledge of the industry, the products, and the latest technology. They talked about the industry the way we talked about baseball. They seem to know the competitive products cold, and could rattle off the latest energy efficiencies and technological innovations.

Our company had maintained an unacknowledged caste system, where employees in technology, research, manufacturing, and design had little power or leadership status, nor did they have an office in "mahogany hall." Our senior management team was populated with prototypical leadership personalities from sales, IT, finance, and HR, some of whom who had little or no air-conditioning experience.

The Japanese, on the other hand, were more collaborative and craftsman-like; even their management systems ensured constant collaboration among the functions as well as among young and old. Daikin follows an old Japanese tradition of craftsmanship or *mono-zukuri*, which implies making things or manufacturing.

As it was explained to me, monozukuri is far more than simply making things. The word combines two concepts: *mono* is the thing itself, the product; and *zukuri* which roughly translated means the "doing"[1] or crafting the product. Working in this way develops a sense of ownership and pride, not only restoring dignity to the work, but creating an environment for waste elimination, through creativity and improvement. In this way, without a sense of monozukuri, there can be no *kaizen*.[2] This monozukuri model also focuses on learning through the master-to-apprentice relationship.

Just as in the Paul Bakery on the Left Bank, the master does not take time to formally "teach" the apprentice. The Parisian rascals, like the Japanese apprentices, learn by watching. In both environments, the apprentices start with menial jobs and gradually gain responsibility. They learn skills by doing, and being part of the shop, metaphorically sweeping up information consciously and unconsciously. In fact, a Japanese master will say it is the apprentice's job to "steal the art."[3]

Daikin's home is Osaka, a commercial city which was decimated during the Second World War. Daikin is proud of its Japanese heritage and its history of growth from very humble beginnings. After learning a little of their history, it was no surprise to me that they are now the largest air conditioning company in the world. Founded in 1924, Daikin has stayed extraordinarily focused on its core business of designing, manufacturing, and selling air conditioning equipment. Is it a hedgehog[4] organization, doing the same thing day after day, and becoming very, very good at that one big thing. Its success and dominance seem just and deserved, because they are earned through the dedication to, and expertise in, the craft of making something. Daikin stood in contrast to McQuay, whose success was largely the result of an expertise in leveraged buyouts and financial engineering, by a lone American hero who bought the company with ninety-eight percent debt.[5]

Back in Minneapolis that winter, the demographic transition I had read about was getting real. Many of the longer term employees (and my friends) were being asked to take an early retirement package or find a new job. As the management team was slowly being replaced, I took the opportunity to move toward something I wanted to do, no longer compelled to "be somebody," nor to be in the "right place." With my coaching experience in the Middle East still fresh, I knew what I wanted to do. I sought the experience of lift, through coaching and consulting.

I enjoyed living in Minneapolis, but I decided to move closer to my family and to a destination of my choice, where I could finally settle down. Having worked and briefly lived in Virginia at a McQuay facility, I had dreamed of moving back to the Shenandoah Valley one day. That day had come. Starting my own firm was a big step, but I trusted my metis and the research, and was getting very positive results and feedback from clients.

Central Virginia is now home, and I am learning to become part of a wonderful, real community. I founded a consulting and coaching firm which leverages my metis and experience in the Middle East and Europe, with a specialty in helping organizations develop their own internal Expert Coaches, using the principles and practices in this book.

My own practice as a consultant and coach has benefited from the research in social science and psychology as examined in this book, particularly the use of positive psychology and the correlation between meaningful work and employee engagement. I continue my research to this day.

Psychology & Coaching

The theories and concepts used in conventional leadership and transformational coaching today are a little like those used in energy analysis in the nineteenth century. If you recall from our discussion of the physics of transformation in the first chapter, before Herman von Helmholtz and James Joule established and then proved the first law of thermodynamics (energy cannot be created nor destroyed – only changed into different forms of energy),[6] many tried to explain heat and energy. Some theorized that heat was a kind of magical fluid, called a caloric, and others, including even the great Sir Isaac Newton, believed in a divine living energy inside of moving objects. In other words, coaching theory is still struggling with the basics.

At the heart of the issue for some is the art-versus-science debate; many coaches and transformational consultants simply deny their use of the science of psychology. The argument generally involves the following points: coaches explain they only work with the present and the future, or a "possible future," while psychologists work with the past. These coaches may contend they work to make healthy clients more effective, while psychologists work with pathology and illness. The coaches also claim they work primarily with the conscious mind, and specifically just the client's views, perspectives, and assessments. Some coaches feel it is their unique role to find the perspectives or limiting beliefs (as with the myth of the four-minute mile) hidden to the client.

Practicing clinical psychologists[7] interviewed for this book suggest they may do exactly what the coaches claim to do depending on the situation, with the proviso that they use scientifically tested theory and consistent methods. Clinical psychologists point to basic definitions of psychology, calling it, "the scientific study of thought and behavior,"[8] or explaining that "...psychologists study how human beings relate to each other and how to work to improve these relationships,"[9] and that "studying psychology not only makes you more aware of how people work in general, but also makes you more aware of how you work. ...Understanding others' thoughts, feelings and motives – as well as your own – may help you be a more effective doctor, lawyer, businessperson or friend."[10]

However, some psychologists take a different position. Dr. Steven Berglas is one such psychologist, also an executive coach, who sees untrained executive coaches as dangerous to an organization. Berglas practiced psychology at the Harvard Medical School before launching into a career as an executive coach. In a 2002 article in the Harvard Business Review, he outlines his belief that there are an "...alarming number of situations, [in which] executive coaches who lack rigorous psychological training do more harm than good."[11]

Professor Martin Seligman, a former president of the American Psychological Association, has this view of coaching today:

> As coaching stands now...its scope of practice is without limits... It uses an almost limitless array of techniques: affirmations, visualizations, aromatherapy, feng shui, meditation, counting your blessings, and on and on. The right to call oneself a coach is unregulated and this is why scientific and theoretical backbones are urgent.[12]

Dr. Seligman's depiction of coaching may be a little far-reaching and condescending, particularly for those of us who have studied hard to become business coaches, but he does address important points that cannot be ignored. There is neither an agreed-upon scientific backbone or curriculum, nor a widely-accepted accreditation process. Leadership coaching seems to get all the press, and much of it is not good.

Meanwhile, good science and research are slowly rooting out and exposing the various hoaxes and myths peddled by the LGAT–derived so-called transformational technologies which are, in fact, neither.

Positive Psychology

What is exciting for coaching is the use of the science of positive psychology. The coaching program at Georgetown University does in fact include specific aspects of positive psychology. Positive psychology uses its tried-and-true methods of measurement, of experiments, of longitudinal research, and of random-assignment placebo-controlled outcome studies to evaluate which interventions actually work and which are bogus.[13]

This type of psychology differs from the more conventional in both the theoretical approach and in the group of people to which it offers support. Seligman, the father of positive psychology, explains that a statistical majority of people employed in corporate America are healthy, functional men and women. Their psychological well-being is normally distributed as a bell curve, with most falling under the central portion of the curve. Those who are not as psychologically healthy and who may struggle in their job or career are typically located on the left tail of the bell curve. Those at the other tail of the bell curve are highly functional and successful. As Seligman points out, our current systems are focused on those people who are not as psychologically healthy or functioning normally. Psychologists can, and often do, spend their careers working with unhappy and dysfunctional people in the hope that intervention and treatment can make them less so. Like most modern healthcare systems, the attention is on those who are ill or not functioning well. This is the dysfunctional focus of coaching described earlier.

But Seligman, like Robert Hogan and Donald Clifton before him,[14] is interested in working with the healthy, successful people who populate the large central portion of the bell curve, to improve their strengths and increase their well-being. Unfortunately for all of us, Seligman's 2003 book, *Authentic Happiness*, was widely appreciated and became a best seller. It's unfortunate because it branded

Seligman and the positive psychology movement with the label of the "Happy Psychology," which did not seem to suit corporate America, particularly during the financial recession.

Seligman is not a New-Age healer, nor a particularly happy–motivational kind of guy; he started at Princeton, with a bachelor's degree in philosophy summa cum laude. Then to the University of Pennsylvania, where he earned a PhD in psychology and went on to create a department there in Applied Positive Psychology. The focus of his work is helping healthy and functional people flourish in their lives and their careers. The goal is to move a C player to a B player, and a B player to an A player.

With further study of Happiness Theory, Seligman and his team found that the surveys used in their research did not accurately measure this thing called happiness, but more accurately reflected a person's mood *at the time the survey was taken*, not an overall or longer-term stasis of increased happiness.

So, in his 2013 bestseller *Flourish,* Seligman offers a more robust theory of positive psychology which maintains the key elements of Happiness Theory but pushes further and adds two more objective elements to complete the theory.

This is important because the new theory, called "Well-Being Theory," addresses points central to LIFT and Expert Coaching. Seligman's research revealed what craftsmen have come to believe and practice for centuries.

It's important to go into some detail here, because Well-Being Theory includes two essential ideas we've addressed in this book. The first is that we experience well-being from doing something well for its own sake, for the sake of accomplishment, and for the satisfaction derived from simply doing it. Secondly, we experience well-being because the work is meaningful to us, and is work which we can see contributes to a larger purpose.

Well-Being Theory has five key elements, three derived from Happiness Theory – positive emotion, engagement, and meaning – and two additional elements, accomplishment and positive relationships.[15]

For Expert Coaching, Seligman's framework offers a more complete and objective way to measure and manage well-being, which can be an important aspect of a positive inner work life.[16]

Finding Meaning in Work

Founded as the Minnesota Mining and Manufacturing Company in a small town in northern Minnesota, 3M deeply believes in ensuring its employees have time to work on projects that are interesting and meaningful to them. Since 1948, they have allowed engineers and scientists fifteen percent free time to work on projects and ideas they believe in; and to follow their own instincts. This not-so-new innovation has propelled them to more than 22,800 patents and $20 billion in annual revenue.[17]

Bill McKnight, who started at 3M in 1907, and served as 3M's Chairman from 1949–1966, best explained the logic:

> Encourage experimental doodling. If you put fences around people, you get sheep. Give people the room they need.[18]

Today Google executives are of the same mind, and offer engineers twenty percent of their time to devote to projects of interest and importance to them, and presumably related to Google's work.

They understand that they get the best performance from people who are given the opportunity to work on ideas of their own, in which they find meaning. So much so that, "back in 2004, with only 2,500 people, Larry [Page] and Serge [Brin] felt we were becoming so big they could not get an intuitive sense of how happy people were just by walking around and talking to people…"[19] So they developed what soon became the survey called the Googlegeist, which taps into how people feel, and uses the data to check their well-being and happiness.

Finding meaning in their work is a challenge to most people, even those who believe they do meaningful jobs. Meaning is not a "thing" which can be found, nor does it have to be profound. Meaning seems to emerge from action, from doing something in which you feel you are making progress and contributing to someone or something greater than your own happiness.

Astrophysicist and modern-day Expert Coach Neil DeGrasse Tyson said it well:

> The problem, often not discovered until late in life, is that when you look for things in life like love, meaning, motivation, it implies they are sitting behind a tree or under a rock. The most successful people in life recognize, that in life they create their own love, they manufacture their own meaning, they generate their own motivation.[20]

In the context of Expert Coaching, meaning is manufactured and developed by working on your skills and by coaching. When people can see evidence that their progress and growth is appreciated and acknowledged by management, they feel their work is more meaningful. And, as Simon Sinek would say, when they can see how it connects to a bigger purpose – or a bigger *why*, they feel as though what they're doing has meaning.[21]

In this book and in my work, I build a case for working in a way consistent with our natural experiences and strengths, both as individuals and in groups. Lift is one such natural experience that emerges not from controlling our minds, or trying to create new mindsets or contexts, but from acting in harmony with nature and our natural human needs and desires. This is not an original thought, and again we can look back to the wisdom of the ancient Greeks.

Many scholars believe that living in accordance with nature means to live and behave aligned with how "nature" has uniquely designed and shaped each of us, building on our individual strengths and, as social creatures, sharing our social strengths of collaboration and community.[22] To the Stoics, human nature is the expression of your very best self; "its central organizing concern is about what we ought to do or be to live well – to flourish."[23]

In fact, Stoicism's reverence for nature has come full circle and is entirely consistent with the blossoming field of biomimicry. According to author Janine Benyus, the science of biomimicry examines three fundamental areas: First, "nature as model, ...a new science that studies nature's models and then imitates or takes inspiration from these designs and processes to solve human problems."[24]

Second, "nature as measure, [using] an ecological standard to judge the 'rightness' of our innovations. After 3.8 billion years of evolution, nature has learned: What works. What is appropriate. What lasts."[25]

Finally, "nature as mentor...[introducing] an era based not on what we can extract from the natural world, but on what we can learn from it."[26]

In the last century, however, our interest has been in mind control and the domination of our minds over nature. In fact, the human potential movement of the 1960s and 70s mocked the Stoics, using tenuously supported fragments of Friedrich Nietzsche's writing.[27]

After years of fighting it, I have found many great benefits to working with human nature, not against it. I recall President Ronald Reagan (quoted earlier), who in his folksy American way affirmed the Stoics when he said, "It is easier to ride a horse in the direction that the horse wants to go."

In the final chapter, I pull together the key elements of the case and propose a way forward: the Craft of Expert Coaching.

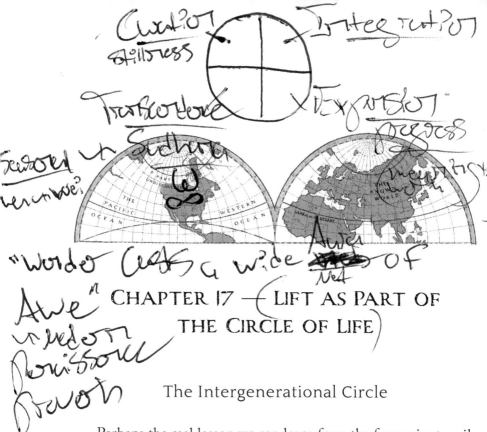

Creation?
Stillness

Integration

Transcendence

Expansion
process

"Wonder casts a wide ... of
Awe
Net

Awe
Wisdom
Reverence
Gratitude

CHAPTER 17 — LIFT AS PART OF
THE CIRCLE OF LIFE

The Intergenerational Circle

Perhaps the real lesson we can learn from the four-minute mile is the use of the very natural human competency of collaboration. Bannister's two pacers influenced his behavior and improved his performance from the outside in, just as the popcorn bucket, the wine bottle labels, and the overweight friends did. In the same way, including an Expert Coach in the environment can influence behavior in an organization, the coach's very presence providing essential behavioral cues, in a version of the home-field advantage.[1]

As we discussed in Chapter Nine on metaphor, an organization has a metaphorical mood, or a climate.[2] The collective mood of an organization can also behave metaphorically like gravity: without active resistance, it will pull people down. Gossip – and what may seem like insignificant banter critical of the organization – can add weight to these issues, creating a greater gravitational pull downward. So, an important responsibility of the Expert Coach is to be tuned into the organizational climate and mood, routinely checking them with managers and teammates.

This craft of coaching operates on the principle that an Expert Coach is an active collaborator in the work community, focused on progress and the benefits of a positive inner work life.[3] Like masters before them, these Expert Coaches are passing on skills and advice as well as the subtler aspects of metis. It is this combination that ultimately helps the apprentices and journeymen learn and grow as they navigate the rough waters ahead (as foretold in *The Iliad*).

In this relationship, the Expert Coach (master), takes on the team member (apprentice), and sees to it that he or she makes it, applying the same kind of unconditional resolve as a good parent would. This involves more than simply asking good questions or offering good advice, and it creates some of the most rewarding and important relationships in a person's working life.

The Expert Coach is more like the family doctor than the specialist surgeon who swoops in, meets only a few members of the team behind closed doors, and then flies out. An important part of the Expert Coach's job is to get a sense of the goings-on, and the coach needs enough time in the environment to sweep up information, consciously and unconsciously.

In addition, an Expert Coach in the construction and air conditioning businesses, for example, also knows the different organizational moods during different business and seasonal cycles. The coach knows from experience how team members and customers react during the hottest days of the summer – the cooling season – and how to coach accordingly.

In this way, the coach understands how the environment influences human nature. The goal is not to resist human nature and invent a new "reality," but to live and work as part of what is. Take Leonardo's example. Art experts know that da Vinci would paint only naturally accurate and appropriate landscape vegetation and geological elements. He did not try to depict some ideal or fictitious landscape, but sought to reproduce nature's beauty as it actually existed.

More recently, Steve Jobs, a modern day Leonardo, understood that Apple needed to develop products that allowed people to interact with them, in the ways they naturally lived and worked.[4] He saw the importance of working with human nature, and like da Vinci, Jobs seemed to be out of step with his contemporaries in his tenacious drive for this merging of human nature, technology, and craftsmanship. It's difficult to overstate how much Jobs influenced the way millions, perhaps billions, of people work, and how they view their work. To Jobs, a competence in your work was the source of meaning and fulfillment, and created a life worth living. In his famous commencement speech at Stanford in 2005, he illustrated this craftsman-like belief when he said:

> Your work is going to fill a large part of your life, and the only way to be truly satisfied is to do what you believe is great work. And the only way to do great work is to love what you do. If you haven't found it yet, keep looking. Don't settle. As with all matters of the heart, you'll know when you find it.

Real satisfaction and well-being come from this dedication, and from the commitment to working with others who also appreciate what you do and how you do it.

Steve Jobs – like Leonardo da Vinci – quite literally changed the world. As mere mortals, they were far from perfect. But, it was Jobs, a modern-day master craftsman, who influenced the way I thought about doing my work – as a craft.

His work, and the lessons from all the men and women whose work I've studied, have provided important material, which I've tied together in the context of the craftsman model. Although LIFT is not a "how to" book, its principles can be summarized in the following practices.

Four Practices of The Expert Coach

(ONE)

STUDY & RESPECT THE ENVIRONMENT OF YOUR BUSINESS, INDUSTRY, CRAFT, OR FIELD.

Because mastery is context dependent, it is important to deeply learn the environment, its influence, and the universal laws of nature that also apply. One of these, the conservation of energy, states that, in a closed system, energy and matter cannot be created from nothing nor reduced to nothing. In short, we cannot get something for nothing.

Our minds and bodies learn and "know" a great deal more than we may be aware. Have patience and learn to trust your experience, over time, in your environment, as ~~Sully did~~. He was able to suppress his panic response because he knew his environment: his conscious mind and his subconscious were not overwhelmed. Similarly, Expert Coaches must intimately understand the business and industry to accurately respond to the environment.

An important aspect of this practice is the use of our natural power of observation and our ability to sense someone's disposition or state. Trust your natural instinct to sense a something for nothing situation.

As we've discussed, ~~shifting~~ demographics will exert intense pressure to bring new team members up to speed. Coaching therefore needs to be immersive and close at hand, available for rapid response and intervention. The in-house Expert Coach, with mastery of the environment, will be in place to provide the lift when a Second-in-Command requires it, ~~the way Sully did for Skiles~~.

(TWO)

PRACTICE DOING
GOOD WORK

Demonstrate, reward, and encourage quality work. Use my modern version of the craftsman model to transfer current business and technology skills as well as collaboration and management competencies and, at the right time, leadership.

Benefit the next generations with Expert Coaching from the men and women who have learned and excelled within the company's context, technology, values, and history.

The second practice focuses on improving what you do, creating meaning from the work itself. Working in this way, we earn the respect of others and the personal satisfaction and confidence of mastery. Practice doing good work in all areas, including team collaboration, conflict resolution, virtual team management, social media market research, and presentation and speaking skills. Also learn to conduct brief, effective meetings, and become adept at using the IT systems specifically adapted to your business.

(THREE)

STUDY & UNDERSTAND HUMAN
NATURE – YOURS & OTHERS'

Learn the most common biases and heuristics which trip you (and others) up. This will help you separate what really happened – the data – from the drama of a good story.

Because we make sense of the world through stories, we need a way to separate what actually happened from the story we told ourselves or bought into. Acquire a basic working knowledge of statistics, the importance of sample size, and the Law of Small Numbers.

Part of our cognitive machinery wants an easy shortcut and wants to believe something because it sounds good, looks good, is top of mind, or has a happy ending. Perhaps the most important reason to use this science is because we are all different, and what may lift and inspire one person may not do so for another. Good science helps us understand nature, including human nature.

FOUR

FOCUS ON PROGRESS & SMALL STEPS EVERY DAY

Coach for steady progress, as with Jim Collins's flywheel metaphor. Coach in real time, lift team members when they are down, and work on a fast recovery. Coach individuals based on their specific personality using validated personality assessments.

Generally, we merely want a lift. We just want to get free or unstuck so we're able to get back to work and make progress. With this process, we intuitively know we will reap the natural rewards of putting in a good day's work.

The fourth practice relies on the use of valid assessment instruments and data. The assessments allow the coach to have stable baselines and accurate reference points – comparing them to hundreds of thousands or even millions of others.

Expert Coaches train and develop collaboration and management skills required for the job, in harmony with the client's natural talents and strengths. Individuals interested in improving their performance, competency, and effectiveness will appreciate the guideposts available from well-researched analysis and training.

The progress principle is effective because it is simple, and helps someone get back on track. This, however requires from the Expert Coach a breadth and depth of knowledge of the business and industry.

Expert Coaching will boost engagement as we learn to do good work, build self-confidence, and develop ownership in our work.

The Paradox of Progress Revisited

In the preface, I touched on the paradox of progress. Now I'd like to wrap up LIFT with a look back at that paradox, which, I believe can now be a useful spur to action.

You've probably heard the expression, "You have to be cruel to be kind." That's an example of a paradox: a sentence or phrase made of two statements which appear to be contradictory but, taken together may communicate wisdom.

Here's the paradox of progress:

> Technology is displacing a growing number of higher skilled workers, while at the same time creating more powerful, complex, and smart systems capable of putting more humans in potentially disastrous situations.

How can we avert future catastrophes – like Flight 1549 might have been, but for the metis of Captain Sully? I argue that it is the metis – an appreciation for it, and a culture of passing it on – which is needed. Perhaps Sully's extraordinary Miracle on the Hudson is prophesy, foretelling how we will need to address this twenty-first-century paradox.

Plenty of data now support the first statement of the paradox:

> Technology is displacing a growing number of higher skilled and experienced workers.[6]

What of the second part of the paradox?

We are creating more powerful, complex, and smart systems capable of putting more humans in potentially disastrous situations.

Look no further than Captain Sully's own industry for an example of smart technology that is putting us in harm's way. Commercial air travel is introducing larger, 400-plus seat commercial planes that are more highly automated, requiring fewer and less-experienced pilots while carrying more passengers. Add to that the complexity of coordinating hundreds of thousands of autonomous cars, trucks, subways, and railroads on high-speed freeways and urban roadways, with pedestrians, bicycles, and commercial and recreational drones. Very soon, we'll be living with an increasing risk of massive destruction from malicious actors or even Canada geese, and we will need the deep knowledge and metis from the men and women who have earned it.

But today those same skilled experienced workers being displaced are struggling with a far more lethal threat. As uncomfortable as it may be to discuss in a business book, it's important to deal with the reality that death from suicide even surpassed the number of deaths from motor vehicle accidents in 2009. Suicide for the gen-X and baby boomer cohorts is often the result of depression and addiction, which can be exacerbated by external factors like the loss of a career.

After the Miracle on the Hudson, in his book, *Highest Duty*, Captain Sullenberger authentically shared his feelings of not being appreciated. After twenty plus years and a pristine record, he was rewarded by having his pension taken away, his salary reduced, and his judgment questioned in the increasingly compliance- and technology-driven aviation industry. Also, tragically, he carries emotional scars as a survivor of the nightmare of his father's mental illness and suicide at the age of forty-five.

The human cost central to this issue hangs in the balance. The effect on real people like you and me, our moms and dads, brothers, sisters, and our friends and neighbors over forty is becoming impossible to ignore and is far outside any margin of error from a reasonable base rate.

Meanwhile, a mountain of research points to an impending labor shortage in the United States. Eighty percent of these unstaffed positions will require complex skills like problem solving, judgment, relationship building, communication, and collaboration.[7] These are the kinds of skills of successful senior managers, experienced tradespeople, and executives: our modern-day masters.

The concept of embedded Expert Coaches relies on a pre-Industrial Revolution classical view of a working community, one which naturally evolved because of its utility. In this way, the Craft of Expert Coaching opens the door to a much larger pool of Expert Coaches. Many of the senior staff now being forced to retire have the content expertise and domain knowledge that make them invaluable as Expert Coaches in their fields over the next few decades.

So our paradox boils down to this:

> Technology is displacing our experienced skilled workers, while its increasing power and scale threaten us with disaster.

Technology will continue to march forward as it has for generations in free and competitive markets. But technology and innovation do not have to create a zero-sum game, costing the lives and livelihoods of so many.

Does a technologically driven society have to be cruel to be kind? Is that what we have in mind when we design increasingly sophisticated systems that require fewer humans to manage and operate?

Is it inevitable that technology designed to free us of dull, routine, or inhumane working conditions will only displace jobs?

Or can we use the knowledge and metis built into our workforce, in the form of Expert Coaches, to help integrate technology into a way of working that serves an organization's employees and the community as much as its shareholders?

Craftsmanship is more than a mindset. It is a way of living, learning, and working which evolved with us and has not left us: Steve Jobs and Sully are the proof. Craftsmanship – the desire to do good work and make beautiful things – is making its way back into both the supply and demand sides of the economy.

As discussed earlier, skill and metis have been transferred, over countless generations, inside a master-to-apprentice structure through doing, interaction, and imitation. While common sense and the data both suggest you need a certain number of hours of deliberate practice to master a new skill, every master will tell you that he or she also learned from one or more key Expert Coaches (mentors).

Aristotle, arguably one of the finest masters and teachers, didn't write textbooks and assign readings. In fact, he left almost no written work. Instead, there's plenty of evidence that the learning process in ancient Greece involved "following around" the masters.[8]

Chris Andersen, the current curator of TED Talks, passionately raises the possibility of accelerated learning through a kind of virtual online following around, interaction, and imitation. Andersen sees a future many of us are just bringing into focus. He's witnessed the extraordinary accomplishments and brilliance of people free to use technology to help them follow a dream.

So, if the process of learning for an apprentice or journeyman is done by following around a master, how could this proven practice be adopted in the current and future economies? With fewer large corporations offering anything like apprenticeships, how is that to be accomplished?

I propose a way forward using the Craft of Expert Coaching, in which corporations design and develop internal Expert Coaching programs, using current science and evidence-based programs, with the existing substantial population of Expert Coaches and managers, to leverage the available technology. If we are willing to think longer-term and not be fooled by the Law of Small Numbers, we can do as Isaac Newton did, and stand on the shoulders of those who came before us.

Using Expert Coaching to facilitate the intergenerational transfer of metis, we can deliberately transmit important behavioral practices and values in our communities and organizations. These interactions and relationships will help to lift the apprentice, the Expert Coach, and the organization.

Conclusion

As I've introduced the Craft of Expert Coaching, I have built a case for craftsmanship, the benefits of DOING good (craft-like) work, and the value of Expert Coaching in service of developing your craft.

Working in this way, you develop your own unique strengths while remaining aware of your natural human biases and the associated potential pitfalls. With a healthy inner work life and the benefits of making progress every day, you can work harmoniously with your human nature, not try to control or abbreviate it.

We've drawn parallels between the Renaissance craft culture in fifteenth-century Europe and the gen-X and millennial culture today – in particular their preference for a collaborative work environment and their appreciation for working in a community. We also saw that then and now men and women simply want to do work where they are skillful, can see their progress, and can find meaning.

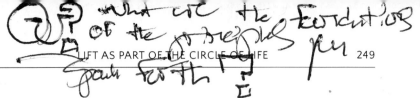

The Craft of Expert Coaching is not asking you to "try on" a new way of thinking, to create new contexts, "possibilities," or new mental models. Instead, it rests on, and believes in, our human nature, and our natural abilities to be creative and productive when we work in alignment with our strengths and passions. I've made the case that real satisfaction comes from working in this way, not from avoiding work.

In fact, it's a familiar story that when some people do finally avoid work and retire, they see nothing left to live for. Perhaps this helps to explain why we have rampant depression and dis-ease among those who no longer work or who contemplate a life without work.

But wait a minute – everyone knows the goal is to not work. Isn't that why we invent all these machines, and spend our lives working for forty or fifty years, so we can have a few good years left…to *not* work?

The extraordinary progress we've made since the Industrial Revolution has freed us from the toil of manual labor – and more recently intellectual labor – through our ever-more-perfected machines.

However, it seems we are *not* moving closer to self-fulfillment, well-being, or tranquility, even as we supposedly recline in leisure and let the machines run the show. The emotional lift of the human spirit that comes from engaging in communities of productive and creative work eludes us.

What if doing your work is a source of your well-being, and provides the most genuine form of self-satisfaction and fulfillment? And what if, as we are coaching, we receive a positive emotional experience – a lift?

The lift metaphor is useful here because it, too, is derived from nature, not from myth or magic. Lift requires action to force the air over the wings or the sail. Lift cannot be abbreviated (or faked), as da Vinci pointed out, nor can it be forced, or bought.

When there is no action (no doing), there is no lift; instead there may be a depression – a term also derived from the physical metaphor for the opposite of lift.

As the boomers approach what is typically assumed to be "retirement" age, they will need courage and action to assert themselves as Expert Coaches. The pre-Industrial Revolution master-to-apprentice model evolved naturally; since then, however, we've developed organizational structures that no longer include intergenerational learning or Expert Coaching.

For those of you who do muster the courage and take the necessary action to become Expert Coaches, know that the rewards are great and well worth the struggle. Take solace in the knowledge that the years and years you worked hard to become masters – even when no one was watching – will be appreciated by those eager to build a career and to learn what you know. In fact, your Expert Coaching will be genuinely appreciated in the most rewarding and authentic way, because the apprentices are also constantly sweeping up cues looking for ways to grow and improve. As discussed, authenticity is sensed and somehow "known" and communicated, so when you coach in areas over which you have mastery, you will communicate your metis, and it will both transfer and inspire. With this interaction comes perhaps the most fulfilling of all human experiences, the phenomenon of lift that results from helping lift another.

In my own journey toward mastery, year after year I came up short, failing to measure up to the lone heroic leader I thought I should be, unable to consistently control my willpower and "transform" into someone more confident, less anxious, and better in relationships. It was only when I ceased fighting, and shifted my attention from who I thought I should be, that I began to pay attention and bring respect to what I was doing in the moment. It was only then that I began to appreciate the person I was becoming.

Experience has taught me to accept and be grateful for human nature – mine and others'. By acknowledging my nature, not trying to numb it or fix it or transform it, I appreciate the struggles we all face in simply being human. Through the practice of Expert Coaching, and through the phenomenon of lift, I am on a path to a wonderful new way of living and working. I have found my place, where I enjoy a meaningful, satisfying way to live and work.

I hope this book has informed and inspired you to create lift and to use nature's gift to create your own place and a fulfilling work life through the craft of Expert Coaching.

In this light, the words of Carl Jung, a true master of his craft of human psychology, can be appreciated in a new way. Jung taught that we don't need to paper over or rid ourselves of our own human nature,

> ... rather to experience what it means, what it has to teach, what its purpose is. We should even learn to be thankful for it, otherwise we miss the opportunity of getting to know ourselves as we really are.[9]

– END –

Appendix A — The Run for the Four-Minute Mile

Pre-IAAF Professionals' Times

Time	Athlete	Nation-ality	Date	City
4:28	Charles Westhall	UK	26 Jul 1855	London
4:28	Thomas Horspool	UK	28 Sep 1857	Manchester
4:23	Thomas Horspool	UK	12 Jul 1858	Manchester
4:22¼	Siah Albison	UK	27 Oct 1860	Manchester
4:21¾	William Lang	UK	11 Jul 1863	Manchester
4:20½	Edward Mills	UK	23 Apr 1864	Manchester
4:20	Edward Mills	UK	25 Jun 1864	Manchester
4:17¼	William Lang	UK	19 Aug 1865	Manchester
4:17¼	William Richards	UK	19 Aug 1865	Manchester
4:16 1/5	William Cummings	UK	14 May 1881	Preston
4:12¾	Walter George	UK	23 Aug 1886	London

IAAF Winning Times[1]

In 1913, the International Amateur Athletic Federation (IAAF) first recognized the men's four-minute mile world record. In 2001, the organization changed its name to International Association of Athletics Federations.

Time	Athlete	Nationality	Date	City
4:14.4	John Paul Jones	US	31 May 1913	Allston, Mass.
4:12.6	Norman Taber	US	16 Jul 1915	Allston, Mass.
4:10.4	Paavo Nurmi	Finland	23 Aug 1923	Stockholm
4:09.2	Jules Ladoumègue	France	4 Oct 1931	Paris
4:07.6	Jack Lovelock	New Zealand	15 Jul 1933	Princeton, N.J.
4:06.8	Glenn Cunningham	US	16 Jun 1934	Princeton, N.J.
4:06.4	Sydney Wooderson	UK	28 Aug 1937	Motspur Park
4:06.2	Gunder Hägg	Sweden	1 Jul 1942	Gothenburg
4:06.2	Arne Andersson	Sweden	10 Jul 1942	Stockholm
4:04.6	Gunder Hägg	Sweden	4 Sep 1942	Stockholm
4:02.6	Arne Andersson	Sweden	1 Jul 1943	Gothenburg
4:01.6	Arne Andersson	Sweden	18 Jul 1944	Malmö
4:01.4	Gunder Hägg	Sweden	17 Jul 1945	Malmö
3:59.4	Roger Bannister	UK	6 May 1954	Oxford
3:58.0	John Landy	Australia	21 Jun 1954	Turku
3:57.2	Derek Ibbotson	UK	19 Jul 1957	London
3:54.5	Herb Elliott	Australia	6 Aug 1958	Dublin
3:54.4	Peter Snell	New Zealand	27 Jan 1962	Wanganui

Time	Athlete	Nationality	Date	City
3:54.1	Peter Snell	New Zealand	17 Nov 1964	Auckland
3:53.6	Michel Jazy	France	9 Jun 1965	Rennes
3:51.3	Jim Ryun	US	17 Jul 1966	Berkeley, Cal.
3:51.1	Jim Ryun	US	23 Jun 1967	Bakersfield, Cal.
3:51.0	Filbert Bayi	Tanzania	17 May 1975	Kingston
3:49.4	John Walker	New Zealand	12 Aug 1975	Gothenburg
3:49.0	Sebastian Coe	UK	17 Jul 1979	Oslo
3:48.8	Steve Ovett	UK	1 Jul 1980	Oslo
3:48.5	Sebastian Coe	UK	19 Aug 1981	Zürich
3:48.40	Steve Ovett	UK	26 Aug 1981	Koblenz
3:47.33	Sebastian Coe	UK	28 Aug 1981	Brussels
3:46.32	Steve Cram	UK	27 Jul 1985	Oslo
3:44.39	Noureddine Morceli	Algeria	5 Sep 1993	Rieti
3:43.13	Hicham El Guerrouj	Morocco	7 Jul 1999	Rome

IAAF Times Expanded 12 Aug 1975 to 22 May 2017 Sorted Chronologically[2]

The IAAF publishes all recorded results for the men's outdoor four-minute mile world record.

Time	Athlete	Nationality	Date
3:49.4h	John Walker	NZL	12 Aug 1975
03:49.0	Sebastian Coe	GBR	17 Jul 1979

Time	Athlete	Nation-ality	Date
3:48.8h	Steve Ovett	GBR	1 Jul 1980
03:49.2	Steve Ovett	GBR	11 Jul 1981
03:48.5	Sebastian Coe	GBR	19 Aug 1981
03:48.4	Steve Ovett	GBR	26 Aug 1981
03:47.3	Sebastian Coe	GBR	28 Aug 1981
03:49.5	Mike Boit	KEN	28 Aug 1981
03:48.8	Sydney Maree	USA	9 Sep 1981
03:48.5	Steve Scott	USA	26 Jun 1982
03:48.8	Sydney Maree	USA	26 Jun 1982
03:49.3	David Moorcroft	GBR	26 Jun 1982
03:47.7	Steve Scott	USA	7 Jul 1982
03:49.1	John Walker	NZL	7 Jul 1982
03:49.4	Sydney Maree	USA	13 Jul 1982
03:49.5	Steve Scott	USA	9 Jul 1983
03:49.2	Steve Scott	USA	17 Aug 1983
03:46.3	Steve Cram	GBR	27 Jul 1985
03:47.8	José Luis González	ESP	27 Jul 1985
03:49.2	Sebastian Coe	GBR	27 Jul 1985
03:46.9	Said Aouita	MAR	21 Aug 1985
03:48.3	Steve Cram	GBR	5 Jul 1986
03:48.7	Steve Scott	USA	5 Jul 1986
03:49.5	Steve Cram	GBR	12 Sep 1986
03:46.8	Said Aouita	MAR	2 Jul 1987
03:49.1	Said Aouita	MAR	13 Jul 1987
03:48.8	Steve Cram	GBR	2 Jul 1988
03:49.2	Peter Elliott	GBR	2 Jul 1988
03:49.2	Jens-Peter Herold	GDR	2 Jul 1988
03:49.4	Abdi Bile	SOM	2 Jul 1988
03:49.3	Joe Falcon	USA	14 Jul 1990
03:49.5	Peter Elliott	GBR	6 Jul 1991

Time	Athlete	Nation-ality	Date
03:49.1	Noureddine Morceli	ALG	10 Jul 1991
03:48.4	William Kemei	KEN	21 Aug 1992
03:47.8	Noureddine Morceli	ALG	10 Jul 1993
03:46.8	Noureddine Morceli	ALG	27 Aug 1993
03:47.3	Noureddine Morceli	ALG	3 Sep 1993
03:44.4	Noureddine Morceli	ALG	5 Sep 1993
03:48.9	Vénuste Niyongabo	BDI	22 Jul 1994
03:48.7	Noureddine Morceli	ALG	26 Jul 1994
03:45.2	Noureddine Morceli	ALG	16 Aug 1995
03:48.7	Hicham El Guerrouj	MAR	16 Aug 1995
03:48.3	Noureddine Morceli	ALG	1 Sep 1995
03:48.1	Noureddine Morceli	ALG	5 Jul 1996
03:49.1	Noureddine Morceli	ALG	30 Aug 1996
03:44.9	Hicham El Guerrouj	MAR	4 Jul 1997
03:47.6	Laban Rotich	KEN	4 Jul 1997
03:47.9	John Kemboi Kibowen	KEN	4 Jul 1997
03:48.3	Vénuste Niyongabo	BDI	4 Jul 1997
03:48.6	Noureddine Morceli	ALG	16 Jul 1997
03:45.6	Hicham El Guerrouj	MAR	26 Aug 1997
03:46.4	Daniel Komen	KEN	26 Aug 1997
03:46.7	Vénuste Niyongabo	BDI	26 Aug 1997
03:47.9	Daniel Komen	KEN	3 Sep 1997
03:44.6	Hicham El Guerrouj	MAR	16 Jul 1998
03:49.0	Hicham El Guerrouj	MAR	29 Jul 1998
03:43.1	Hicham El Guerrouj	MAR	7 Jul 1999
03:43.4	Noah Ngeny	KEN	7 Jul 1999
03:47.1	Hicham El Guerrouj	MAR	7 Aug 1999
03:46.2	Hicham El Guerrouj	MAR	28 Jul 2000
03:47.9	William Chirchir	KEN	28 Jul 2000
03:46.0	Hicham El Guerrouj	MAR	5 Aug 2000

Time	Athlete	Nation-ality	Date
03:47.7	Noah Ngeny	KEN	5 Aug 2000
03:47.9	Hicham El Guerrouj	MAR	25 Aug 2000
03:48.2	William Chirchir	KEN	25 Aug 2000
03:49.3	Benjamin Kipkurui	KEN	25 Aug 2000
03:45.0	Hicham El Guerrouj	MAR	29 Jun 2001
03:47.3	Bernard Lagat	KEN	29 Jun 2001
03:48.4	Andrés Manuel Díaz	ESP	29 Jun 2001
03:48.2	Ali Saidi-Sief	ALG	13 Jul 2001
03:48.6	Bernard Lagat	KEN	13 Jul 2001
03:49.4	Hicham El Guerrouj	MAR	22 Jul 2001
03:48.3	Hicham El Guerrouj	MAR	12 Jul 2002
03:49.5	William Chirchir	KEN	12 Jul 2002
03:48.2	Paul Korir	KEN	8 Aug 2003
03:48.0	Daham Najim Bashir	QAT	29 Jul 2005
03:48.4	Bernard Lagat	USA	29 Jul 2005
03:48.5	Daniel Kipchirchir Komen	KEN	29 Jul 2005
03:48.9	Alan Webb	USA	29 Jul 2005
03:49.0	Craig Mottram	AUS	29 Jul 2005
03:48.3	Daniel Kipchirchir Komen	KEN	10 Jun 2007
03:46.9	Alan Webb	USA	21 Jul 2007
03:49.4	Andrew Baddeley	GBR	6 Jun 2008
03:48.5	Asbel Kiprop	KEN	7 Jun 2009
03:48.8	Haron Keitany	KEN	7 Jun 2009
03:49.0	Deresse Mekonnen	ETH	3 Jul 2009
03:49.3	Ilham Tanui Özbilen	KEN	3 Jul 2009
03:49.1	Haron Keitany	KEN	4 Jun 2011
03:49.4	Silas Kiplagat	KEN	4 Jun 2011
03:49.4	Asbel Kiprop	KEN	2 Jun 2012
03:49.2	Asbel Kiprop	KEN	7 Jun 2012
03:49.5	Silas Kiplagat	KEN	1 Jun 2013

Time	Athlete	Nation-ality	Date
03:47.3	Ayanleh Souleiman	DJI	31 May 2014
03:47.9	Silas Kiplagat	KEN	31 May 2014
03:48.6	Aman Wote	ETH	31 May 2014
03:49.1	Abdelaati Iguider	MAR	31 May 2014
03:49.4	James Kiplagat Magut	KEN	31 May 2014
03:49.5	Ayanleh Souleiman	DJI	11 Jun 2014
03:49.0	Ronald Kwemoi	KEN	27 May 2017
03:49.1	Elijah Motonei Manangoi	KEN	27 May 2017

Four-Minute Mile Progression, 1852 to 1999

Based on IAAF Data 1852 to 1999 – the data used in the regression analysis in Figure 6.0 and Appendix B.[3]

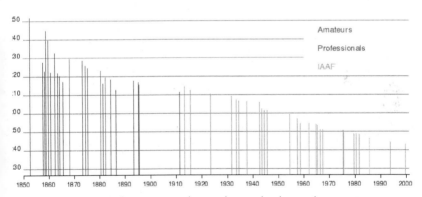

Figure A.0 demonstrates the trend toward a slow and constant improvement over time. Graph courtesy Wikipedia.

Historical Account
From *Runner's World* Article[4]

- 1835 — James Metcalf, tailor and "pedestrian" (professional runner), breaks four and a half minutes for the first time in history, between two milestones on a dirt road, and wins one thousand guineas.

- 1868 — Walter Chinnery, Cambridge, England, on a track of just over three laps to the mile, is the first gentleman amateur to break four and a half minutes (4:29.6).

- 1885 — The fastest amateur in history, pharmacy assistant Walter George (4:18.8), gives up his amateur status and beats the professional record holder, William Cumming (4:16.5) in the "Mile of the Century," with an epoch-making 4:12.75.

- 1915 — Norman Taber, thirty years later breaks George's time with 4:12.6.

- 1923 — Paavo Nurmi, in a decade of world long-distance dominance that has never been equaled, leaves the mile world record at 4:10.4.

- 1936 — New Zealander Jack Lovelock's Olympic 1500m victory sets a world record at Berlin, with a barrier-breaking 55.7 last lap, which would convert to a 4:05 mile.

- 1941 — *The New York Times* reports that America has found "the man who is going to run the mile in four minutes." Leslie MacMitchell, a student at NYU, sets an indoor record of 4:07.4.

- 1941–1945 — Arne Andersson and Gundar Hägg – in Sweden, and not in the war – make progress, with Hägg providing the next record of 4:01.4.

- 1952 — Australian John Landy takes on coach Emil Zatopek (an Expert Coach and three-time gold medalist at the 1952 Olympics), begins an innovative interval training and is getting closer and closer to breaking the four-minute mark.

- 1954 — On May 6 at Oxford University, Englishman Roger Bannister, broke the record, and ran 3:59.4.

- 1954 — June 21. In Turku, Finland, John Landy runs three-quarters of a mile in 2:57.2, three seconds faster than Bannister. Landy took the world 1500m record (3:41.8) and reached the mile in 3:58.0.

- 1954 — August 7. At the British Empire Games in Vancouver, Canada, in an extraordinary Bannister–Landy head-to-head race, both men broke four minutes. Bannister ran a 3:58.8 and Landy 3:59.6. The "Miracle Mile" Statue at Hastings Park in Vancouver, Canada near Empire Stadium, helps perpetuate the myth.

APPENDIX B — FOUR-MINUTE MILE DATA ANALYSIS METHODS

For the World Record Times
Following the Four-Minute Mile Achievement

The following figure displays men's world records recorded since 1852.[1] The horizontal axis shows the year each record was set, the vertical axis shows what the record was, and the points are colored by competitive category. The line through the points reflects the rate at which the world records were changing each year. It was fit using a statistical method known as piecewise linear regression, which allows the slope of the line to change after the first 4-minute mile was recorded (marked with the vertical dashed line). The fact that the slope after the milestone is indistinguishable in the figure from the slope before the milestone indicates that world records did not change at a rate that was any different after the Bannister accomplishment. For the statistically savvy, the p-value associated with the difference in slopes before and after the milestone was 0.978, effectively indicating no statistical support for the notion that world record times improved more quickly after the so-called psychological barrier was removed.

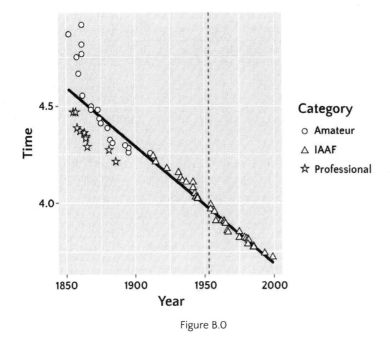

Figure B.0

Technical Explanation

The regression model fit to the data was

$$\hat{Y} = b_0 + b_1 \text{Year} + b_2 D \cdot \text{Spline,}$$

where D is a dummy variable taking on a value of 0 before 1953 and 1 thereafter, and Spline is a variable equal to zero before 1953 and [1953 minus the year] for the years 1954 to 1999. This specification allows for a piecewise change in the slope, if such a change is evidenced by the data. The remaining terms are the estimated regression coefficients. The results of the least-squares solution to the model are:

Results from Piecewise Linear Regression
of World Record on Year

	Estimate	Std. Error	t value	Pr(> |t|)
(Intercept)	15.7609140	0.8389936	18.7854993	0.0000000
Year	-0.0060357	0.0004423	-13.6457914	0.0000000
Spline	-0.0000001	0.0000052	-0.0273029	0.9783073

The Year estimate shows that, for every new year before 1953, the world record was getting smaller by 0.006 minutes, or 0.36 seconds (). Put differently, the world record would be expected to improve by 3.6 seconds every ten years and 36 seconds every 100 years. The small standard error and p-values indicate that this estimate is very precisely estimated.

The coefficient estimate for the Spline variable indicates how much the rate of change shifts after 1953. This change is essentially zero (it is only non-zero at the 7th decimal place), and the p-value is very large. These results indicate that there was no perceptible difference in the rate of change in world records after the 4-minute milestone was achieved.

—*Analysis provided by Jeremy J. Albright, PhD, December 7, 2016. Methods Consulting 27 East Cross Street, Ypsilanti, Michigan. http:// www.methodsconsultants.com.*

Appendix C — Metaphors Explored

Weather & Water Metaphors

Organizational climate reflects the morale, mood, or the current prevailing disposition of an organization. The word climate is a metaphor comparing the prevailing weather condition to the mood in an organization. The climate may be dark and toxic, or sunny, clear, and crisp. It may flow and change quickly or it may just aimlessly drift. Temperature is used metaphorically as well, when someone claims they feel they are left out in the cold. Or when a division or a sales team is hot.

In his 2014 book, *What Happened to Goldman Sachs*, Steven Mandis, of the Columbia Business School, describes the organizational drift of Goldman Sachs as the slow and thoughtless movement away from the very high principles on which its reputation was built.[1] Organizational drift tends toward less discipline and less principled behavior. Because the drift is slow and steady, it is hard to perceive. Without direction and motivation, people will get caught up in the drift.

An organization's culture[2] or climate often uses the water metaphor to explain the behavior of individuals in the culture or climate. Not just useful in commencement speeches, water is an important metaphor, particularly in organizational behavior. Also, fluids metaphors are used with Expert Coaching and knowledge transfer. Thomas Davenport, a professor at Boston College, has researched and written extensively on knowledge management and the transfer of organizational knowledge. He says, " 'viscosity' refers to the richness (or thickness) of the knowledge transfer in organizations. ... Knowledge transfer by means of a long apprenticeship or mentoring relationship is likely to have a high viscosity: the receiver will gain a tremendous amount of detail and subtle knowledge over time."[3]

Honey is more viscous than water, and, using this metaphor, Expert Coaching is like honey – more densely packed with information than the more watery platitude-filled motivational theories in leadership. Expert Coaching, by contrast, includes language, images, sounds, feelings, and smells as well as metaphorical and conceptual experiences. One can hear the fluid metaphors used in everyday expressions:

- The organization has undergone wave after wave of layoffs.

- Our finances are under water.

- We were swept up in the financial crisis.

- Our people are drowning.

Orientation Metaphors

These metaphors identify orientation, like up / down, in front of / behind, above / below, and inside / outside. These orientation metaphors operate outside of consciousness but influence behavior in consistent ways:

- More is better.

- High status is up. Low status is down.

- Happy is up.

- Good health and fitness is up. Poor health is down.

- Progress is up (elevation).

- In a theological frame, heaven is up and hell is down.

Object or Entity Metaphors

Another important set of metaphors compares events and actions to objects.

- Organizations are machines (entities).[4]

- Organizations and businesses are ships.[5]

- Organizations are humans.

- Organizations are containers.

- Business is war.

- Business is a farm or a garden.

- Economy is an aircraft.

- Inflation is an entity.

- Ideas are boxes.

- Ideas are people.

- Ideas are products.

Additional Metaphors in Business

- Theories are buildings.

- Products are tools.

- Products are living organisms.

- Software is a building.

- Careers are ladders. (And it's hard to switch paths when you're on the ladder: the ladder is straight and does not allow changing direction, so you have only two options: promotion up the ladder, or demotion down.)

- Careers are paths.

- Strategy is a game, like chess.

- Processes are journeys.

- Processes are chains.

- Processes are cycles.

The Polarity Metaphor

One of the most effective coaching and managing metaphors appears in polarity management, credited to Barry Johnson in the 1970s. The general idea is that we are always operating between poles, like the positive and negative poles of a magnet. In his book, *Polarity Management: Identifying and Managing Unsolvable Problems*,[6] Johnson offers the example of opposing operating states: working independently versus working in teams.

Working independently and working in groups are the mutually repellent poles, because they can't both be sustained at the same time. Many people find the polarity metaphor useful because it can be shown on a diagram, with the entire dynamic process mapped out visually, not just linguistically. This metaphor is coherent with a real physical object: a magnet, not just an abstraction.

Polarity management does not choose between one polarity or another to fix the problem. Instead, it manages the dynamic behavior between polarities. That unsolvable problem, referred to in the subtitle of the book, is the false choice of operating at either extreme.

To address this in an effective and methodical way, coaching and polarity management experts prefer to use "and," rather than the "either / or" of opposite poles. Simply put, you need to be able to operate effectively at and between both poles. The resulting wide range of behaviors offers more ways to operate, and provides more options and better effectiveness. The goal of polarity management is to get the best of both poles, while steering clear of their limits and weaknesses. Polarity management recognizes that, in organizations, the operating state is rarely static; instead it's always moving between different ways of operating.

NOTES

Notes to Preface

1. Thrust in jet aircraft is typically expressed in pounds of thrust, not horsepower. The approximate horsepower here is calculated from the manufacturer's thrust data, to give an idea of the relative magnitude of power generated by the engines.

2. At the front of traditional propellers, long wing-shape blades create lift as they spin around. In aircraft with these traditional propellers, the Bernoulli Principle is one of the key principles used by the propellers to "propel" the plane forward (horizontal lift) – essentially pulling the plane through the air. The Bernoulli Principle also helps to explain why the wing uses lift. While lift has been well comprehended since the early twentieth century, it is still commonly misunderstood. For this book about coaching, what's important is that lift is one of nature's most useful and powerful forces. Understanding and working with, not against nature is a fundamental and consistent message in this book. While lift may be challenging to calculate (the Eulerian formulation is complex), you only need to understand two of Newton's three laws and the Bernoulli Principle to understand both why and how lift works.

However, to effectively use Newton's second law, F=ma, we need to consider convective acceleration, fluid flow around bodies, and the deformation of a fluid. I recommend Doug McLean's book, *Understanding Aerodynamics: Arguing from the Real Physics* (Hoboken: Wiley & Sons Ltd., 2013) Section 7.3.3, 286–357.

3. Colin Pask provides a more accurate phrasing of Newton's third law in his lovely book, *Magnificent Principia: Exploring Isaac Newton's Masterpiece* (Amherst: Prometheus Books, 2013), 126. "To every action there is always opposed an equal reaction; or, the mutual actions of two bodies upon each other are always equal, and directed to contrary parts."

4. Newton's third law is useful to understand the pushing force from the fan and jet engine. However, it is often used inaccurately when referring to lift; the idea that the wing is pushing down on the air, and the air pushing back is just not correct. The mischief lies in the use of the application of the third law. The third law is about forces exchanged by bodies and fluids, not motion. Force is being exerted on the wing by the fluid, but the third law does not explain how or why. Lift is a function of a force, a force is derived from acceleration – and it is Newton's second law, not the third, which deals with accelerations. See McLean's *Understanding Aerodynamics* for more.

5. In addition to the force from the fan blades, the turbo-fan also creates a force from the combustion of fuel. The word turbo, in turbo-fan, is derived from the word turbine, which is just a machine that converts the explosive energy from the combustion of fuel into a rotating force. Turbines are good for powering things that spin around, like the fans providing most (approximately seventy to eighty percent) of the thrust for the A-320. These fan blades push the air into each engine at eleven thousand cubic feet per second – that's the volume of air in a small bedroom, every second. Most of this incoming air bypasses the interior jet core of the engine, and therefore it is called "high-bypass." However, the air not bypassed enters the jet core. In the core, this air cascades over and spins an array of short, fat windmill blades lined up like rows of dominos, and as Newton determined, creates an equal and opposite reaction which

powers an internal air compressor, further compressing the incoming air. This compressed air contains lots of oxygen (good for burning and exploding), and then bursts into what is called the combustion chamber further downstream. There, the rapidly expanding air meets a spray of jet fuel and fire, creating a continuous explosion (combustion) of high-temperature expanding gas. The explosion also creates a pushing action backward and, again, an equal and opposite action helps thrust the plane forward. But, ingeniously, these engines also recruit and use some of this combustion energy which spins another set of short, fat windmill-like blades also lined up like dominos. These blades convert the energy from the explosions into a rotating force that spins the fan blades visible from the front of the engine.

6.   Robert Kolker, "'My Aircraft': Why Sully May be the Last of His Kind," *New York Magazine*, February 1, 2009, http://nymag.com/news/features/53788/.

7.   Rainer Strack, Jens Baier, Matthew Marchingo, and Shailesh Sharda, "The Global Workforce Crisis: $10 Trillion at Risk," Boston Consulting Group, July 2, 2014, https://www.bcg.com/publications/2014/people-organization-human-resources-global-workforce-crisis.aspx.

8.   Chesley Burnett Sullenberger and Jeffrey Zaslow, *Highest Duty: My Search for What Really Matters* (New York: Harper, 2010), 214.

9.   Ibid., 189.

10.   Ibid., 230.

11.   The water landing of an Ethiopian Airlines Boeing 767 260ER was caught on video in 1996 and can be seen on YouTube. One of the wingtips touched the water, cartwheeling and breaking apart the airplane. Of the 175 souls on board, 125 died that day.

12.   Lorentz E. Wittmers, MD, PhD and Margaret V. Savage, PhD, "Cold Water Immersion," in *Medical Aspects of Harsh Environments*, ed. Kent B. Pandalf, PhD and Robert E. Burr, MD, vol. 1 (Falls

Church, VA: Office of The Surgeon General, Department of the Army, 2002), 531–553.

13. Jason Paur, "Sullenberger Made the Right Move Landing on the Hudson," *Wired*, May 05, 2010, https://www.wired.com/2010/05/ntsb-makes-recommendations-after-miracle-on-the-hudson-investigation/.

14. Sullenberger and Zaslow, *Highest Duty*, 159.

15. Janine M. Benyus, *Biomimicry: Innovation Inspired by Nature*. 1st ed. (New York: Harper Perennial, 1997), 3. The name biomimicry is derived from the Greek words, bios, for life, and mimesis, for imitation.

16. Ibid., 2.

17. In this book, the natural physical metaphors of nature are based on classical mechanics, not subatomic behavior. My assertion is we created metaphors based on the world in which we have lived for generations and not the subatomic world, the nature of which is still not entirely agreed upon.

18. Gallup, Inc. "State of the American Workplace." Gallup.com. February 15, 2017, http://news.gallup.com/reports/178514/state-american-workplace.aspx.

19. Richard Sennett, *The Craftsman* (New Haven: Yale University Press, 2008. 129–130

20. Ibid., 197. It took a while for surgeons and anatomists to adopt the available technology for sharpened metal knives and scissors. In the early 1500s, a master surgeon in Europe would simply stand over the patient and provide a descriptive running commentary while an assistant, typically a barber, "hacked away. Dissection was done by peeling away layers of skin and tissue, using the ancient Greek principles of Galen of Pergamon." (Quoting Sennett, *The Craftsman*, 197.) Although sharp knives capable of precisely slicing through tissue had already been available in the late 1400s, it was not until the 1540s that Andrea Vesalius, a Brussels physician considered to

be the founder of modern anatomy, began experimenting with the sharpened knives. Through trial and error, he used sharp blades to slice through tissue to reveal a rich new substrate of anatomy.

21. "Jiggling Atoms," in *Richard Feynman: Fun to Imagine*, BBC TV, 1983, http://www.bbc.co.uk/archive/feynman/.

Notes to Introduction

1. "The Last Journey of a Genius," on *NOVA*, PBS TV, January 24, 1989, first broadcast on *Horizon*, BBC TV, November 23, 1981.

2. Newton didn't mathematically prove the motion of the sun, moon, and earth until he was in his late twenties or early thirties. See Michael J. Crowe, *Mechanics from Aristotle to Einstein* (Santa Fe: Green Lion Press, 2007) 114.

3. Newton and others experimented with other heavy metals, not just lead.

4. Doug McLean is one of the most knowledgeable men in the world when it comes to the physics of lift. McLean, a Technical Fellow (retired) at Boeing, holds a PhD in aeronautical engineering from Princeton, and is the author of *Understanding Aerodynamics*.

5. Newton's second law of motion pertains to the behavior of objects for which all existing forces are not balanced. The second law states that the acceleration of an object is dependent upon two variables: the net force acting upon the object and the mass of the object. The acceleration of an object depends directly upon the net force acting upon the object, and inversely upon the mass of the object. In other words, as the force acting upon an object is increased, the acceleration of the object is increased. As the mass of an object is increased, the acceleration of the object is decreased.

6. While the propeller blade operates like a wing under lift, operating in a non-uniform flow-field, the propeller, more accurately, behaves like a mechanical screw as it moves through the air. Doug McLean,

Understanding Aerodynamics: Arguing from the Real Physics (Hoboken: Wiley & Sons Ltd., 2013). 229–230.

7. Marianne Williamson, *A Return to Love: Reflections on the Principles of A Course in Miracles* (New York: HarperCollins, 1992), 190.

8. Teresa Amabile and Steven Kramer, *The Progress Principle: Using Small Wins to Ignite Joy, Engagement, and Creativity at Work* (Boston: Harvard Business Review Press, 2011), 6–7, 20–29, 32–57.

9. Stephen Colbert, "The Word—Truthiness," in *The Colbert Report*, October 17, 2005.

10. Kurt Andersen, "How America Lost Its Mind: The Nation's Current Post-Truth Moment is the Ultimate Expression of Mind-Sets That Have Made America Exceptional Throughout Its History." *The Atlantic*, September 2017, https://www.theatlantic.com/magazine/toc/2017/09/, 77–80. (Adapted from the Kurt Andersen book *FANTASYLAND: How America Went Haywire—a 500-Year History*. New York: Random House, 2017.)

11. Ibid., 77–80 (emphasis original).

12. and/or a decrease in pressure.

13. *Oxford Advanced Learner's Dictionary of Current English*, 3rd ed., s.v. "transformation."

14. K. Anders Ericsson and Robert Pool, *Peak: Secrets from the New Science of Expertise* (Boston: Houghton Mifflin Harcourt, 2016), 98, 122–124, 130–137.

15. See Ryan Howes's article in *Psychology Today*, http://www.psychologytoday.com/blog/in-therapy/200907/the-definition-insanity-is.

16. "Time Spent Working by Full- and Part-Time Status, Gender, and Location in 2014: The Economics Daily," U.S. Bureau of Labor Statistics, https://www.bls.gov/opub/ted/2015/time-spent-working-by-full-and-part-time-status-gender-and-location-in-2014.htm.

17. Gallup, Inc. "State of the American Workplace."

18. Sennett, *The Craftsman*, 20–21.

Notes to Chapter 1

1. More accurately, in HVAC we are working with a first-order phase transition from a liquid to a gas—however, in thermodynamics, such a first-order phase transition falls under the more general category heading of phase transformation, and will be referred to as transformation.

2. The Khobar Towers, where nineteen American servicemen would be killed by a bomb in 1996, were a few miles south of where I lived, just outside the old town center, between Al Khobar and Dammam.

3. ARAMCO is the Saudi Arabian Oil Company, (formerly Arabian American Oil Company), in Dhahran, beside Al Khobar and Dammam.

4. Al Khafji would later become the site of the infamous 1991 battle during Operation Desert Storm, when US troops routed Saddam Hussein's Iraqi troops who had rolled into Saudi Arabia after invading Kuwait.

5. This idea that we learn naturally in our environment was developed primarily by Maurice Merleau-Ponty, considered one of the greatest French phenomenologists. He essentially says that through movement and the interaction of our body and our environment, we learn, or come to gain knowledge. See Maurice Merleau-Ponty, *Phenomenology of Perception*, trans. Donald A. Landes (London: Routledge, 2014).

6. The term "heat pump" is a simple metaphor used to describe the process by which all air conditioning systems work. Although it can describe a system that does both heating and cooling, the heat pump metaphor also accurately describes the physical principles behind a cooling-only unit like a window air conditioner.

7. Changing the pressure of the refrigerant gas changes the temperature at which it boils, or turns to vapor. By reducing the pressure, you are also reducing the temperature at which it boils. This is why water boils at 193.2 degrees Fahrenheit in Leadville, Colorado, the city with the highest elevation in the US. However, when the pressure is increased, the temperature at which the gas turns into a liquid (or condenses) also decreases. For this reason, the part of your home air conditioning system outside can condense the gas refrigerant at low temperatures. Even on cold days, the compressed gas will condense, or turn into a liquid and give up the heat it has pumped from inside your home. Air conditioning systems require a lot of energy to increase and reduce the pressures to allow for the natural process of evaporation (or vaporization) and condensation to take place.

8. Erich Fromm, *The Anatomy of Human Destructiveness* (New York: Holt, Rinehart and Winston, 1973), 366.

9. Fausto Tazzi and Cinzia de Rossi, *Biomimicry in Organizations: Business Management Inspired by Nature.* Translated by Meaghan Toohey. 3rd ed. (Paris: CreateSpace Independent Publishing Platform, 2017), 16.

10. For non-subatomic motion and energy flow.

11. Except perhaps in subatomic space.

12. H. Young et al., *Sears and Zemansky's University Physics: With Modern Physics* (Reading: Pearson Higher Education, 2004), 274.

13. Richard M. Warren, Roslyn Pauker Warren, and Hermann Ludwig Ferdinand Von Helmholtz, *Helmholtz on Perception: Its Physiology and Development* (New York: Wiley, 1968), 4–5.

14. Theoretically, Joule determined.

15. Even the label on your home air conditioner reflects the law of conservation of energy, where it indicates the unit's capacity in BTUs (and perhaps tons). A typical air conditioning system uses units of heat energy called British Thermal Units, or BTU. One BTU is the amount of heat energy required to raise the temperature of one

pound of water by one Fahrenheit degree, and one ton is 12,000 BTU, based on the cooling energy created by 2,000 pounds of ice melting for a twenty-four-hour period, at a constant pressure (in the metric system that unit of heat is referred to as the calorie).

16. A thorough analysis would take into account all the losses due to inefficiencies of the air conditioning system and leakage in the building envelope.

17. The caloric was thought to be a kind of self-repelling substance which flowed from hot to cold objects—it was also thought of as a weightless, odorless gas that could pass in and out of porous membranes in solids and liquids. Phlogiston was thought to be an elemental part of matter, which was released upon oxidation (burning or rusting).

18. Scott D. Anthony, "What Do You Really Mean by Business 'Transformation'? " *Harvard Business Review*, February 29, 2016, https://hbr.org/2016/02/what-do-you-really-mean-by-business-transformation.

19. Ibid.

20. First described in a 1979 *Harvard Business Review* article, http://www.isc.hbs.edu/strategy/business-strategy/Pages/the-five-forces.aspx.

21. Properties of a fluid (density, viscosity, specific heat, enthalpy, and entropy) can be measured and studied – usually in mechanical engineering programs – in the branch of physics called Fluids.

22. George Lakoff and Mark Johnson, *Metaphors We Live By* (Chicago: University Press, 1980), 3–4.

23. As I was writing this book and discussing aspects of it, inevitably the philosophy of science came up, focusing on the question of what is science. These discussions became controversial when they crossed into fields like ontology and epistemology. LIFT does not attempt to address the psychology of science, coherentism, or foundationalism, but rather is interested in a subset that includes only the observable

principles in the laws of motion and basic thermodynamics (principles outside of proposed quantum physics principles).

Notes to Chapter 2

1. Harper, the supporting character Rhoda on *The Mary Tyler Moore Show* from 1970 to 1974, later starred in the spinoff, *Rhoda*. Harper won four Emmy Awards, and during her 1975 Emmy acceptance speech, she publicly thanked and acknowledged Werner Erhard.

2. Vikki G. Brock, *Sourcebook of Coaching History*, 2nd ed. (CreateSpace Independent Publishing Platform, 2012), 44.

3. Ibid., 40–47.

4. Ibid., 84–85.

5. Fernando Flores and Marianne Flores Letelier, *Conversations for Action and Collected Essays: Instilling a Culture of Commitment in Working Relationships* (CreateSpace Independent Publishing Platform, 2013), 17–30.

6. Thomas Gordon was an American psychologist known for his research in communications, conflict resolution, and educational training. He developed Parent Effectiveness Training (P.E.T.), and wrote a widely appreciated book offering a parenting philosophy, in the context of elementary education. This became so popular, he was compelled to develop a program and write a book for teachers, in 1974, called the Teacher Effectiveness Training (T.E.T.). He later used much of the same material to develop a Leaders Effectiveness Training program.

7. Later in the book we will review engineered environments in more detail.

8. Solomon Elliott Asch, *Social Psychology* (Upper Saddle River, NJH: Prentice Hall, 1952b), 7–9.

9. Solomon E. Asch, "Studies of Independence and Conformity: I. A Minority of One against a Unanimous Majority.," *Psychological*

Monographs: General and Applied 70, no. 9 (1956): 1–70, doi:10.1037/h0093718.

10. Mihaly Csikszentmihalyi, *Flow: The Psychology of Optimal Experience* (New York: Harper Row, 2009), 4, 17.

11. Luke Rhinehart, Werner Erhard, and Joe Vitale, *The Book of est* (Lulu.com: Hypnotic Marketing, Inc., 2010), xii.

12. Steven Pressman, *Outrageous Betrayal: The Dark Journey of Werner Erhard from est to Exile* (New York: St. Martins Press, 1993), 29.

13. Ibid., 28–29.

14. Ibid., 26.

15. Ibid., 34.

16. Ibid., 23–25.

17. Rhinehart, Erhard, and Vitale, *The Book of est*, xi–xii.

18. Maya Angelou, *The Complete Collected Poems of Maya Angelou* (New York: Random House, 1994).

19. US President John F. Kennedy remarked anecdotally at the conclusion of his speech at the dedication of the Aerospace Medical Health Center in San Antonio on 21 November 1963: "Frank O'Connor, the Irish writer, tells in one of his books how, as a boy, he and his friends would make their way across the countryside, and when they came to an orchard wall that seemed too high and too doubtful to try and too difficult to permit their voyage to continue, they took off their hats and tossed them over the wall—and then they had no choice but to follow them. This nation has tossed its cap over the wall of space and we have no choice but to follow it."

"John F. Kennedy Speeches," John F. Kennedy Presidential Library and Museum, https://www.jfklibrary.org/Research/Research-Aids/JFK-Speeches/San-Antonio-TX_19631121.aspx.

Notes to Chapter 3

1. Another beautiful metaphor is the string quartet, which has four instruments, often a violin, a viola, a cello, and a bass; and by varying the tempo, volume, pace, and tones, these four beautiful instruments could make extraordinary music. See Zachary Golper, Peter Kaminsky, and Thomas Schauer, *Bien Cuit: The Art of Bread* (New York: Regan Arts, 2015), 15.

2. Robert J. Jeffers and Henk Aertsen, *Historical Linguistics 1989* (Amsterdam: J. Benjamins, 1993), 207.

3. Golper, Kaminsky, and Schauer, *Bien Cuit*, 12.

4. In the Christian tradition, for example, in the book of John, Christ multiplies loaves of bread—he cares about the physical needs of people, but is more concerned about their spiritual needs. So, he reprimands the people for seeking Him only for physical nourishment (John 6:26). He tells the people, "I am the bread of life. Your fathers ate the manna in the wilderness, and they died...I am the living bread that came down out of heaven; if anyone eats of this bread, he will live forever; and the bread also which I will give for the life of the world is My flesh" (John 6:48–51). Jesus was referring to His death and resurrection. Today we memorialize this act of grace by eating the bread of communion. The physical "piece" of sustenance represents the spiritual "peace" we can have through Jesus Christ, the Bread of Life. See Mischelle Sandwich, "One of the Great Metaphors: The Bread of Life," *Reformed Health*, June 16, 2016, https://reformedhealth.net/one-of-the-great-metaphors-the-bread-of-life/.

5. William Hollingsworth Whyte, *The Organization Man* (New York: Simon and Schuster, 1956), 88.

6. Richard Florida, *The Rise of the Creative Class: And How It's Transforming Work, Leisure, Community and Everyday Life* (New York: Basic Books, 2006), 48–55.

7. Yuval Noah Harari, *Sapiens: A Brief History of Humankind* (New York: Harper, 2015), 114–118.

8. Sennett, *The Craftsman*, 9.

9. Marcel Detienne and Jean-Pierre Vernant, *Cunning Intelligence in Greek Culture and Society* (Chicago: University of Chicago Press, 1991), 3–4.

10. Ibid., 4.

11. Library of Matthew Carter, Charlottesville, Virginia, Non-copyright translation, 2017, *Iliad*.

12. Ibid., *Iliad* 23.304–318.

13. Ibid., *Iliad* 23.304–318.

14. Ibid., *Iliad* 23.304–306.

15. Frank Marshall and Allyn Stewart (Producers), Clint Eastwood (Director). September 9, 2016. *Sully* [Motion picture]. USA: Warner Bros.

16. Laurie Taylor, "Craft works: Laurie Taylor interviews Richard Sennett," *New Humanist*, March 3, 2008, https://newhumanist.org.uk/articles/1733/craft-works-laurie-taylor-interviews-richard-sennett.

17. Detienne and Vernant, *Cunning Intelligence*, 3–4.

18. True to the ancient Greek model, Captain Sully has become much more than an airline captain. He is a dedicated expert pilot and an inspirational father, husband, and leader of his communities.

19. Florida, *Rise of the Creative Class*, 45.

20. Ibid., 38–39.

21. Ibid., 54.

22. Ibid., 56.

23. Edith Hamilton, *The Greek Way* (New York: W.W. Norton & Co., 1993).

24. Sennett, *The Craftsman*, 326–327.

25. Hamilton, *The Greek Way*, 23.

26. Ibid., 24.

27. Ibid., 44.

28. Robert Fulghum, *All I Really Need to Know I Learned in Kindergarten: Uncommon Thoughts on Common Things* (New York: Ballantine Books, 2003), 11–17.

29. Timothy D. Wilson, *Strangers to Ourselves: Discovering the Adaptive Unconscious* (Cambridge: Belknap Press, 2004), 24–25.

30. Diana Coutu and Carol Kauffman, *What Can Coaches Do for You?* (Boston: Harvard Business Review Press, 2009).

Notes to Chapter 4

1. The Leadership Circle 360; the Hogan HDS, HPI, and MVPI; the ESCI (Emotional and Social Competency Inventory); and the Clifton StrengthsFinder assessment.

2. Meeting standards for test development by one or all of the following: American Psychological Association, the American Educational Research Association, and the National Council on Measurement in Education (1999).

3. As estimated by The International Coach Federation. John LaRosa, "U.S. Personal Coaching Industry Tops $1 Billion, and Growing," February 12, 2018, https://blog.marketresearch.com/us-personal-coaching-industry-tops-1-billion-and-growing.

4. Brock, *Sourcebook of Coaching History*, 44.

5. Ibid., 153. Landmark was a successor program after *est.*

6. Rick Karlgaard, "Peter Drucker on Leadership," *Forbes*, November 19, 2004, https://www.forbes.com/2004/11/19/cz_rk_1119drucker.html#2699730e6f48.

7. Gallup, Inc., "State of the American Workplace."

8. Ibid.

9. "2016 Employee Viewpoint Survey Results Summary," National Archives and Records Administration, August 29, 2016, https://www.archives.gov/files/about/plans-reports/employee-survey/survey-results-2016-summary.pdf.

10. Gallup, Inc., "State of the American Workplace." Between 2000 and 2008, Gallup conducted its employee engagement research on the US working population via the Gallup Panel, with sample sizes ranging from 991 to 23,572 full- and part-time workers. From 2009 to 2012, Gallup collected these data using Gallup Daily tracking, with sample sizes ranging from 2,182 to 151,290 full- and part-time workers. Gallup's historical client database contains information from clients who took the Q12 survey between 1996 and 2012. It holds data from 25 million respondents from 2.8 million workgroups and 1,110 clients in 195 countries and 16 major industries.

11. Barbara Kellerman, *Hard Times: Leadership in America* (Stanford: Stanford Business Books, 2015).

12. Jeffrey Pfeffer, *Leadership BS: Fixing Workplaces and Careers One Truth at a Time* (New York: HarperBusiness, 2015), 6–7.

13. Liquid water.

14. Fritjof Capra, *The Science of Leonardo* (New York: Random House, 2007), 11–12.

15. Ibid., 11–12.

16. Ibid., 10–12.

17. Ibid., 11-12.

18. Ibid., 11.

19. W. Chalmers Brothers, *Language and the Pursuit of Happiness: A New Foundation for Designing Your Life, Your Relationships & Your Results* (Naples: New Possibilities Press, 2005), 87, 153–283.

20. Steven Pinker, *The Language Instinct: How the Mind Creates Language* (New York: Harper Collins, 1994), 63–64.

21. Peter Haldeman, "The Return of Werner Erhard, Father of Self-Help," *The New York Times*, November 28, 2015, https://www.nytimes.com/2015/11/29/fashion/the-return-of-werner-erhard-father-of-self-help.html.

22. Robert A. Hargrove, *Masterful Coaching,* 3rd ed. (Pfeiffer, 1995).

James Flaherty, *Coaching Evoking Excellence in Others*, 3rd ed. (London: Routledge, 1998).

W. Chalmers Brothers, *Language and the Pursuit of Happiness: A New Foundation for Designing Your Life, Your Relationships & Your Results* (Naples: New Possibilities Press, 2005).

John Whitmore, *Coaching for Performance: GROWing Human Potential and Purpose: The Principles and Practice of Coaching and Leadership*, 4th ed. (London: Nicholas Brealey, 2009).

Henry Kimsey-House et al., *Co-active Coaching Changing Business, Transforming Lives*, 3rd ed. (Boston: Nicholas Brealey Publishing, 2011). (Henry Kimsey-House also founded "the oldest and largest in-person coach training program.")

23. Rhonda Byrne, *The Secret* (New York: Simon and Schuster, 2006).

24. The *Harvard Business Review* in 1997 identified *The Fifth Discipline* as one of the seminal management books of the previous 75 years. Cited in http://mitsloan.mit.edu/faculty-and-research/faculty-directory/detail/?id=41415.

25. Ericsson and Pool, *Peak*, 11.

26. Isaiah Berlin, *The Hedgehog and the Fox: An Essay on Tolstoy's View of History*, ed. Henry Hardy, 2nd ed., (Princeton: Princeton University Press, 2013), 1–3.

27. Jim Collins, *Good to Great: Why Some Companies Make the Leap... and Others Don't* (London: Random House, 2001), 14.

28. Ibid., 8–10.

29. In Chapter Nine and Appendix C we go into more detail about the power and influence of metaphors.

Notes to Chapter 5

1. Then we'll analogize to the idea that our view of consciousness and willpower also moved from inside of us to outside ourselves.

2. Despite the fact that the Greeks knew the earth was a sphere, a myth used in transformational material says that the early explorers thought the earth was flat – and this limiting belief stopped them from sailing.

3. Pask, *Magnificent Principia*, 67–69.

4. Nicolaus Copernicus, Polish mathematician and astronomer (1473–1543), Galileo Galilei, Italian astronomer, physicist, mathematician, engineer, and philosopher (1564–1642), Johannes Kepler, German astronomer and mathematician (1571–1630).

5. Pask, *Magnificent Principia*, 45–46.

6. Ibid., 67–69.

7. Gert-Jan Lokhorst, "Descartes and the Pineal Gland," Stanford Encyclopedia of Philosophy, September 18, 2013, https://plato. stanford.edu/entries/pineal-gland/.

8. John Searle, "Our shared condition—consciousness," TED: Ideas Worth Spreading, https://www.ted.com/talks/ john_searle_our_shared_condition_consciousness.

9. Alva Noë, *Out of Our Heads: Why You Are Not Your Brain, and Other Lessons from the Biology of Consciousness* (New York: Hill and Wang, 2009), 10.

10. Ibid., 8–9.

11. Alva Noë, "Beyond Brain Reading: Making Sense Of Brain Behavior," NPR, December 17, 2010, http:// www.npr.org/sections/13.7/2010/12/17/132115540/ beyond-brain-reading-making-sense-of-brain-behavior.

12. Chris Argyris, "Teaching Smart People How to Learn." *Harvard Business Review*, https://hbr.org/1991/05/ teaching-smart-people-how-to-learn.

13. Albert Einstein and Alice Calaprice, *The Ultimate Quotable Einstein* (Princeton: Princeton University Press, 2010), 474. This particular quote is from the section "Misattributed to Einstein."

14. Elizabeth Loftus and Katherine Ketcham, *The Myth of Repressed Memory: False Memories and Allegations of Sexual Abuse* (New York: St. Martins Press, 1996), 4.

15. The Hawthorne effect describes the alteration of behavior by the subjects of a study which produces improved results solely because the subjects are aware of being observed.

16. Ellen Bass and Laura Davis, *The Courage to Heal: A Guide for Women Survivors of Child Sexual Abuse: 20th Anniversary Edition* (New York: Collins, 2008), xxiv.

17. Ibid., xxix.

18. Ibid., 4–6.

19. Loftus and Ketcham, *The Myth of Repressed Memory*, 4.

20. "About." Innocence Project, https://www.innocenceproject.org/About.

21. "Eyewitness Misidentification." Innocence Project. https://www.innocenceproject.org/causes/eyewitness-misidentification.

22. This is essentially the problem Professor Argyris revealed with single and double loop learning, when he wrote the *Harvard Business Review* article "Teaching smart people how to learn." *Harvard Business Review*, https://hbr.org/1991/05/teaching-smart-people-how-to-learn.

23. Daniel Kahneman, *Thinking, Fast and Slow* (New York: Farrar, Straus and Giroux), 2011.

24. Wilson, *Strangers to Ourselves*, 167–169.

25. Kahneman, *Thinking, Fast and Slow*, 8.

26. Brothers, *Language and the Pursuit of Happiness*, 88.

27. Rodney Warrenfeltz and Trish Kellett, *Coaching the Dark Side of Personality* (Tulsa: Hogan Press, 2017), 57.

Notes to Chapter 6

1. Kahneman, *Thinking, Fast and Slow*, 137.

2. Jerome S. Bruner, *Actual Minds, Possible Worlds* (Cambridge: Harvard Univ. Press, 1987), 13.

3. Matthew B. Crawford, *The World Beyond Your Head: On Becoming an Individual in an Age of Distraction* (New York: Farrar, Straus and Giroux, 2015), 24–25.

4. "The Bannister Effect—Breaking Through the Four Minute Mile," Orrin Woodward on LIFE & Leadership, http://orrinwoodwardblog.com/2011/01/24/the-bannister-effect-breaking-through-the-four-minute-mile/.

5. "12th IAAF World Championships in Athletics: IAAF Statistics Handbook. Berlin 2009" (Monte Carlo: IAAF Media & Public Relations Department, 2009), http://www.iaaf.org/mm/document/competitions/competition/05/15/63/20090706014834_httppostedfile_p345-688_11303.pdf Pages 546, 549–50. Archived from the original (PDF) on June 29, 2011. See, also the National Union of Track Statistics www.nuts.uk.com. See, also Appendix A and Appendix B for more details.

6. Kahneman, *Thinking, Fast and Slow*, 112–113.

7. Roger Robinson, "Four Minute Everest: The Story and the Myth An epic narration of the historic first sub-four mile," *Runners World*, May 1, 2004. https://www.runnersworld.com/running-times-info/four-minute-everest-the-story-and-the-myth.

8. Even twenty years ago, access to data made an analysis like the one in Figure 6.0 inaccessible to most, but today one can gather this data and perform the analysis in a matter of hours. See, also Appendix A and Appendix B for more details.

9. Neal Bascomb, *The Perfect Mile: Three Athletes, One Goal, and Less Than Four Minutes to Achieve It* (Boston: Houghton Mifflin Co., 2004).

10. Jean-Christophe Rohner and Anders Rasmussen, "Recognition Bias and the Physical Attractiveness Stereotype," *Scandinavian Journal of Psychology* 53, no. 3 (2012), doi:10.1111/j.1467-9450.2012.00939.x, 239–246.

11. Kahneman, *Thinking, Fast and Slow*, 249–256.

12. Ibid., 250–254.

13. Matthew D. Lieberman, *Social: Why Our Brains Are Wired to Connect* (New York: Crown, 2013), 8.

Notes to Chapter 7

1. Dubai was given this nickname because of the massive gold trade there.

2. Wilson, *Strangers to Ourselves*, 24.

3. Albert Mehrabian, *Silent Messages: Implicit Communication of emotions and Attitudes* (Belmont: Wadsworth Pub. Co., 1971), 286.

4. Paul Ekman and Wallace V. Friesen, *Unmasking the Face: A Guide to Recognizing Emotions from Facial Expressions* (Cambridge: Malor Books, 2003), 17–18.

5. Paul Ekman, "Facial Expression and Emotion.," *American Psychologist* 48, no. 4 (1993): 384–392, doi:10.1037//0003-066x.48.4.384.

6. Wilson, *Strangers to Ourselves*, 20–21.

7. Marvin Minsky, *The Society of Mind* (New York: Simon and Schuster, 1985), 17.

8. Ibid.

9. In tennis, a player gets two attempts to start the point by "serving" into the court – if the player misses both consecutive serves it's called a double fault.

10. Malcolm Gladwell, *Blink: The Power of Thinking Without Thinking* (New York: Back Bay Books, 2015), 49–50.

11. Implicit learning is not a completely agreed upon field and is far more complex than what I have presented.

12. Wilson, *Strangers to Ourselves*, 14.

13. A. David Redish, *The Mind Within the Brain: How We Make Decisions and How Those Decisions Go Wrong,* reprint ed. (New York: Oxford University. Press, 2015), 7.

14. Bernard J. Baars, "In the Theater of Consciousness: Global Workspace Theory, A Rigorous Scientific Theory of Consciousness," *Journal of Consciousness Studies* 4, no. 4 (1997), 292.

15. Redish, *The Mind Within the Brain*, 145–159.

16. Keith Humphreys, Janet C. Blodgett, and Todd H. Wagner, "Estimating the Efficacy of Alcoholics Anonymous without Self-Selection Bias: An Instrumental Variables Re-Analysis of Randomized Clinical Trials," *Alcoholism: Clinical and Experimental Research* 38, no. 11 (2014): 2688–2694, doi:10.1111/acer.12557.

Notes to Chapter 8

1. Jim Krane, *City of Gold: Dubai and the Dream of Capitalism* (New York: Picador, 2010), 12–13.

2. John Julius Norwich, *A History of Venice* (New York: Knopf, 1985), 282–284.

3. The proverb existed already, but it was Shakespeare who made it famous in his 1596 play, *The Merchant of Venice.*

4. New Thought, a uniquely American movement involving mind over matter and mind-healing. It is based on religious, spiritual, and metaphysical thinking. There is no governing group or a central tenet or dogma. The Editors of Encyclopædia Britannica, "New Thought," Encyclopædia Britannica, https://www.britannica.com/event/New-Thought.

5. Allen introduced the term, "law of attraction," in his 1902 book, *As a Man Thinketh*. *Thought Vibration, or The Law of Attraction in the Thought Worlds*, (1906) by William M. Atkinson is also cited as in influence in the book and movie versions of *The Secret*.

6. Byrne, *The Secret*, 4.

7. Ibid., 11.

8. Ibid., 10–11.

9. Michael Shermer, "The (Other) Secret," *Scientific American* 296, no. 6 (2007): doi:10.1038/scientificamerican0607-39.

10. The inverse square law essentially says the strength of a wave energy or signal decreases based on 1 divided by the square of the distance from the electric current. So, for example a measurement at one inch (or whatever unit of distance) from the source would give an energy reading of, say, 100. But when moved two inches from the source, the measurement would be 100 divided by two inches squared, or one quarter, so the energy diminishes from 100 to 25. At three inches away, the calculation would be 100 divided by three inches squared, or one ninth, and the energy reading decreases from 100 to 11. The inverse square law is formidable.

11. Wilson, *Strangers to Ourselves*, 38–39.

12. Richard P. Feynman and Ralph Leighton, *Surely You're Joking, Mr. Feynman! (Adventures of a Curious Character)* (New York: W.W. Norton & Company, 2010), 1–21.

13. Ibid., 9–15.

14. Leonard Susskind and Art Friedman, *Quantum Mechanics: The Theoretical Minimum* (New York: Basic Books, 2014), 103–108.

15. Kahneman, *Thinking, Fast and Slow*, 142–145.

16. Chip Heath and Dan Heath, *Made to Stick: Why Some Ideas Survive and Others Die*, 1st ed. (New York: Random House, 2007), 14–19.

17. Byrne, *The Secret*, 51.

18. Ibid., 13, quoting Bob Doyle.

19. "What Oprah Learned from Jim Carrey | Oprah's Life Class | Oprah Winfrey Network," YouTube, October 13, 2011, https://www.youtube.com/watch?v=nPU5bjzLZX0.

20. Sennett, *The Craftsman*, 58.

Notes to Chapter 9

1. H. Anna Suh, *Leonardo's Notebooks: Writing and Art of the Great Master* (New York: Black Dog & Leventhal, 2013), 354–357.

2. Capra, *The Science of Leonardo*, 169–170.

3. Excerpt from David Foster Wallace's "This is Water," his 2005 Kenyon commencement address. The full text can be found at http://bulletin-archive.kenyon.edu/x4280.html.

4. Ibid.

5. A tribute to Shakespeare's character in *Hamlet*: a dead royal jester, Yorick.

6. *Wall Street*, dir. Oliver Stone, by Oliver Stone and Stanley Weiser, perf. Michael Douglas, Charlie Sheen, Daryl Hannah, Martin Sheen, and Hal Holbrook (United States: Twentieth Century Fox Film Corporation, 1987).

7. Lakoff and Johnson, *Metaphors We Live By*, 3–5.

8. Steven Pinker, *The Stuff of Thought: Language as a Window into Human Nature*, 1st ed. (New York: Viking Adult, Penguin Books, 2007), 114–116.

9. Lakoff and Johnson, *Metaphors We Live By*, 3.

10. Ibid., 10–11.

11. Gerald Zaltman and Lindsay H. Zaltman, *Marketing Metaphoria: What Deep Metaphors Reveal About the Minds of Consumers* (Boston: Harvard Business School Press, 2008), 11–14.

12. Ibid., xv.

13. Ibid., xv–xvi.

14. Ibid., 22, 68–70.

15. Ibid., 98.

16. For more background on Collins's metaphors of the hedgehog and the flywheel, see Chapter Four.

17. Peter M. Senge, *The Fifth Discipline: The Art and Practice of the Learning Organization* (New York: Doubleday, 1990), 58–61.

18. Ibid., 57.

19. Kahneman, *Thinking, Fast and Slow*, 85.

20. Douglas R. Hofstadter and Emmanuel Sander, *Surfaces and Essences: Analogy as the Fuel and Fire of Thinking* (New York: Basic Books, 2013), 257.

21. Lakoff and Johnson, *Metaphors We Live By*, 19.

Notes to Chapter 10

1. John Julius Norwich, *The Middle Sea: A History of the Mediterranean* (New York: Vintage Books, 2007), 219.

2. District cooling is an ideal system for a city, but difficult to use in older cities where underground access is restricted. This same system is used in many of the larger university campuses or hospitals in North America, and often combined with steam used for heating. In Dubai, these district cooling plants were small buildings, typically four to five stories high, and one-third the footprint of a typical office building. They are simply mechanical rooms with up to 30,000 tons, using water cooled in 3,000–5,000-ton chillers inside and in cooling towers mounted on the roof. Typically, three or four such plants are built in a loop to provide redundancy and expansion capabilities.

3. It is more efficient because it uses fewer machines operating at a constant output. Traditionally each building has its own system, therefore there would be far smaller machines and because each machine has moving parts, and with more moving parts, there are more energy losses due to friction and other inefficiencies. Perhaps the most valuable benefit, particularly in hot climates, is that these plants are monitored and maintained round-the-clock by highly trained operators and mechanics.

4. "Home | District Energy Initiative," District Energy Initiative, http://www.districtenergyinitiative.org/.

5. Future of American Fiction: Authors David Foster Wallace, Jonathan Franzen and Mark Leyner debate the future of American fiction and the appeal it has to the younger generation," Charlie Rose, September 19, 2010, https://charlierose.com/videos/15361.

6. Lieberman, *Social*, 33–34.

7. Ibid., 8–9.

8. Richard Fry, "Millennials Overtake Baby Boomers as America's Largest Generation," Pew Research Center, April 25, 2016, http://www.pewresearch.org/fact-tank/2016/04/25/millennials-overtake-baby-boomers/.

9. Strobe Talbott, The Great Experiment: The Story of Ancient Empires, Modern States, and the Quest for a Global Nation (New York: Simon & Schuster, 2009) 1st ed., 24–25.

10. Crawford, *The World Beyond Your Head*, 26–27.

11. David Brooks, *The Social Animal: The Hidden Sources of Love, Character, and Achievement* (New York: Random House, 2011), 283–284.

12. Henry Mintzberg, *Managing* (San Francisco: Berrett-Koehler, 2011), 9.

13. Brooks, *The Social Animal*, 149.

14. Daniel Goleman, *Emotional Intelligence: Why It Can Matter More than IQ* (London: Bloomsbury, 2010).

Notes to Chapter 11

1. Ronald Abadian Heifetz, Alexander Grashow, and Martin Linsky, *The Practice of Adaptive Leadership: Tools and Tactics for Changing Your Organization and the World* (Boston: Harvard Business Press, 2009), 7, 155.

2. Robert D. Putnam, *Bowling Alone: The Collapse and Revival of American Community* (New York: Simon & Schuster, 2007), 22–26.

3. Neil Howe, William Strauss, and Robert J. Matson, *Millennials Rising: The Next Great Generation* (New York: Vintage Books, 2000), 215–216.

4. "The Growing Contingent Workforce and Coworking," Coworking Labs, May 25, 2011, http://genylabs.typepad.com/coworking_labs/2011/05/the-growing-contingent-workforce-and-coworking.html.

5. "Bottega" also implies a teaching workshop.

6. Piero Formica, "The Innovative Coworking Spaces of 15th-Century Italy," *Harvard Business Review*, April 27, 2016, https://hbr.org/2016/04/the-innovative-coworking-spaces-of-15th-century-italy.

7. Eric Weiner, "Renaissance Florence Was a Better Model for Innovation than Silicon Valley Is," *Harvard Business Review*, https://hbr.org/2016/01/renaissance-florence-was-a-better-model-for-innovation-than-silicon-valley-is.

8. Ibid.

9. Ibid.

10. Pfeffer, *Leadership BS*, 12–14.

11. Mintzberg, *Managing*, 9.

12. Kathleen O'Brien and NJ Advance Media for NJ.com, "Suicides on the Rise Among Baby Boomer Men: Rutgers Study," NJ.com, August 19, 2014, http://www.nj.com/healthfit/index.ssf/2014/08/suicides_on_the_rise_.

13. Anne Case and Angus Deaton, "Rising Morbidity and Mortality in Midlife Among White Non-Hispanic Americans in the 21st Century," *Proceedings of the National Academy of Sciences* 112, no. 49 (November 02, 2015), doi:10.1073/pnas.1518393112, 2. See Figure 1, http://www.pnas.org/content/112/49/15078.figures-only.

14. Curtin et al., *Increase in Suicide in the United States, 1999–2014.*

15. Ibid.

16. Jeanne C. Meister and Karie Willyerd, *The 2020 Workplace: How Innovative Companies Attract, Develop, and Keep Tomorrow's Employees Today* (New York: Collins Business, 2010), 20.

17. Darren Staloff, *Hamilton, Adams, Jefferson: The Politics of Enlightenment and the American Founding* (New York: Hill & Wang, 2005), 3.

18. Michael J. Crowe, *Mechanics from Aristotle to Einstein* (Santa Fe: Green Lion Press, 2007), 2–25.

19. Brian Wansink, *Mindless Eating: Why We Eat More Than We Think*, 1st ed. (New York: Bantam Books, 2006), 25.

20. Ibid., 1.

21. Ibid., 18.

22. Ibid.

23. Wilson, *Strangers to Ourselves.*

24. Nicholas A. Christakis and James H. Fowler, *Connected: The Amazing Power of Social Networks and How They Shape Our Lives* (New York: Back Bay Books, 2009), 107.

25. Ibid., 109.

26. Lakoff and Johnson, *Metaphors We Live By*, 124–130.

Notes to Chapter 12

1. Andersen, *FANTASYLAND*, 23.

2. Immanuel Kant, "An Answer to the Question, What is Enlightenment?" in *The Longman Anthology of World Literature*, by April Alliston, 2nd ed., vol. D (New York: Pearson Longman, 2009), 599–604.

3. Kant defines nonage as "the inability to use one's own understanding without another's guidance. This nonage is self-imposed if its cause lies not in lack of understanding but in indecision and lack of courage to use one's own mind without another's guidance." "An Answer to the Question, What Is Enlightenment?" 599.

4. Kant, "An Answer to the Question, What Is Enlightenment?" 599–604.

5. Putnam, *Bowling Alone*, 24.

6. Leonard Robert Sayles, *Leadership: What Effective Managers Really Do—and How They Do It* (New York: McGraw-Hill, 1979), 6.

7. Karlgaard, "Peter Drucker on Leadership."

8. Peter Haldeman, "The Return of Werner Erhard."

9. Ibid.

10. Dennis Tourish, *The Dark Side of Transformational Leadership: A Critical Perspective* (Hove, East Sussex: Routledge, 2013).

11. Tom Rath, *StrengthsFinder 2.0* (New York: Gallup Press, 2007).

12. J. McKay and M. Greengrass, "People: March 2003," *Monitor on Psychology*, March 2003, 87.

13. Gallup Organization, CliftonStrengths website. https://www.gallupstrengthscenter.com/Home/en-US/CliftonStrengths-How-it-Works.

14. Ibid.

15. Harari, *Sapiens*, 30–39.

16. Lieberman, *Social*, 8–10.

17. Ibid., 243.

18. Quoted in Frank J. Holuch, "Negotiating." Donald W. Dobler, Harold E. Fearon, Kenneth H. Killen, editors, National Association of Purchasing Management, corporate author, *Purchasing Handbook* (New York: McGraw-Hill, 1993), 5th ed., 242.

Notes to Chapter 13

1. Organizational health as a metaphor is not addressed in any detail in this book; however as defined by Patrick Lencioni, the metaphor is extremely important and valuable.

2. Michael Bungay Stanier, *The Coaching Habit: Say Less, Ask More & Change the Way You Lead Forever* (Toronto, Ontario, Canada: Box of Crayons Press, 2016).

3. Teresa M. Amabile and Steve J. Kramer. "What Really Motivates Workers." *Harvard Business Review* 88 (1–2), January–February 2010: 44–45. (#1 in Breakthrough Ideas for 2010.)

4. Amabile and Kramer, *The Progress Principle*, 3.

5. Ibid., 3.

6. Seligman is the author of *Flourish: A Visionary New Understanding of Happiness and Well-Being, and How to Achieve Them.* (New York: Simon & Schuster, Free Press, 2012) and *Authentic Happiness: Using the New Positive Psychology to Realize Your Potential for Lasting Fulfillment* (New York: Simon & Schuster, Free Press, 2004).

7. Dweck wrote *Mindset: The New Psychology of Success* (New York: Ballantine Books, 2007).

8. Daniel H. Pink, *Drive: The Surprising Truth About What Motivates Us* (New York: Riverhead Books, 2012), 71–73.

9. Shelly L. Gable and Jonathan Haidt, "What (and Why) is Positive Psychology?" *Review of General Psychology* 9, no. 2 (2005): doi:10.1037/1089-2680.9.2.103.

10. Martin E. P. Seligman, *Flourish: A Visionary New Understanding of Happiness and Well-Being, and How to Achieve Them* (New York: Simon & Schuster, Free Press, 2012), 2–7.

11. Pink, *Drive*, 71.

12. Amabile and Kramer, *The Progress Principle*, 139.

13. Ibid., 46–47.

14. Ibid., 17.

15. Ibid., 20–22.

16. Wilson, *Strangers to Ourselves*.

17. Talbott, *The Great Experiment*, 24–25.

18. This concept comes from Jonathan Talpin and his book, *Move Fast and Break Things: How Facebook, Google, and Amazon Cornered Culture and Undermined Democracy* (New York: Little, Brown and Company, 2017).

19. C. Wright Mills, *White Collar: The American Middle Classes* (New York: Oxford University Press, 1951), 219–220.

20. Robert M. Pirsig, *Zen and the Art of Motorcycle Maintenance: An Inquiry into Values* (New York: Harper Collins, 1974), 7.

21. Chip Espinoza and Mick Ukleja, *Managing the Millennials: Discover the Core Competencies for Managing Today's Workforce* (Hoboken: John Wiley & Sons, Inc., 2016), 148.

22. Pirsig, *Zen and the Art of Motorcycle Maintenance*, 296.

23. Sennett, *The Craftsman*, 24.

Notes to Chapter 14

1. Richard J. Hackman and Greg R. Oldham, *Work Redesign* (Reading: Addison-Wesley Publishing Company, 1980), 18–20.

2. Ibid., p 32–33.

3. In smaller organizations, this is not generally an issue.

4. Amabile and Kramer, *The Progress Principle*, 5, 81–83, 88.

5. Ibid., 80.

6. Ibid., 134–137.

7. Ibid., 83.

8. Ibid., 81–83.

9. Ibid., 84.

10. Ibid., 84.

11. Gerd Gigerenzer, Ralph Hertwig, and Thorsten Pachur, *Heuristics: The Foundations of Adaptive Behavior* (Oxford: Oxford University Press, 2011), 4, 142.

12. Ibid., xvii.

13. Ibid.

14. Ibid.

15. Ibid., 183.

16. Ibid., 165–183.

17. Ibid., 183–184.

18. Collins, *Good to Great*, 14.

19. Amabile and Kramer, *The Progress Principle*, 20.

Notes to Chapter 15

1. Paulo Coelho, *By the River Piedra I Sat Down and Wept*, 3rd Printing ed. (San Francisco: Harper Brothers, 1996), 180.

2. "Bin" Rashid indicated the son of Rashid.

3. The Kleindienst website, www.thefloatingvenice.com/.

4. Burj, roughly translated, means tower.

5.   Abu Dhabi is generally considered more conservative than Dubai.
     Some say it can afford to be, as it has far more than Dubai of the
     world's gas and oil reserves—something like five and ten percent
     respectively—in a city of about one and a half million people.
     That's almost three times more oil reserves than the entire United
     States. Although Abu Dhabi has grown more slowly than Dubai, its
     extraordinary modern architecture, glamorous Formula One Racing,
     and world-class schools and museums are as spectacular as anything
     in the world.

6.   The literal translation of Bur, is mainland. This part of Dubai, north
     of the creek, was considered the mainland.

7.   Steven Jobs, "Text of Steve Jobs' Commencement address (2005),"
     Stanford News, https://news.stanford.edu/2005/06/14/jobs-061505/.

8.   "The Last Journey of a Genius," on *NOVA*, PBS TV, January 24,
     1989.

9.   Bryan Dik and Ryan Duffy, *Make Your Job a Calling: How
     the Psychology of Vocation Can Change Your Life at Work* (West
     Conshohocken: Templeton Press, 2012), 31.

10. Ibid., 30–32.

11. Dik and Duffy, *Make Your Job a Calling*, 256, quoting Ágnes Heller,
     Renaissance Man (London: Routledge and Kegan Paul, LLC., 1984)
     cited in Lee Hardy, *The Fabric of This World: Inquiries into Calling,
     Career Choice, and The Design of Human Work* (Grand Rapids:
     William B. Eerdmans Publishing Company, 2003).

12. Dik and Duffy, *Make Your Job a Calling*, 30–31.

13. Friedrich Engels, *The Part Played by Labour in the Transition from Ape
     to Man* (London: Electric Book Co., 2001). The unfinished article
     was first published in *Die Neue Zeit* 1895-06 and was translated
     from the German by Clemens Dutt and first published in English by
     Progress Publishers, Moscow, 1934. Transcribed: by director@marx.
     org, Jan 1996. https://www.marxists.org/archive/marx/works/1876/
     part-played-labour/index.htm.

14. Ibid.

15. Ibid.

Notes to Chapter 16

1. Eoin O'Sullivan, "A Review of International Approaches to Manufacturing Research," (Cambridge: University of Cambridge Institute for Manufacturing, 2011), 61.

2. Kaizen means improvement or change for the better, and is a widely understood detailed process.

3. Patricia Pringle, "Monozukuri – Another Look at a Key Japanese Principle," Japan Intercultural Consulting (July 23, 2010), http://www.japanintercultural.com/en/news/default.aspx?newsid=88.

4. Jim Collins's metaphor of the hedgehog, in *Good to Great*, represents the company that focuses on one big thing, and does that one big thing very well, over and over.

5. In 1982 Dick Snyder borrowed $27.2M on a purchase price of $27.7M – a leveraged acquisition with more than 98% debt – from Singer's air conditioning division, Climate Control, Inc. Snyder then went on to build the company through a series of highly leveraged acquisitions, finally selling to the Malaysia-based OYL Industries, part of Hong Leong Group, in 1994.

6. In a closed system.

7. Interviews with psychologists, 2011–2015. The names of interviewees are available upon written request to the author.

8. Gregory J. Feist and Erika L. Rosenberg, *Psychology: Perspectives and Connections* (New York: McGraw-Hill Higher Education, 2012), 6–8.

9. Ibid., 7.

10. Ibid., 6–8.

11. Steven Berglas, "The Very Real Dangers of Executive Coaching," *Harvard Business Review*, 3, https://hbr.org/2002/06/the-very-real-dangers-of-executive-coaching.

12. Seligman, *Flourish*, 70–77.

13. Ibid., 71.

14. We met Clifton, the founder of StrengthsFinder, in Chapters 4 and 12.

15. Additionally, each of these five elements must display three properties: first, that it contributes to well-being; second, that it is pursued for its own sake and is not contingent upon other elements, and third, that it can be defined and measured independently of the other elements.

16. As defined by Theresa Amabile and Steven Kramer in *The Progress Principle*.

17. Vijay Govindarajan and Srikanth Srinivas, "The Innovation Mindset in Action: 3M Corporation," *Harvard Business Review*, https://hbr.org/2013/08/the-innovation-mindset-in-acti-3.

18. Ibid.

19. Laszlo Bock, *Work Rules!: Insights from Google That Will Transform How You Live and Lead* (New York: Hachette Book Publishing, 2015), 138.

20. Neil DeGrasse Tyson on Reddit, 2012, https://www.reddit.com/r/IAmA/comments/qccer/i_am_neil_degrasse_tyson_ask_me_anything/c3wgffy/.

21. Simon Sinek is a British-American author known for his best-selling book, *Start with Why: How Great Leaders Inspire Everyone to Take Action*. (London: Portfolio/Penguin, 2013)

22. Benyus, *Biomimicry*, 36.

See, also, William B. Irvine, *A Guide to the Good Life: The Ancient Art of Stoic Joy* (Oxford: Oxford University Press, 2008) 1st ed.

23. Benyus, *Biomimicry*, 35.

24. Ibid., epigraph.

25. Ibid.

26. Ibid.

27. In his book, *Beyond Good and Evil*, published in 1886, Nietzsche (1844–1900) wrote: "You desire to live 'according to Nature'? Oh, you noble Stoics, what fraud of words! Imagine to yourselves a being like Nature, boundlessly extravagant, boundlessly indifferent, without purpose or consideration, without pity or justice, at once fruitful and barren and uncertain: imagine to yourselves indifference as a power – how could you live in accordance with such indifference?" Nietzsche's writings about the Stoics were selectively exploited by the human potential movement to support their belief in relativism and the absolute power of language.

Notes to Chapter 17

1. Revisit Chapter 11 to review those influences.

2. Benjamin Schneider, *Organizational Climate and Culture* (San Francisco: Jossey-Bass, 1990), 17–22. This concept of organizational climate and its influence on behavior has been around since the 1930s, and was one of the central interests of a very early positive psychologist, Kurt Lewin. Also, in the late 1950s, Chris Argyris, a psychologist influential in coaching theory whose work we discussed earlier, wrote in some detail about the influence of organizational climate on individual behavior and collective mood.

3. As defined by Theresa Amabile and Steven Kramer in *The Progress Principle*.

4. For example, it's more natural or intuitive to point and click than to enter a key code like Ctrl-Alt-Delete. From Cameron Shelley, "The Nature of Simplicity in Apple Design," Taylor & Francis Online, *The Design Journal*, Vol. 18, Issue 3, http://www.tandfonline.com/doi/abs/10.1080/14606925.2015.1059609.

5. Jobs, commencement address.

6. Derek Thompson, "A World Without Work," *The Atlantic*, July–August 2015, https://www.theatlantic.com/magazine/archive/2015/07/world-without-work/395294/.

7. Ibid.

8. Hamilton, *The Greek Way*, 29–31.

9. Carl G. Jung, "The State of Psychotherapy Today" (1934), in *Collected Works of Carl Jung*, ed. Gerhard Adler, Michael Fordham, Herbert Read, William McGuire (Princeton, NJ: Princeton Univ. Press, 2014) Vol. 10, Civilization in Transition, 170.

Notes to Appendix A

1. "12th IAAF World Championships in Athletics: IAAF Statistics Handbook."

2. Retrieved from https://www.iaaf.org/records/all-time-toplists/middlelong/one-mile/outdoor/men/senior?regionType=world&page=1&bestResultsOnly=false&firstDay=1899-12-31&lastDay=2018-03-15 on 15 March 2018.

3. "Mile Run World Record Progression," Wikipedia, https://en.wikipedia.org/wiki/Mile_run_world_record_progression.

4. Roger Robinson, "Four Minute Everest."

Notes to Appendix B

1. "Mile Run World Record Progression," Wikipedia.

Notes to Appendix C

1. Steven G. Mandis, *What Happened to Goldman Sachs?: An Insider's Story of Organizational Drift and Its Unintended Consequences* (Boston, MA: Harvard Business Review Press, 2013).

2. Organizational cultures pertain to larger-scale organizations like a country or state. Culture includes the dress, style, tools (artifacts), values, and norms. In the practice of a craft, it is the masters or elders who pass on the important cultural elements of the craft.

3. Thomas A. Davenport and Laurence Prusak, *Working Knowledge: How Organizations Manage What They Know* (Cambridge, MA: Harvard Business Review Press, 2000) 2nd ed., 102–104.

4. These can be traced back to Descartes' seventeenth-century automatons and then later to the work of Frederick W. Taylor in the early 1900s. When businesses started doing what Taylor called mechanistic work, changes in organizational structures and job specifications resulted.

5. This is demonstrated by L. David Marquet's best-selling business book, *Turn the Ship Around!: A True Story of Turning Followers into Leaders* (2013).

6. Barry Johnson, *Polarity Management: Identifying and Managing Unsolvable Problems* (Amherst, MA: HRD Press, Inc., 2014).

SOURCES CONSULTED

"2016 Employee Viewpoint Survey Results Summary." National
Archives and Records Administration. August 29, 2016.
https://www.archives.gov/files/about/plans-reports/employee-
survey/survey-results-2016-summary.pdf.

Amabile, Teresa, and Steven Kramer. *The Progress Principle: Using
Small Wins to Ignite Joy, Engagement, and Creativity at Work.*
Boston: Harvard Business Review Press, 2011.

Amabile, Teresa M., and Steve J. Kramer. "What Really Motivates
Workers." *Harvard Business Review* 88, nos. 1/2, January–
February 2010: 44–45. (#1 in Breakthrough Ideas for 2010.)

Andersen, Kurt. *FANTASYLAND: How America Went Haywire—a
500-Year History.* New York, NY: Random House, 2017.

Andersen, Kurt. "How America Lost Its Mind: The Nation's
Current Post-Truth Moment is the Ultimate Expression
of Mind-Sets that Have Made America Exceptional
Throughout Its History." *The Atlantic*, September 2017.
https://www.theatlantic.com/magazine/toc/2017/09/. Cover

Title: BELIEVE: Conspiracy Theories, Fake News, magical Thinking. How America Went Haywire.

Angelou, Maya. *The Complete Collected Poems of Maya Angelou.* New York: Random House, 1994.

Anthony, Scott D. "What Do You Really Mean By Business 'Transformation?'" *Harvard Business Review*, February 29, 2016. https://hbr.org/2016/02/ what-do-you-really-mean-by-business-transformation.

Argyris, Chris. "Teaching Smart People How to Learn." *Harvard Business Review.* https://hbr.org/1991/05/ teaching-smart-people-how-to-learn.

Asch, Solomon E. "Studies of Independence and Conformity: I. A Minority of One Against a Unanimous Majority." *Psychological Monographs: General and Applied* 70, no. 9 (1956): 1–70. doi:10.1037/h0093718.

Asch, Solomon Elliott. *Social Psychology.* Upper Saddle River, NJ: Prentice Hall, 1952b.

Baars, Bernard J. *A Cognitive Theory of Consciousness.* Cambridge: Cambridge Univ. Press, 1988.

Baars, Bernard J. "In the Theater of Consciousness: Global Workspace Theory, A Rigorous Scientific Theory of Consciousness," *Journal of Consciousness Studies* 4, no. 4 (1997).

"The Bannister Effect—Breaking Through the Four Minute Mile," Orrin Woodward on LIFE & Leadership. January 24, 2011. http://orrinwoodwardblog.com/2011/01/24/ the-bannister-effect-breaking-through-the-four-minute-mile/.

Bascomb, Neal. *The Perfect Mile: Three Athletes, One Goal, and Less than Four Minutes to Achieve It*. Boston: Houghton Mifflin Co., 2004.

Bass, Ellen, and Laura Davis. *The Courage to Heal: A Guide for Women Survivors of Child Sexual Abuse: 20th Anniversary Edition*. New York: Collins, 2008.

Benyus, Janine M. *Biomimicry: Innovation Inspired by Nature*. 1st ed. New York: Harper Perennial, 1997.

Berglas, Steven. "The Very Real Dangers of Executive Coaching." *Harvard Business Review*. https://hbr.org/2002/06/the-very-real-dangers-of-executive-coaching.

Berlin, Isaiah. *The Hedgehog and the Fox: An Essay on Tolstoy's View of History*. 2nd ed. Princeton: Princeton University Press, 2013.

Bock, Laszlo. *Work Rules!: Insights from Google That Will Transform How You Live and Lead*. New York: Hachette Book Publishing, 2015.

Brock, Vikki G. *Sourcebook of Coaching History*. 2nd ed. CreateSpace Independent Publishing Platform, 2012.

Brooks, David. *The Social Animal: The Hidden Sources of Love, Character, and Achievement*. New York: Random House, 2011.

Brothers, W. Chalmers. *Language and the Pursuit of Happiness: A New Foundation for Designing Your Life, Your Relationships & Your Results*. Naples: New Possibilities Press, 2005.

Brown, Theodore L. *Making Truth: Metaphor in Science*. Urbana: University of Illinois Press, 2003.

Bruner, Jerome S. *Actual Minds, Possible Worlds*. Cambridge: Harvard Univ. Press, 1987.

Byrne, Rhonda. *The Secret*. New York: Simon and Schuster, 2006.

Capra, Fritjof. *The Science of Leonardo*. New York: Anchor Books, 2008.

Case, Anne, and Angus Deaton. "Rising Morbidity and Mortality in Midlife Among White Non-Hispanic Americans in the 21st Century." *Proceedings of the National Academy of Sciences* 112, no. 49 (November 02, 2015): 15078-5083. doi:10.1073/pnas.1518393112.

Christakis, Nicholas A., and James H. Fowler. *Connected: The Amazing Power of Social Networks and How They Shape Our Lives*. New York: Back Bay Books, 2009.

Coelho, Paulo. *By the River Piedra I Sat Down and Wept*. 3rd Printing ed. San Francisco: Harper Brothers, 1996.

Colbert, Stephen. "The Word—Truthiness." In *The Colbert Report*. October 17, 2005.

Collins, Jim. *Good to Great: Why Some Companies Make the Leap... and Others Don't*. London: Random House, 2001.

Coutu, Diana, and Carol Kauffman. *What Can Coaches Do for You?* Boston: Harvard Business Review Press, 2009.

Crawford, Matthew B. *Shop Class as Soulcraft: An Inquiry into the Value of Work*. New York: Penguin Press, 2009.

Crawford, Matthew B. *The World Beyond Your Head: On Becoming an Individual in an Age of Distraction*. New York: Farrar, Straus and Giroux, 2015.

Crowe, Michael J. *Mechanics from Aristotle to Einstein*. Santa Fe: Green Lion Press, 2007.

Csikszentmihalyi, Mihaly. *Flow: The Psychology of Optimal Experience*. New York: Harper Row, 2009.

Curtin, Sally C., Margaret Warner, and Holly Hedegaard. "Increase in Suicide in the United States, 1999–2014." Centers for Disease Control, NCHS Data Brief No. 241, April 2016. https://www.cdc.gov/nchs/products/databriefs/db241.htm.

Davenport, Thomas H., and Laurence Prusak. *Working Knowledge: How Organizations Manage What They Know*. 2nd ed. Boston: Harvard Business School Press.

Detienne, Marcel, and Jean-Pierre Vernant. *Cunning Intelligence in Greek Culture and Society*. Chicago: University of Chicago Press, 1991.

Dik, Bryan J., and Ryan D. Duffy. *Make Your Job a Calling: How the Psychology of Vocation Can Change Your Life at Work*. West Conshohocken: Templeton Press, 2012.

Dweck, Carol S. *Mindset: The New Psychology of Success*. New York: Ballantine Book, 2007.

Einstein, Albert, and Alice Calaprice. *The Ultimate Quotable Einstein*. Princeton: Princeton University Press, 2010.

Ekman, Paul. "Facial Expression and Emotion." American Psychologist 48, no. 4 (1993): 384-92. doi:10.1037//0003-066x.48.4.384.

Ekman, Paul, and Wallace V. Friesen. *Unmasking the Face: A Guide to Recognizing Emotions from Facial Expressions*. Cambridge: Malor Books, 2003.

Encyclopædia Britannica, The Editors of. "New Thought." Encyclopædia Britannica. https://www.britannica.com/event/New-Thought.

Engels, Friedrich. *The Part Played by Labour in the Transition from Ape to Man*. London: Electric Book Co., 2001.

Ericsson, K. Anders, and Robert Pool. *Peak: Secrets from the New Science of Expertise*. Boston: Houghton Mifflin Harcourt, 2016.

Espinoza, Chip, and Mick Ukleja. *Managing the Millennials: Discover the Core Competencies for Managing Today's Workforce*. Hoboken: John Wiley & Sons, Inc, 2016.

"Eyewitness Misidentification." Innocence Project. http://www.innocenceproject.org/causes/eyewitness-misidentification.

Feist, Gregory J., and Erika L. Rosenberg. *Psychology: Perspectives and Connections*. New York: McGraw-Hill Higher Education, 2012.

Feynman, Richard P., and Ralph Leighton. *Surely You're Joking, Mr. Feynman! (Adventures of a Curious Character)*. New York: W.W. Norton & Company, 2010.

"The Five Forces." Institute For Strategy & Competitiveness. *Harvard Business Review* https://www.isc.hbs.edu/strategy/business-strategy/Pages/the-five-forces.aspx.

Flaherty, James. *Coaching Evoking Excellence in Others*. 3rd ed. London: Routledge, 1998.

Flores, Fernando, and Marianne Flores Letelier. *Conversations for Action and Collected Essays: Instilling a Culture of Commitment in Working Relationships*. CreateSpace Independent Publishing Platform, 2013.

Florida, Richard. *The Rise of the Creative Class: And How It's Transforming Work, Leisure, Community and Everyday Life*. New York: Basic Books, 2006.

Formica, Piero. "The Innovative Coworking Spaces of 15th-Century Italy." *Harvard Business Review.* April 27, 2016. https://hbr.org/2016/04/the-innovative-coworking-spaces-of-15th-century-italy.

Fromm, Erich. *The Anatomy of Human Destructiveness.* New York: Holt, Rinehart and Winston, 1973.

Fry, Richard. "Millennials Overtake Baby Boomers as America's Largest Generation." Pew Research Center. April 25, 2016. http://www.pewresearch.org/fact-tank/2016/04/25/millennials-overtake-baby-boomers/.

Fulghum, Robert. *All I Really Need to Know I Learned In Kindergarten: Uncommon Thoughts on Common Things.* New York: Ballantine Books, 2003.

"Future of American Fiction: Authors David Foster Wallace, Jonathan Franzen and Mark Leyner debate the future of American fiction and the appeal it has to the younger generation." Charlie Rose. September 19, 2010. https://charlierose.com/videos/15361.

Gable, Shelly L., and Jonathan Haidt. "What (and Why) is Positive Psychology?" *Review of General Psychology* 9, no. 2 (2005): 103-10. doi:10.1037/1089-2680.9.2.103.

Gallup, Inc. "State of the American Workplace." Gallup.com. February 15, 2017. http://news.gallup.com/reports/178514/state-american-workplace.aspx.

Gallup Organization, CliftonStrengths website. https://www.gallupstrengthscenter.com/Home/en-US/CliftonStrengths-How-it-Works.

Gigerenzer, Gerd, Ralph Hertwig, and Thorsten Pachur. *Heuristics: The Foundations of Adaptive Behavior*. Oxford: Oxford University Press, 2011.

Gladwell, Malcolm. *Blink: The Power of Thinking Without Thinking*. New York: Back Bay Books, 2015.

Goleman, Daniel. *Emotional Intelligence: Why It Can Matter More than IQ*. London: Bloomsbury, 2010.

Golper, Zachary, Peter Kaminsky, and Thomas Schauer. *Bien Cuit: The Art of Bread*. New York: Regan Arts, 2015.

Gottlieb, Anthony. *The Dream of Enlightenment: The Rise of Modern Philosophy*. 1st ed. New York: Liverlight, 2016.

Govindarajan, Vijay, and Srikanth Srinivas. "The Innovation Mindset in Action: 3M Corporation." *Harvard Business Review*. https://hbr.org/2013/08/the-innovation-mindset-in-acti-3.

"The Growing Contingent Workforce and Coworking." Coworking Labs. May 25, 2011. http://genylabs.typepad.com/coworking_labs/2011/05/the-growing-contingent-workforce-and-coworking.html.

Hackman, Richard J., and Greg R. Oldham. *Work Redesign*. Reading: Addison-Wesley Publishing Company, 1980.

Haldeman, Peter. "The Return of Werner Erhard, Father of Self-Help." *The New York Times*. November 28, 2015. https://www.nytimes.com/2015/11/29/fashion/the-return-of-werner-erhard-father-of-self-help.html.

Hamilton, Edith. *The Greek Way*. New York: W.W. Norton & Co., 1993.

Harari, Yuval Noah. *Sapiens: A Brief History of Humankind*. New York: Harper, 2015.

Hardy, Lee. *The Fabric of This World: Inquiries into Calling, Career Choice, and the Design of Human Work*. Grand Rapids: William B. Eerdmans Publishing Company, 2003.

Hargrove, Robert A. *Masterful Coaching*. 3rd ed. Pfeiffer, 1995.

Heath, Chip, and Dan Heath. *Made to Stick: Why Some Ideas Survive and Others Die*. 1st ed. New York: Random House, 2007.

Heifetz, Ronald Abadian, Alexander Grashow, and Martin Linsky. *The Practice of Adaptive Leadership: Tools and Tactics for Changing Your Organization and the World*. Boston: Harvard Business Press, 2009.

Heller, Ágnes. *Renaissance Man*. London: Routledge and Kegan Paul, LLC., 1984.

Hindle, Tim. *Guide to Management Ideas and Gurus*. London: Profile Books, 2008.

Hobbes, Thomas. *Philosophical Rudiments Concerning Government and Society*. Aalen: Scientia, 1962.

Hofstadter, Douglas R., and Emmanuel Sander. *Surfaces and Essences: Analogy as the Fuel and Fire of Thinking*. New York: Basic Books, 2013.

Holuch, Frank J. "Negotiating." In *Purchasing Handbook* edited by Donald W. Dobler, Harold E. Fearon, Kenneth H. Killen, with National Association of Purchasing Management, corporate author. New York: McGraw-Hill, 1993, 5th ed.

"Home | District Energy Initiative." District Energy Initiative. http://www.districtenergyinitiative.org/.

Howe, Neil, William Strauss, and Robert J. Matson. *Millennials Rising: The Next Great Generation.* New York: Vintage Books, 2000.

Howes, Ryan, PhD, ABPP. "The Definition of Insanity Is..." Psychology Today. July 27, 2009. https://www.psychologytoday.com/us/blog/in-therapy/200907/the-definition-insanity-is.

Humphreys, Keith, Janet C. Blodgett, and Todd H. Wagner. "Estimating the Efficacy of Alcoholics Anonymous without Self-Selection Bias: An Instrumental Variables Re-Analysis of Randomized Clinical Trials." *Alcoholism: Clinical and Experimental Research* 38, no. 11 (2014): 2688-2694. doi:10.1111/acer.12557.

Innocence Project. "About." https://www.innocenceproject.org/About.

"Institute For Strategy & Competitiveness." The Five Forces—Institute For Strategy And Competitiveness—Harvard Business School. http://www.isc.hbs.edu/strategy/business-strategy/Pages/the-five-forces.aspx.

Irvine, William Braxton. *A Guide to the Good Life: The Ancient Art of Stoic Joy.* 1st ed. Oxford: Oxford University Press, 2008.

Jefferson, Thomas. Letter to Benjamin Rush, 16 January 1811, "Founders Online," National Archives, last modified November 26, 2017, http://founders.archives.gov/documents/Jefferson/03-03-02-0231. [Original source: The Papers of Thomas Jefferson, Retirement Series, vol. 3, 12 August 1810 to 17 June 1811, ed. J. Jefferson Looney. Princeton: Princeton University Press, 2006, pp. 304–308.]

"Jiggling Atoms." In *Richard Feynman: Fun to Imagine*. BBC TV. 1983. http://www.bbc.co.uk/archive/feynman/.

Jobs, Steven. "Text of Steve Jobs' Commencement Address (2005)." Stanford News. https://news.stanford.edu/2005/06/14/jobs-061505/.

Johnson, Barry. *Polarity Management: Identifying and Managing Unsolvable Problems*. Amherst: HRD Press, Inc., 2014.

Jung, Carl G. "The State of Psychotherapy Today" (1934), in *Collected Works of Carl Jung*, Vol. 10, Civilization in Transition, edited by Gerhard Adler, Michael Fordham, Herbert Read, William McGuire. Princeton: Princeton Univ. Press, 2014.

Kahneman, Daniel. *Thinking, Fast and Slow*. New York: Farrar, Straus and Giroux, 2011.

Kant, Immanuel. "An Answer to the Question, What is Enlightenment?" In *The Longman Anthology of World Literature*, by April Alliston, 599–604. 2nd ed. Vol. D. New York: Pearson Longman, 2009.

Karlgaard, Rick. "Peter Drucker on Leadership." *Forbes*, November 19, 2004. https://www.forbes.com/2004/11/19/cz_rk_1119drucker.html#2699730e6f48.

Kellerman, Barbara. *Hard Times: Leadership in America*. Stanford: Stanford Business Books, 2015.

Kennedy, John F. "John F. Kennedy Speeches." John F. Kennedy Presidential Library and Museum. https://www.jfklibrary.org/Research/Research-Aids/JFK-Speeches/San-Antonio-TX_19631121.aspx.

Kimsey-House, Henry, Karen Kimsey-House, Phillip Sandahl, and Laura Whitworth. *Co-active Coaching: Changing Business, Transforming Lives.* 3rd ed. Boston: Nicholas Brealey Publishing, 2011.

Kolker, Robert. " 'My Aircraft': Why Sully May be the Last of His Kind." *New York Magazine*, 2009. https://nymag.com/news/features/53788/.

Kornbluth, Jesse. "The Fuhrer Over est: Werner Erhard of est: How the king of the brain-snatchers created his private empire." *New Times: The Feature News Magazine*, March 19, 1976. https://culteducation.com/group/908-est/6130-the-fuhrer-over-est.html.

Krane, Jim. *City of Gold: Dubai and the Dream of Capitalism.* New York: Picador, 2010.

Lakoff, George, and Mark Johnson. *Metaphors We Live By.* Chicago: University Press, 1980.

LaRosa, John. "U.S. Personal Coaching Industry Tops $1 Billion, and Growing," February 12, 2018. https://blog.marketresearch.com/us-personal-coaching-industry-tops-1-billion-and-growing.

"The Last Journey of a Genius." On NOVA, PBS TV, January 24, 1989, first broadcast on *Horizon*, BBC TV, November 23, 1981.

Lieberman, Matthew D. *Social: Why Our Brains Are Wired to Connect.* New York: Crown, 2013.

Lipner, Julius J. *Hindus: Their Religious Beliefs and Practices.* London: Routledge, 2010.

Locke, John. *The Clarendon Edition of the Works of John Locke.* Edited by Peter Harold Nidditch. Oxford: Clarendon Press, 1975.

Locke, John. "Two Treatises of Government," (1690) [(http://www.gutenberg.org/dirs/etext05/trgov10h.htm) (10th edition)]. Project Gutenberg. Retrieved January 21, 2009.

Loftus, Elizabeth, and Katherine Ketcham. *The Myth of Repressed Memory: False Memories and Allegations of Sexual Abuse.* New York: St. Martins Press, 1996.

Lokhorst, Gert-Jan. "Descartes and the Pineal Gland." Stanford Encyclopedia of Philosophy. September 18, 2013. https://plato.stanford.edu/entries/pineal-gland/.

Mandis, Steven G. *What Happened to Goldman Sachs?: An Insider's Story of Organizational Drift and Its Unintended Consequences.* Boston, MA: Harvard Business Review Press, 2013.

Marquet, L. David. *Turn the Ship Around!: A True Story of Turning Followers into Leaders.* New York: Portfolio/Penguin, 2012.

McKay, J., and M. Greengrass. "People: March 2003." *Monitor on Psychology*, March 2003, 87.

McLean, Doug. *Understanding Aerodynamics: Arguing from the Real Physics.* Hoboken: Wiley & Sons Ltd., 2013.

Mehrabian, Albert. *Silent Messages: Implicit Communication of Emotions and Attitudes.* Belmont, CA: Wadsworth, 1972.

Meister, Jeanne C., and Karie Willyerd. *The 2020 Workplace: How Innovative Companies Attract, Develop, and Keep Tomorrow's Employees Today.* New York: Collins Business, 2010.

Merleau-Ponty, Maurice. *Phenomenology of Perception*. Translated by Donald A. Landes. London: Routledge, 2014.

"Mile Run World Record Progression." Wikipedia. https://en.wikipedia.org/wiki/Mile_run_world_record_progression.

Mills, C. Wright. *White Collar: The American Middle Classes*. New York: Oxford University Press, 1951.

Minsky, Marvin. *The Society of Mind*. New York: Simon and Schuster, 1985.

Mintzberg, Henry. *Managing*. San Francisco: Berrett-Koehler, 2011.

Newsweek Staff. "The Sorrows of Werner." *Newsweek*. http://www.newsweek.com/sorrows-werner-205506.

Noë, Alva. "Beyond Brain Reading: Making Sense of Brain Behavior." NPR. December 17, 2010. http://www.npr.org/sections/13.7/2010/12/17/132115540/beyond-brain-reading-making-sense-of-brain-behavior.

Noë, Alva. *Out of Our Heads: Why You Are Not Your Brain, and Other Lessons from the Biology of Consciousness*. New York: Hill and Wang, 2009.

Norwich, John Julius. *A History of Venice*. New York: Knopf, 1985.

Norwich, John Julius. *The Middle Sea: A History of the Mediterranean*. New York: Vintage Books, 2007.

O'Brien, Kathleen. "Suicide Rates Higher Among Baby Boomer Men, Study Finds," *Huffington Post*, August 20, 2014. https://www.huffingtonpost.com/2014/08/20/suicide-men_n_5694921.html

O'Brien, Kathleen and NJ Advance Media for NJ.com. "Suicides on the Rise among Baby Boomer Men: Rutgers Study." NJ.com. August 19, 2014. http://www.nj.com/healthfit/index. ssf/2014/08/suicides_on_the_rise_among_baby_boomer_men_rutgers_study.html.

O'Sullivan, Eoin. "A Review of International Approaches to Manufacturing Research." Cambridge: University of Cambridge Institute for Manufacturing, 2011.

Pask, Colin. *Magnificent Principia: Exploring Isaac Newton's Masterpiece.* Amherst: Prometheus Books, 2013.

Paur, Jason. "Sullenberger Made the Right Move Landing on the Hudson." Wired. May 05, 2010. https://www.wired.com/2010/05/ntsb-makes-recommendations-after-miracle-on-the-hudson-investigation/.

Pfeffer, Jeffrey. *Leadership BS: Fixing Workplaces and Careers One Truth at a Time.* New York: HarperBusiness, 2015.

Phillips, E. M. *Plans for Vocational Education in Minnesota. Under the Provisions of the Federal Law Known as the Smith-Hughes Act. Adopted by the State High School ... for Vocational Edition December 18, 1917.* Paperback ed. April 28, 2017. Leopold Classic Library, 2017.

Phillips, Julie A., Ashley V. Robin, Colleen N. Nugent, and Ellen L. Idler. "Understanding Recent Changes in Suicide Rates among the Middle-Aged: Period or Cohort Effects?" *Public Health Reports* 125, no. 5 (2010): 680-88. doi:10.1177/003335491012500510.

Pink, Daniel H. *Drive: The Surprising Truth about What Motivates Us.* New York: Riverhead Books, 2012.

Pinker, Steven. *The Language Instinct: How the Mind Creates Language*. New York: Harper Collins, 1994.

Pinker, Steven. *The Stuff of Thought: Language as a Window into Human Nature*. 1st ed. New York: Viking Adult, Penguin Books, 2007.

Pirsig, Robert M. *Zen and the Art of Motorcycle Maintenance: An Inquiry into Values*. New York: Harper Collins, 1974.

Pressman, Steven. *Outrageous Betrayal: The Dark Journey of Werner Erhard from est to Exile*. New York: St. Martins Press, 1993.

Pringle, Patricia. "Monozukuri – Another Look at a Key Japanese Principle," Japan Intercultural Consulting, July 23, 2010, http://www.japanintercultural.com/en/news/default.aspx?newsid=88.

Putnam, Robert D. *Bowling Alone: The Collapse and Revival of American Community*. New York: Simon & Schuster, 2007.

Rath, Tom. *StrengthsFinder 2.0.* New York: Gallup Press, 2007.

Redish, A. David. *The Mind Within the Brain: How We Make Decisions and How Those Decisions Go Wrong*. Reprint ed. New York: Oxford University Press, 2015.

Rhinehart, Luke, Werner Erhard, and Joe Vitale. *The Book of est*. Lulu.com: Hypnotic Marketing, Inc., 2010.

Richards, David A. J. *Foundations of American Constitutionalism*. Oxford: Oxford University Press, 1989.

Robinson, Roger. "Four Minute Everest: The Story and the Myth. An epic narration of the historic first sub-four mile." *Runners World*. May 1, 2004. https://www.runnersworld.com/running-times-info/four-minute-everest-the-story-and-the-myth.

Rohner, Jean-Christophe, and Anders Rasmussen. "Recognition Bias and the Physical Attractiveness Stereotype." *Scandinavian Journal of Psychology* 53, no. 3 (2012): 239–246. doi:10.1111/j.1467-9450.2012.00939.x.

Sandwich, Mischelle. "One of the Great Metaphors: The Bread of Life." *Reformed Health,* June 16, 2016. https://reformedhealth. net/one-of-the-great-metaphors-the-bread-of-life/.

Sayles, Leonard Robert. *Leadership: What Effective Managers Really Do—and How They Do It.* New York: McGraw-Hill, 1979.

Schneider, Benjamin. *Organizational Climate and Culture.* San Francisco: Jossey-Bass, 1990.

Searle, John. "Our Shared Condition—Consciousness." TED: Ideas worth spreading. https://www.ted.com/talks/ john_searle_our_shared_condition_consciousness.

Seligman, Martin E. P. *Authentic Happiness: Using the New Positive Psychology to Realize Your Potential for Lasting Fulfillment.* New York: Simon & Schuster, Free Press, 2004.

Seligman, Martin E. P. *Flourish: A Visionary New Understanding of Happiness and Well-Being, and How to Achieve Them.* New York: Simon & Schuster, Free Press, 2012.

Senge, Peter M. *The Fifth Discipline: The Art and Practice of the Learning Organization.* New York: Doubleday, 1990.

Sennett, Richard. *The Craftsman.* New Haven: Yale University Press, 2008.

Shelley, Cameron. "The Nature of Simplicity in Apple Design." *The Design Journal* 18, no. 3 (2015): 439–56. doi:10.1080/1460 6925.2015.1059609.

Shermer, Michael. "The (Other) Secret." *Scientific American* 296, no. 6 (2007): 39. doi:10.1038/scientificamerican0607-39.

Staloff, Darren. *Hamilton, Adams, Jefferson: The Politics of Enlightenment and the American Founding*. New York: Hill & Wang, 2005.

Stanier, Michael Bungay. *The Coaching Habit: Say Less, Ask More & Change the Way You Lead Forever*. Toronto, Ontario, Canada: Box of Crayons Press, 2016.

Steffes, Tracy L. "Smith-Hughes Act," Encyclopædia Britannica, https://www.britannica.com/topic/Smith-Hughes-Act.

Strack, Rainer, Jens Baier, Matthew Marchingo, and Shailesh Sharda. "The Global Workforce Crisis: $10 Trillion at Risk." Boston Consulting Group, July 2, 2014, https://www.bcg.com/publications/2014/people-organization-human-resources-global-workforce-crisis.aspx.

Suh, H. Anna. *Leonardo's Notebooks: Writing and Art of the Great Master*. New York: Black Dog & Leventhal, 2013.

Sullenberger, Chesley Burnett., and Jeffrey Zaslow. *Highest Duty: My Search for What Really Matters*. New York: Harper, 2010.

Susskind, Leonard, and Art Friedman. *Quantum Mechanics: The Theoretical Minimum*. New York: Basic Books, 2014.

Talbott, Strobe. *The Great Experiment: The Story of Ancient Empires, Modern States, and the Quest for a Global Nation*. New York: Simon & Schuster, 2009.

Taplin, Jonathan. *Move Fast and Break Things: How Facebook, Google, and Amazon Cornered Culture and Undermined Democracy*. New York: Little, Brown and Company, 2017.

Taylor, Laurie. "Craft works: Laurie Taylor interiews Richard Sennet," *New Humanist,* March 3, 2008, https://newhumanist.org.uk/articles/1733/craft-works-laurie-taylor-interviews-richard-sennett.

Tazzi, Fausto and Cinzia de Rossi. *Biomimicry in Organizations: Business Management Inspired by Nature.* Translated by Meaghan Toohey. 3rd ed. Paris: CreateSpace Independent Publishing Platform, 2017.

Thompson, Derek. "A World Without Work." *The Atlantic.* https://www.theatlantic.com/magazine/archive/2015/07/world-without-work/395294/.

"Time Spent Working by Full- and Part-Time Status, Gender, and Location in 2014: The Economics Daily." U.S. Bureau of Labor Statistics. https://www.bls.gov/opub/ted/2015/time-spent-working-by-full-and-part-time-status-gender-and-location-in-2014.htm.

Tocqueville, Alexis De. *Democracy in America.* Translated by Harvey C. Mansfield and Delba Winthrop. 1st ed. Chicago: University of Chicago Press, 2000.

Tourish, Dennis. *The Dark Side of Transformational Leadership: A Critical Perspective.* Hove, East Sussex: Routledge, 2013.

Tyson, Neil DeGrasse, on Redditt, 2012. https://www.reddit.com/r/IAmA/comments/qccer/i_am_neil_degrasse_tyson_ask_me_anything/.

Wall Street. Directed by Oliver Stone. By Oliver Stone and Stanley Weiser. Performed by Michael Douglas, Charlie Sheen, Daryl Hannah, Martin Sheen, and Hal Holbrook. United States: Twentieth Century Fox Film Corporation, 1987.

Wallace, David Foster. This is Water—Alumni Bulletin—Kenyon College. http://bulletin-archive.kenyon.edu/x4280.html.

Wansink, Brian. *Mindless Eating: Why We Eat More Than We Think*. 1st ed. New York: Bantam Books, 2006.

Warren, Richard M., Roslyn Pauker Warren, and Hermann Ludwig Ferdinand Von Helmholtz. *Helmholtz on Perception: Its Physiology and Development*. New York: Wiley, 1968.

Warrenfeltz, Rodney and Trish Kellett. *Coaching the Dark Side of Personality*. Tulsa: Hogan Press, 2017.

Weiner, Eric. "Renaissance Florence Was a Better Model for Innovation than Silicon Valley Is." *Harvard Business Review*. https://hbr.org/2016/01/renaissance-florence-was-a-better-model-for-innovation-than-silicon-valley-is.

"What Oprah Learned from Jim Carrey | Oprah's Life Class | Oprah Winfrey Network." YouTube. October 13, 2011. https://www.youtube.com/watch?v=nPU5bjzLZX0.

Whitmore, John. *Coaching for Performance: GROWing Human Potential and Purpose: The Principles and Practice of Coaching and Leadership*. 4th ed. London: Nicholas Brealey, 2009.

Whyte, William Hollingsworth. *The Organization Man*. New York: Simon and Schuster, 1956.

Williamson, Marianne. *A Return to Love: Reflections on the Principles of A Course in Miracles*. New York: HarperCollins, 1992.

Wilson, Timothy D. *Strangers to Ourselves: Discovering the Adaptive Unconscious*. Cambridge: Belknap Press, 2004.

Wittmers, Lorentz E., MD, PhD, and Margaret V. Savage, PhD. "Cold Water Immersion." In *Medical Aspects of Harsh Environments*, edited by Kent B. Pandalf, PhD and Robert E. Burr, MD, 531-53. Vol. 1. Falls Church, VA: Office of The Surgeon General, Department of the Army, 2002.

Woodward, Orrin. "The Bannister Effect—Breaking Through the Four Minute Mile." Orrin Woodward on LIFE & Leadership. http://orrinwoodwardblog.com/2011/01/24/the-bannister-effect-breaking-through-the-four-minute-mile/.

Young, H., R. Freedman, F. W. Sears, M. W. Zemansky, and A. Ford. *Sears and Zemanskys University Physics: With Modern Physics*. Reading: Pearson Higher Education, 2004.

Zaltman, Gerald, and Lindsay H. Zaltman. *Marketing Metaphoria: What Deep Metaphors Reveal about the Minds of Consumers*. Boston: Harvard Business School Press, 2008.

ABOUT THE AUTHOR

Having lived and worked in the Middle East and Europe for most of his career as a Fortune 100 executive, Bruce Dorey now consults with C-level executives who work and travel among the world's business centers. His lifelong interests in physics, psychology, coaching, and business strategy inspire the creative and practical new methods in his work. LIFT is his first book. In it, he illustrates the types of work he does with senior executives to help build a coaching competency into their organizations by leveraging the existing "Experts" within their senior teams (hence the term, Expert Coaching). The founder of Bruce R Dorey – Consulting LLC, he divides his time between Charlottesville, Virginia and a cabin at Moose Lake, Ontario.

For more information, email info@brucerdorey.com and visit::
brucerdorey.com
instagram.com/bruce_r_dorey
facebook.com/brucerdorey
twitter.com/bruce_r_dorey
linkedin.com/in/brucerdorey

Manufactured by Amazon.ca
Bolton, ON